Nissan
300ZX & 350Z
PORTFOLIO
1984-2003

Pubilshed jointly by

BROOKLANDS BOOKS LTD.
P.O. BOX 146, COBHAM,
SURREY, KT11 1LG. UK
sales@brooklands-books.com

ROAD & TRACK
1499 MONROVIA AVENUE,
NEWPORT BEACH, CA 92663.UUS
www.roadandtrack.com

A-N3ZRT   Printed in China   ISBN 185520 6285

The *Road & Track* Portfolio Series is an exciting new group of publications covering some of the most exciting automobiles for the enthusiast. In each Portfolio, you will find feature stories, road test narratives and complete specifications along with performance data. For the serious enthusiasts, the Portfolio series is an excellent reference for collecting, restoring or buying the car of your dreams. Happy reading!

Thos. L. Bryant
Editor-in-Chief
Road & Track

Contents

PREVIEW...

NISSAN 300-ZX

Remember that you saw it here first

BY RANDOLPH BECKMAN

ILLUSTRATIONS BY MARK STEHRENBERGER

IT STARTED WITH a questionnaire in the mail from a marketing research company in Chicago. This was followed by a phone call. Then another phone call with an invitation to be a member of a panel providing opinions about what was referred to as "a new sports car." I own a Datsun 280ZX 2+2. So I guessed it would be a sports car in that category but at this time there had been no clue as to the make of car we'd be seeing.

As a result of all this I ended up at the Pomona (California) Fairgrounds. In the parking lot there was an assortment of

sporty cars—not only ZXs but Toyota Supras, Mazda RX-7s, Porsche 944s, Chevrolet Corvettes and so on. So whatever it was we were going to look at, an assortment of owners had been invited to offer their opinions.

After filling out a questionnaire keyed to the car we owned we were escorted into one of the fairground's curtained exhibit halls. There, in a semicircle, all painted the same shade of silver, were six cars—Porsche 944, two Toyota Supras (one luxury, one sports version), a new Corvette, Datsun 280ZX 2+2 and, lo and behold, an unfamiliar car we soon came to realize was the new Nissan 300-ZX 2+2!

Aha, we all said, the new Z-car about which we'd heard rumors but nothing more. This was what we'd come here for, obviously. Nissan had this new car and they wanted opinions from people who were familiar with cars of this type.

On the other side of a curtain, beyond which we were not supposed to go, there was another group of cars. The 300-ZX on that side of the curtain was a 2-seater, not a 2+2, and it was

obvious, even at a glance, that it was much less luxurious than the 2+2. The cars supplied for comparison with the 2-seater were the Mitsubishi Starion, Mazda RX-7, Chevrolet Camaro Z28, Datsun 280ZX and 200SX. All these were painted gold.

The obvious question in my mind at this point was whether this was the genuine soon-to-be-seen 300-ZX or if it was merely a styling exercise about which Nissan wanted opinions. For a number of reasons—perhaps the most telling was that the body was steel rather than clay or fiberglass—it's clear this was the real thing. Being steel makes it almost certain that production tooling either already exists or is close to final form. Some minor details may change but, believe me, this is the new 300-ZX.

Running Gear

WITH THAT out of the way, the next thing you want to know about is the engine and suspension, right? Unfortunately, I can't tell you much about these parts of the new Z because almost no information was supplied about them. There is a 3.0-liter engine, of course, which we had already figured out from the 300-ZX designation. But I think we were all surprised to learn that it's a V-6 design rather than an inline-6. No information was forthcoming about this engine's output but it's probably safe to speculate that it will have more horsepower than the current 2.8-liter non-turbo. On the order of 165–175 bhp, say.

There were 5-speed manual transmissions in both of the cars I saw but it's safe to assume that an automatic will be offered.

It was difficult to get much of a look at the suspension but from what I could see, it appeared to have been transplanted from the current ZX to the new car without change. That is, MacPherson struts up front while at the rear there are still the semi-trailing arms whose trailing-throttle oversteer has been criticized by R&T in the past.

Styling

As A package, the new 300-ZX appears to be just about the same size as the current ZX and, to me, the front end looks like a combination of 944 and Camaro. In other words, the hood is flatter (but still with the "power bulge" down the center) and slopes more sharply than the current model. There are pop-up headlights and, like the Pontiac Firebird, the lights are set back from the leading edge. Also like the Firebird, you get a slotted glimpse of the lenses from the front. In the 2+2 there are four rectangular headlights, those inboard being smaller in the manner of the new Mercedes 380SEL. On the 2-seater, from what I could see, there is one pair of round headlights. Unfortunately, the batteries were disconnected (because of fire regulations, we were told) so we weren't able to see exactly how the pop-up mechanism works.

Later, we were shown photos of three different hood scoop treatments and were asked which one we preferred. Two of the three scoops were clearly nonfunctional but they did suggest to me that a turbocharged model was planned for the future. A further hint a turbo was coming was a question as to whether we thought $1200 was a reasonable amount to add for that model.

The wheel wells and fender flares are reminiscent of the current ZX and there is also an inch-wide groove down the side and running the entire length of the car above the fender line. The cowl area appears to be similar to the current ZX, as do the doors, except that the door line doesn't kick up as it nears the B-post. This line is carried to the rear and results in a larger rear quarter window than on the current car. The sides are also much flatter and smoother than on the present ZX and from the rear three-quarter view there's something of the flavor of the Toyota Corolla fastback. The 2+2 is stretched in the middle but from the B-pillar back it looks the same as the 2-seater.

On the 2-seater there were plain-jane steel wheels with rather timid slotted-disc wheel covers while the 2+2 had alloy wheels with Potenza tires. These alloy wheels aren't deep-dish but a disc with holes that give the impression of spokes.

Only from the rear end can you identify the car as a ZX and

this comes mostly from the look of the taillights. These are well integrated into the new design and result in an unmistakable Z-car family resemblance.

The bumpers front and rear are shiny black, as if they were made from the same material as those on the Supra.

My impression of the car from the outside is that the 2+2 looks like a luxury tourer. The overall design is a lot cleaner and different than before but it doesn't have the aggressive look of the original 240Z and doesn't come across like a gutsy sports car the way, for example, I think the sportier of the Supras does.

Interior

INSIDE, THERE is about the same amount of space as in the current ZX. You don't feel as closed in, however, and the field of vision in all directions is very good. The seats are much like the current ones and the steering wheel has a single wide spoke at the bottom with thumb perches at the 10:00 and 2:00 o'clock positions. This wheel was covered by the same plastic material as before and I couldn't help thinking a leather-wrapped wheel would be much more appropriate to the 2+2's luxury-car image. The 2-seater had a less exotic 4-spoke wheel.

On the dash, there are four big air vents, two in the center and two outboard, and in the 2+2 there was dark, plastic-looking fake wood trim along the center console. This area in the 2-seater was unadorned, giving it an almost naked look.

The upscale sound system in the 2+2 had speakers in the lower front corners of the doors and there were large rectangular speakers (approximately 6 x 9 in.) over the spring towers in the rear. One of the questions asked was whether a graphic equalizer would be important.

In the 2+2 there was digital instrumentation with push-button controls in a steering-wheel surround similar to those found on the new Mazda 626 and Isuzu Impulse. In the 2-seater there were analog dials and gauges with tacky-looking Day-Glo orange on the pointers and numbers.

In the rear compartment the spring towers intrude in the same way as in the ZX and there's still the nicely carpeted luggage area. On the right there's a panel concealing the stand-up inflatable spare tire, on the left there's a cubbyhole for the jack and under the carpet a toolbox is recessed into the floor. One change I did note was that where there used to be two hidey holes at the front of the luggage compartment there is now one, full width.

Prices

IT WAS apparent from looking at the two versions that the 2-seater we saw was going to be offered with more modest trim so it could compete in the market place with the likes of the RX-7 and Camaro Z28. Sure enough, on a specifications sheet we were shown the price was given as $12,500. This seems reasonable because the spec sheet on the RX-7 gave its price as $12,250.

For the 2+2 model, which was obviously more expensive throughout, the price given was $18,000.

Finally

THROUGHOUT THE whole process, which took more than two hours, our opinions were sought on a very wide variety of subjects, most of which were flattering in their assumption that we knew what we were talking about. To give you an idea of the thorough nature of the session, we filled out three different questionnaires adding up to what must have been a total of 400 to 500 questions. We were also handed an envelope containing a $20 bill. For which we signed a receipt.

What's my overall opinion of the car? I like the idea of the new, larger, more powerful V-6 engine. Performance per dollar has always been one of the Z-car's most endearing features. Also, the new body gives the Z a completely new look.

I like the new 300-ZX. It's an exciting car to look at, a well integrated and very clean design that's going to take its place among the best looking cars available today.

The Z-car Story Thus Far...

Original 240Z, launched in 1970, had diverse styling influences but solid market concept.

260Z of 1974 had minor displacement increase but no significant changes to appearance.

Next displacement increase, another 200 cc, came in 1975 on 280Z, still with original lines.

All-new body of 280ZX was larger, more angular, but kept distinctive Z-car form and proportions.

Driving Impressions:

I TOO WAS invited to take part in the market research described earlier and, what's more, I had a chance later to drive the new 300-ZX and some of its competitors.

The cars supplied for comparison were two of the new 300-ZXs (a 2-seater and a 2+2 Turbo), a new Corvette, Porsche 944 and Toyota Supra. Curiously enough, a Mazda RX-7, the car I regularly drive, wasn't included. The driving took place in a huge parking lot and we put all five cars through their paces—acceleration, panic stops, over bumps and rough pavement, a wiggle-waggle slalom course and so on. A good, impartial wring-out even though we didn't get to time anything for exact comparisons, or drive them at high speed.

Both the 2-seater ZX and the 2+2 Turbo were impressive. On the slalom-type S-turns where you snake through a row of pylons, the real differences in the handling of the five cars became apparent. The stars were the Vette and 944. But the 2+2 Turbo with its fine suspension package was fast and precise and beautifully maneuverable, even at 55 or so in 2nd. The 2-seater ZX didn't embarrass itself either.

But, compared to the Supra, for instance, it felt much lighter in the rear and less precise about ending up exactly where I aimed it. How does it compare to the RX-7? I wish I knew. I think it was a mistake not to have one there because it's going to be the 2-seater ZX's most nearly direct competitor.

In the acceleration runs, the turbocharged 2+2 ZX seemed very close to the 944 in power and from about 15 mph on up there was no perceptible turbo lag. The non-turbo ZX is no slouch, either. It doesn't perform with the Corvette or 944 but there's no doubt that it'll blow the doors off the cars that are in its price class such as the Mazda RX-7 and Mitsubishi Starion.

Over bumps, the driver of the 2+2 Turbo just cranks up the ride he wants with a shock-control button on the console—soft, medium or hard. (I felt that both medium and hard were still too soft over these particular undulations.) The driver of the 2-seater ZX can make no such adjustment but it still acquitted itself well.

We did two controlled and a number of informal stopping tests. In a full-out panic stop the ZXs' rear brakes tended to lock, making the rear end want to come around. So I'd suggest that some more development

work is needed on the front/rear brake proportioning at this point.

Both ZXs were exceptionally quiet over pavement that varied from slightly to very rough—with the exception of rattles from an add-on ducktail spoiler on the 2+2 Turbo. Which is fixable.

Impressions of the interior? Driving position was good but taller drivers may have a problem with head room. The steering wheel is in the right position, a good size and I like its thumb perches. The shift lever is where it should be (but I did miss 4th gear in a couple of shifts). The 2+2 Turbo dashboard is video arcade time and I enjoyed the g-meter that's mounted in the center of the dash alongside a compass. The 2-seater instrument panel is plain by comparison but certainly adequate. The seats on both versions are good and those on the 2+2 Turbo are elaborately adjustable.

The manufacturer's suggested retail price for the 2-seater ZX will be $12,000 and for the 2+2 Turbo, $17,200 (or $18,000 with T-top). In their two markets, Nissan's 3rd-generation Z-cars look like great competitors to me.

Datsun has done it again.—*Thad Mazakius*

NISSAN 300-ZX

The same—only more so

BY JONATHAN THOMPSON
PHOTOS BY JOHN LAMM

THREE MONTHS AGO we previewed Nissan's all-new 1984 300-ZX in a story by Randolph Beckman. We hadn't seen the car itself but Mr Beckman had participated in a public opinion survey conducted by Nissan in southern California to assess the new ZX's marketability. He was extremely observant and in addition to providing most of the details was able to transmit his visual impressions of its lines through the skills of Mark Stehrenberger, working in "police artist" fashion. Now that we've been to Japan to see and drive the 300-ZX we can report that this preview was essentially accurate (except, perhaps, for the cover painting, which made the car look much leaner than it is).

If you liked the 280ZX, you'll love the 300. As its number suggests, it has a 3.0-liter engine; to make a blanket assessment, we could say that it's a good 10 percent improved in most departments, a bit less so in some. On the other hand, if you were lukewarm about the old ZX the new model is unlikely to turn you around. It's a conservative update, different in every detail but significantly unchanged in character.

The reasons for this are obvious. The 240/260/280Z and 280ZX created and developed the mid-range GT concept into a highly profitable market, retaining sports car behavior but giving more and more emphasis on comfort and luxury. Since 1970 Nissan has sold nearly three-quarters of a million Z and ZX models in the U.S., with annual sales in the 70,000 category (though slipping a bit in 1981–1982). Such cars as the Mazda RX-7 and Toyota Supra, while making technical and performance challenges to the Nissan product, haven't been really close in sales. Nissan management has done what could be reasonably predicted for any successful product line: provide more of the same.

Nissan has kept the size, weight, luxury equipment and basic handling characteristics of the 280ZX while achieving moderate gains in efficiency and refinement; a big improvement in straight-line performance with the V-6 engine, especially in top speed; and an updated appearance, different in contour and detail but retaining the familiar Z-car look. As we neared our magazine deadline, Nissan was still determining the actual mix of 300-ZX models and equipment to be available in the U.S. Because of the import quotas Nissan has decided not to bring in the base 2-seat model, originally targeted at $13,000, understandably preferring to sell more cars in the higher brackets. The GL and GLL models shown to us in Japan have been consolidated under the GS designation, with a base price for the non-turbo 2-seater estimated at $17,000 and a fully optioned 2-seat Turbo at around $21,000. The 2+2 is priced between these two.

Standard on all cars for the U.S., the GS configuration includes air conditioning, electric window lifts, tilt steering wheel, 8-way manually adjustable seats, AM/FM stereo/cassette audio system, cruise control and alloy wheels. Body styles available are the 2-seater, with normally aspirated or turbo engine; and the 2+2, available only with the normally aspirated unit; while either engine can be mated with a 5-speed manual gearbox or 3-speed-plus-overdrive automatic. For the first three months of production (approximately 15,000 units) no T-bar roofs will be made; after that, *all* ZXs will have the T roof, shown in our exclusive cover photo, as standard equipment (collectors take note). The only equipment option is the interior package comprising leather upholstery, digital instrumentation, electric seat control, compass, accelerometer, trip computer (miles-to-empty, instant mpg and average mpg), special audio system, automatic temperature control, rear cargo compartment cover, driver's vanity mirror, woodgrain accent panels and bronze-tinted window glass; exterior features include accent striping and an electronically defogging mirror. The 3-way adjustable shock absorbers come only with the turbo engine.

The biggest change for the 300-ZX is, of course, the V-6 engine (discussed in detail along with the other chassis features in the accompanying engineering analysis by Paul Van Valken-

burgh); this produces significantly more power than the inline 2.8-liter six: 160 bhp in normally aspirated form and a fat 200 with the turbocharger. The acceleration is noticeably improved but the real difference is at the top end; after building up to it we were able to do a full lap of Nissan's 6.5-km (4-mile) Tochigi test track at a steady 135 mph in a Turbo 2-seater. We'll have to wait for a representative road test car before recording hard numbers but there's no doubt that this is a faster machine. Comparing several 300-ZXs (2-seater and 2+2 bodies, turbo and non-turbo) at the track, switching back and forth with examples of the 280ZX provided for comparison, we found the new car offered better ride and handling characteristics. The inner roads of the Tochigi proving ground included extremely twisty sections and a series of abruptly changing road surfaces, such as Belgian paving stones, potholes and freeway strips. These are no doubt important in durability testing but they didn't give us the chance to judge the effectiveness of the adjustable shock absorbers in fast road driving, where undulating surfaces and off-cam-

Pent-roof combustion chamber, with plug at top and valves inclined at 50 degrees to promote swirl, increases burning speed.

NISSAN 300-ZX PRELIMINARY U.S. SPECIFICATIONS

GENERAL

	2-seat Turbo 5-sp	2+2 Auto
Curb weight, lb	3015	3030
Wheelbase, in.	91.3	99.2
Track, front/rear	55.7/56.5	
Length	170.7	178.5
Width	66.5	
Height	51.0	51.6
Fuel capacity, U.S. gal.	19.0	

ENGINE

Type	60-deg sohc V-6
Bore x stroke, mm	87.0 x 83.0
Displacement, cc	2960
Compression ratio	7.8:1 ... 9.2:1
Bhp @ rpm, SAE net	200 ... 160 @ 5200
Torque @ rpm, lb-ft	227 ... 173 @ 3600
Fuel injection	Bosch L-Jetronic

DRIVETRAIN

Transmission	5-sp M	3-sp A+OD
Gear ratios, overall: 5th	2.76:1	
4th	3.54:1	2.55:1
3rd	4.88:1	3.70:1
2nd	7.29:1	5.40:1
1st	11.86:1	9.10:1
Final drive ratio	3.54:1	3.70:1

CHASSIS & BODY

Layout	front engine/rear drive
Brake system	10.8-in. (275-mm) vented discs front, 11.4-in. (290-mm) discs rear; vacuum assisted
Wheels	cast alloy, 15 x 6½ JJ
Tires	P215/60R-15
Steering type	rack & pinion, power assisted
Turns, lock-to-lock	3.6
Suspension, front/rear:	MacPherson struts, lower lateral arms, compliance struts, coil springs, tube shocks, anti-roll bar/semi-trailing arms, coil springs, tube shocks, anti-roll bar

ber turns would provide a truer test. The Tochigi surfaces were either too smooth (banked test track) or too harsh (the infield parts) to appreciate the differences in settings subjectively, other than to note that the 300-ZX seemed better at any setting than the 280ZX.

While Werner Bührer's styling analysis provides a detailed look at the exterior solutions (and can be compared with what he did on the 240Z back in April 1970), the philosophy of Nissan's styling department needs to be mentioned. Given the task of creating an all-new body while retaining the 280ZX concept, the General Manager of Studio No. 2, Isao Sano, was successful in keeping the familiar proportions (so successful that when seen alone from certain angles, especially three-quarter rear, the 300-ZX does not seem much different) while revising every inch of the surface. The new car is more contemporary in appearance (maybe early-Eighties but certainly not mid-Eighties) and has a crisper, more aggressive front end, but it still has the heavy flanks that characterized the older ZX and detract from an effi-cient, really sporting image. But the 300-ZX looks substantial and luxurious and that's what counts.

Summing up this 3rd-generation Z-car, the simplest phrase might be: The same—only more so. It's improved overall and in every detail, but it's unlikely to send any competing designers back to their drawing boards. The 1st-generation Z lasted 8½ years (1970–1978), the 2nd-generation ZX only five, and we wonder how long this conservatively updated 3rd-generation ZX car will last in an ever more competitive market. Its excellent V-6 engine is certainly a strong point, but the car's structure and styling are not up to the state of the art. When we learned that the competitively priced 2-seat SF version wasn't going to be brought into the U.S. we were concerned about what Nissan would do to attract less affluent, younger buyers to its GT line in the future (especially if the quotas are removed), but there is a new version of the 200SX—closer to the ZX in character than the SX is currently—reported to be in the works, and it may serve that purpose. ⌾

ENGINEERING ANALYSIS

THE MOST CURIOUS feature about the new 300-ZX is the similarity to its predecessor. Considering the fact that every panel and almost every component in the car is totally redesigned, it is amazing that all basic dimensions remain essentially identical. The wheelbase is exactly the same as last year on both the 2-seat and 2+2 models. The overall height is exactly the same, as is the width of the body. Spec sheets indicate the new body to be almost 2.5 in. wider, but the engineers insist that is solely a result of trim and rub strip additions. This was a significant point to them, because it supports their contention that there was no drag-inducing increase in frontal area. The front track was increased by 0.8 in. to 55.7 and the rear by 0.8 in. to 56.5. That and the use of wider wheels move the tires out closer to the wheel well openings for slightly better airflow along the sides.

The installation of an all-new V-6 engine did have some effect on dimensions, as 2.3 in. was removed from the nose. The engine room opening is almost 8.0 in. shorter because of the shortening from inline to V-6 configuration. Just for balance and good measure, exactly an inch was taken off the tail also. The reduction overall is 3.3 in ; other than the fact that the base of the windshield is about 5.0 in. farther forward, the silhouettes are much the same.

Weight is also surprisingly similar. Nissan engineers shuffled and redesigned everything, and ended up less than 1 percent from where they started—and not on the lighter side either. Nissan lists the weight distribution as 51 per-cent on the front wheels of every car listed, regardless of seats, options or engine. On the surface it seems like a lot of change for the sake of change. But to bring the mechanicals up to date, practically every bracket and seam in the body had to be changed anyhow.

The all-new V-6 engine is largely a response to the American performance market, where the old inline-6 is being seen more and more as an antique. But the cost of developing a new engine is so great that it must be used in a wide variety of models. So the V-6 was designed from the start to be produced in both 3.0-liter and 2.0-liter versions, although only the larger engine will be seen in America. This is an unusually wide range for one common design, especially at introduction. The indication is that Nissan has really reached some extremes in the dichotomy between durability and power-to-weight ratio. As a 2.0-liter engine it must be incredibly strong, if perhaps heavier than it need be, while as a 3.0-liter it must be stressed fairly close to its limit. With this in mind, I asked what the ultimate eventual displacement limit might be. The engineers' response was that they never intend to enlarge it past 3.0 liters, which is easy to believe, based on the interior layout.

With the 60-degree vee design, there are inherent limitations to the bore and stroke at the point where the pistons meet (or nearly so) between the banks at the bottom of their travel. In other words, if you want to increase the bore, you have to increase the rod length (and deck height) to keep the pistons from interfering with each other. In fact, that is exactly what Nissan does to get the larger displacement as it is. Of course, there are other casting core differences between the two engines, which mean that a 2.0-liter block could never be opened up to 3.0 liters, in spite of identical bore spacing. Because of similar cyl-inder wall thicknesses on both engines, boring out the smaller engine would cut right through into the water jackets. Because of the differences in stroke, there are also changes in the main bearing webs. This "ultimate original displacement" is a somewhat new philosophy in engine engineering. When management walks in next year and says, "We need more power," the engineers are not going to have the convenient alternative of boring and stroking.

One of the major advantages of a V-6 compared with an inline-6 is stiffness per pound. The shorter the engine, the less torque-twisting you get, in both the crank and the block itself. In using computerized "finite element analysis" of the block structure, it was possible to minimize excess material. As it turned out, the final stiffness appeared a little marginal, especially in the turbo version, so a special "cradle frame" main bearing casting is used. This means that all four main bearing caps are cast as a unit, with a bridge, or truss, connecting them. Altogether, engine weight was reduced by 15 percent, or about 90 lb. Another advantage is package dimensions. Not only is it shorter than the old engine, it is lower and actually no wider when you consider accessories.

The crankshaft has such improved stiffness that instead of being forged, as in other high performance engines, it is a ductile iron casting. Still, there should be no question of its durability in normal use, as it is machined using the current technology of "fillet rolling." In other words, in the critical stress area of bearing journal fillets, the last machining operation is a very high-pressure rolling or squeezing of the material into shape, as opposed to cutting. A forged crank should be available within the next year, however, perhaps as racers or management decide they need more power or rpm.

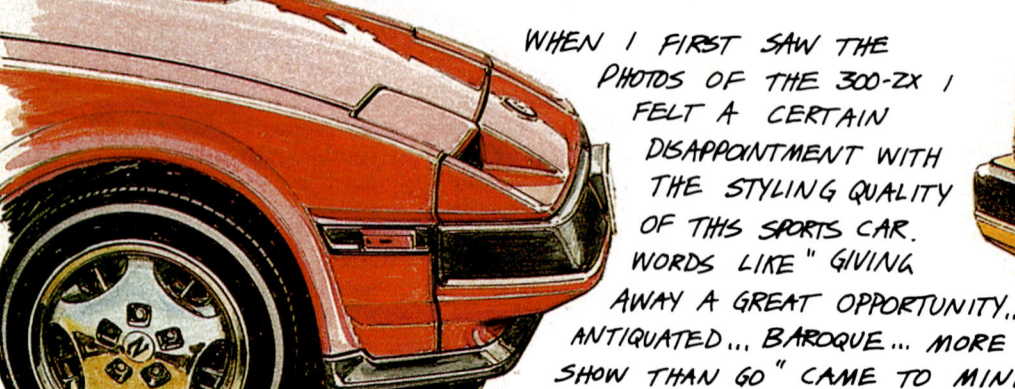

WHEN I FIRST SAW THE PHOTOS OF THE 300-ZX I FELT A CERTAIN DISAPPOINTMENT WITH THE STYLING QUALITY OF THIS SPORTS CAR. WORDS LIKE " GIVING AWAY A GREAT OPPORTUNITY... ANTIQUATED... BAROQUE ... MORE SHOW THAN GO " CAME TO MIND.

300-ZX

IT SEEMS OBVIOUS THAT THE 300-ZX WAS CAREFULLY RESTYLED UPON THE SUCCESSFUL FORMULA OF ITS PREDECESSORS, THE 240Z THROUGH 280ZX (1970-1983), ESPECIALLY IN THE U.S. MARKET. THE OLDER CARS WERE ALSO SOMEWHAT DATED AT THE TIME OF THEIR DEBUTS, LACKING THE IMPACT OF SUCH CARS AS THE PORSCHE, FERRARI AND LOTUS.

BUT THEY MET THE NEED FOR A CERTAIN MARKETABLE EXOTIC TOUCH; FROM THAT POINT OF VIEW THE NISSAN STYLISTS HAVE LEARNED THEIR LESSON WELL.

CRITIQUE: THE FRONT END LOOKS GOOD, BUT NOT THE GREENHOUSE (ROOF AND WINDOWS). THERE'S NO "LINE" HOLDING THE VARIOUS ELEMENTS TOGETHER; TOO MANY DEPRESSIONS AND DECO-LINES ALONG THE SIDE. THE TAIL DESIGN IS MUCH TOO HEAVY.

W. BÜHRER '83

The cylinder heads are not too unconventional for a single-overhead-camshaft cross-flow design. The new pent-roof combustion chamber has a 50-degree angle between the valves, with the sparkplug located very close to the center and favored toward the inlet. The valves may turn out to be the limiting factor in this engine, more so even than the fixed displacement. Although the bore is slightly greater in the new engine, the intake valves are actually smaller, from 44.0 to 42.0 mm, while the exhaust valves are the same at 38.0 mm. The design engineer, Kenichi Sasaki, claims that this is not a problem in ordinary use, because smoother flowing inlet ports with an off-center "swirl" path more than made up the difference. Regardless, valves are so close to each other (actually overlapping in profile) that they will never be made much larger—in this casting at least.

Valve actuation is by a cog belt to the cams, aluminum rockers and hydraulic tappets. Obviously the system was designed primarily for low maintenance and quiet operation, although it is only a few pieces removed from being a very competitive engine. Nominal redline is set at 6300 rpm, with hydraulic tappet valve float to be feared at over 6600. (There is a fuel control rev limiter to help avoid this problem.) Mechanical lifters and a different cam may be made available, though "not soon." The rocker arms are lightweight aluminum forgings with steel rubbing inserts pressed into each end.

The induction system is very similar in operation to last year's 280ZX Nissan/Bosch injector, with timed port injection aimed directly toward the intake valves. However, there is naturally a large difference in plumbing. The new V-6 intake plenum is a clever design, which provides some interesting ram, or tuning, pulses. With a firing order of 1, 2, 3, 4, 5, 6, the intake valves open in sequence left-right-left-right from front to rear of the manifold. The plenum is divided down the center, with intake from the throttle butterfly at the extreme rear. So as the incoming flow alternates from left to right, it creates a series of ram pulses, with a ram tube length greater than could be obtained with a more vertical layout. Of course, the effect will vary with rpm, but a gain of 5 percent is claimed across a wide rpm band.

Fuel control electronics are also similar this year, with one significant improvement. Instead of the old trapdoor vane airflow meter, Nissan will use a hot-wire anemometer flow sensor, as has already been developed for some European Bosch-charged systems. This should give a small reduction in inlet flow blockage, as well as improved response time in the control system.

The turbo version of this engine is modified in roughly the same manner as the inline-6 was. The compression ratio is lowered from 9.0 to 7.8:1 by dishing out the pistons. Externally, the only changes from the base engine are a safety blowoff valve threaded into the manifold plenum, and the installation of a piezoelectric knock sensor. The rest of the add-on turbo plumbing is similar to last year, with a Garrett AiResearch T-5 turbo, which is wategate-limited at 7.0 psi boost. With the new engine the boost starts coming in at a low 1800 rpm and hits its maximum at about 2900 rpm.

The entire driveline is also the same as in the 280—the two 5-speed manual gearboxes (Nissan's own with the normally aspirated engine, the Borg-Warner with the turbo) and the 3-speed-plus-overdrive automatic. The one change is the addition of computer control for the overdrive on the automatic with the non-turbo engine. This was accomplished by placing a 0.69:1 planetary gearset and clutch pack between the old gear case and the converter housing. The computer control, with four sets of logic to control upshift and downshift in economy mode or performance mode, is not a new concept, although it is perhaps a little more refined here. A manual override switch next to the shifter returns control to the driver if so desired.

Just as in the body, every component in the suspension was changed front and rear, with only the most minor effect on geometry. At the front the caster was increased from 5 to 7 degrees, and both the trail and scrub radii were decreased. At the same time the steering geometry was redesigned to reduce bump steer by about 75 percent. Altogether, these changes do produce a noticeable improvement in steering effort and feedback. Anti-dive is also increased, but going from 23 to 25 percent is hardly noticeable.

The new rear trailing arms look essentially the same, except for separation of the formerly concentric coil/shock units. The most significant changes are an increase in the distance between mounting points of both the trailing arms and their crossmember, and an increase in the stiffness of all the rubber bushings. This reduces the problem of trailing-throttle oversteer by minimizing unwanted toe-change deflections. Anti-squat was also increased insignificantly from 65 to 68 percent. Cockpit-adjustable shock absorbers and stiffer anti-roll bars will be available, although those demonstrated at the press preview had a negligible effect on ride or handling, without any undulating roads on which to try them.

Wheels, tires, axles, hubs and brakes are all larger—on just the turbo model. The hubs are peculiar in that both a 4-bolt and a 5-bolt pattern are offered. Ap-

parently turbo power demanded the change, but it was considered too expensive for the base model. The largest alloy wheels will be 15 x 6½ in. While the base package has P195/70R-14 Bridgestone Potenzas on 14 x 5½ steel rims, all other cars get either Potenza or Goodyear Eagle GT P215/60R-15s. In a skid-pad test, the Goodyears out-pulled the Potenzas by 0.777g to 0.710, and the 300-ZX just barely edged out last year's 280ZX on P205/70R-14 Eagles, which achieved 0.762g. Transient response is considerably improved in the new car, however, as noted in both plots of response time and yaw overshoot, and the subjective feel in step-steers and high-g drop-throttle maneuvers.

Aerodynamic drag has been reduced on the new 300-ZX, though perhaps not as much as we would be led to believe. The reported drag coefficient is now 0.30 (0.31 without the optional spoilers). Two reasons why this is suspect are the obvious similarities to last year's body, which has a reported C_x of 0.385, and the inadequate explanation as to how this feat was achieved. The only observable aerodynamic improvements include: semi-concealed headlights, semi-concealed wipers, semi-flush windshield and backlight glass, faired-in mirrors, and an increase in the windshield rake angle from 29.5 to 31 degrees. On the negative side is a blunter nose, which is shorter but has the same MacPherson strut tower height. Regardless, the turbo version would still pull an easy rpm-limited 135 mph on Nissan's 4-mile oval.

Inside the cockpit, there are some notable changes in instrumentation. The base model has a beautifully conventional and functional dial-face speedometer and tachometer, while the luxury package comes with a truly fantastic electronic digital and graphic display. There are digital and bar graph readouts for speedometer, tachometer and fuel gauge, plus bar graph displays for coolant temperature, oil pressure and voltage. In addition there is an electronic compass and a digital accelerometer—the latter is essentially useless as it has a mere 0.5g limit and only 0.1g precision. The whole thing is just the latest example of this faddish preoccupation by carmakers.

In sum, what we have here is an all-new engine in an already popular car, with a chassis that is slightly more competitive than formerly in comparison with its market rivals. To their credit, Nissan engineers have responded to complaints by making detail refinements in every area—although not to the degree that might be possible given state-of-the-art technology. But for all practical purposes (and for the dollar) the car is good enough as it sits—for today at least.

—Paul Van Valkenburgh

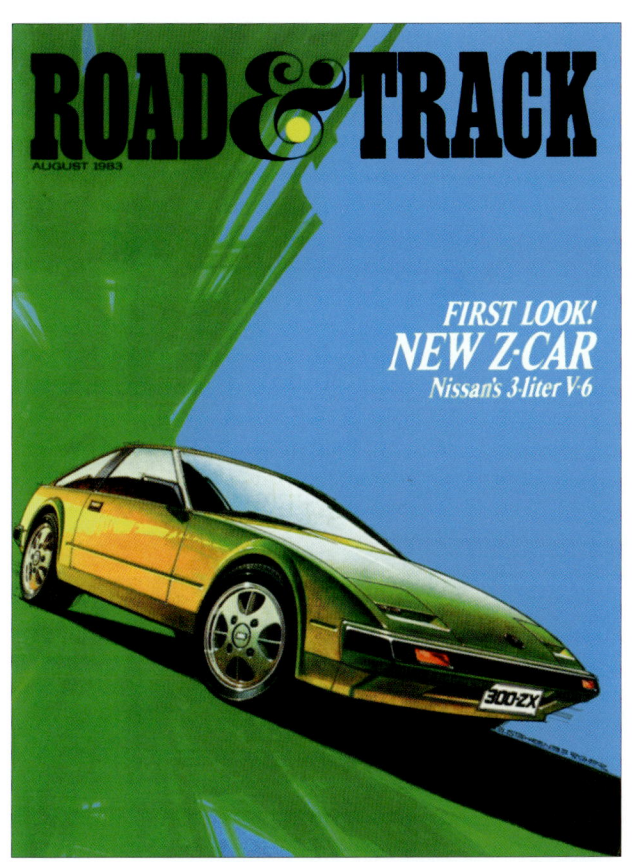

Road & Track cover August 1983

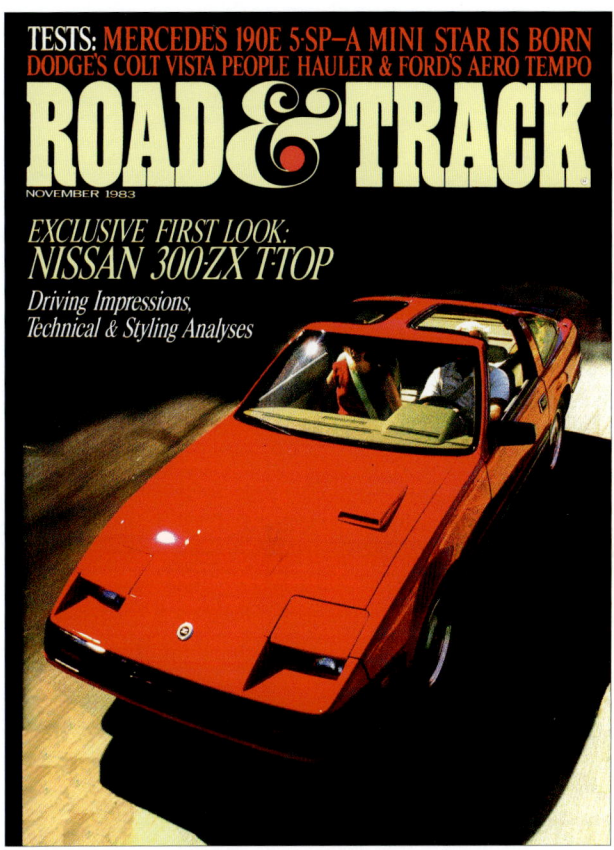

Road & Track cover November 1983

...The Z car has clung tenaciously to its own look in the face of changing trends.

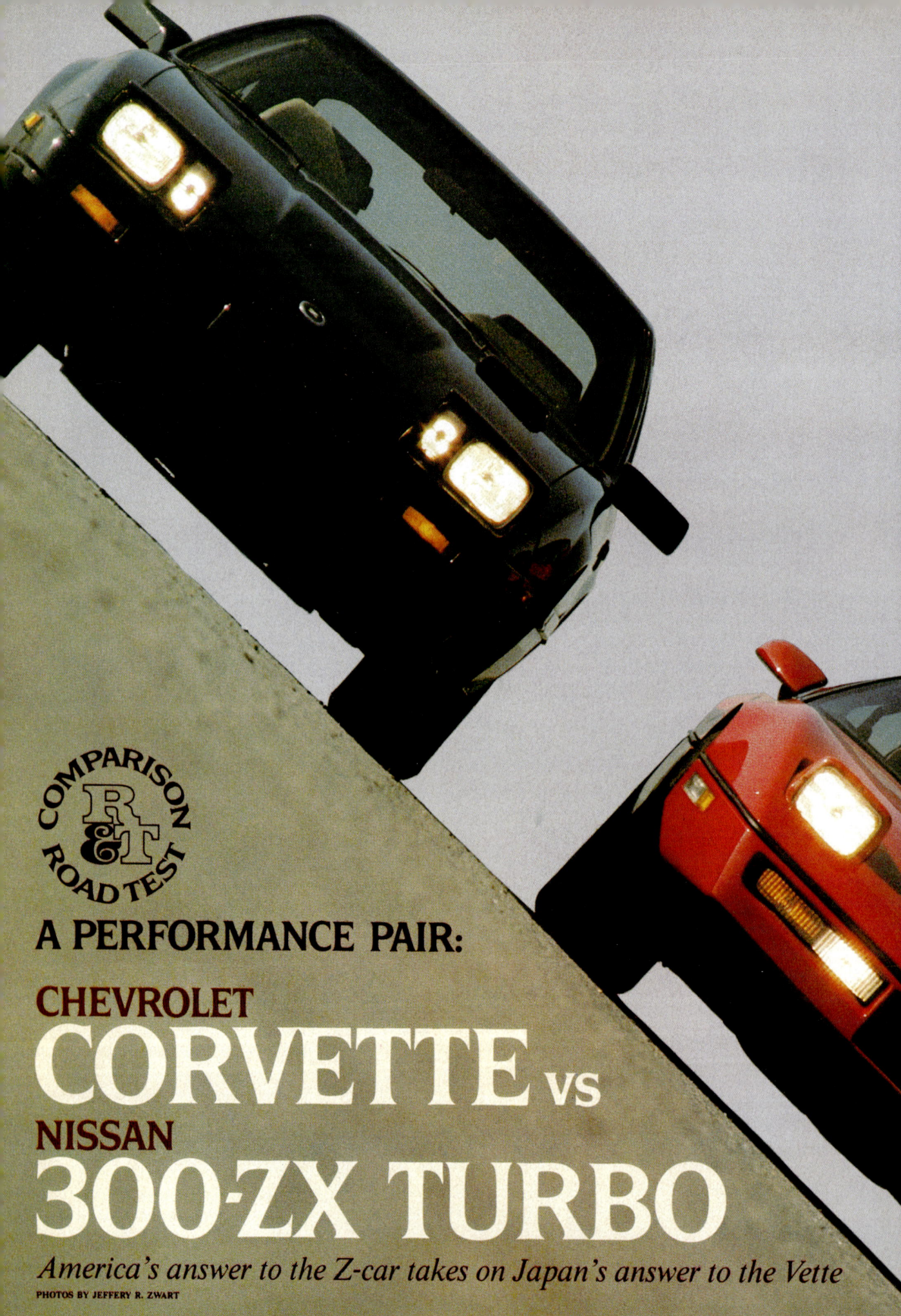

R&T

A PERFORMANCE PAIR:

CHEVROLET

CORVETTE VS

NISSAN

300-ZX TURBO

America's answer to the Z-car takes on Japan's answer to the Vette

PHOTOS BY JEFFERY R. ZWART

COMPARISON TESTS AT *Road & Track* arise in several ways. Sometimes it begins with soul searching to select the most suitable cars in a particular class. Other times, there's a benchmark car used to assess the strengths and weaknesses of a new competitor. Now and again, though, we're completely impulsive: "Hey, have you driven that new Glitzflib? Wow, does it ever knock the Smedley out of the water." Or, perhaps more thoughtfully, "You know, I'm struck by how similar those two are."

This comparison test falls into the last category. It just so happened that Chevrolet's 4+3 Overdrive Corvette and Nissan's 300-ZX Turbo arrived at our offices simultaneously. We drove them on the street, filled their notebooks, gathered our track data and, as we did, the collective impulse arose. Both cars are resplendent with features—and, at another level entirely, gimmicks; both are very quick in today's spectrum; both are recent updates of extremely successful predecessors; their dimensions, weights and overall feel are roughly comparable; and each had us asking, "How do you think this one compares with the other?"

"Set up a route and let's find out." The accompanying tables let you get up to speed on this, and the following comments give you a head start.

Though we've seen the 300-ZX in a couple of settings already (on the sly in August 1983; in Japan by November), this was our first opportunity to live with one for awhile on home ground. We chose the Turbo for said opportunity, which also implied at this point the 3-speed+ OD automatic. "Mixing apples and oranges?" you may say, what with the Vette's manual gearbox. Not really, and we refer you to the accompanying article on the Vette's 4+3 to learn just how smart a manual gearbox can be.

Ah, you're back. Let's continue our analysis of the two. Our Corvette had several elements not available at the time of our August 1983 "Four High Performance Cars" test; specifically, the aforementioned 4+3 Overdrive and a full-house Z51 suspension. The Z51 was of interest as our first experience with a production set of the Bilstein gas-over shocks, as fitted to our prototype Corvette test car (March 1983).

Each of our test cars was loaded with features such as cruise control, air conditioning, electric window lifts, AM/FM stereo/cassette, adjustable steering wheel (the ZX's, for rake; the Vette's, rake and reach), electrically adjustable mirrors (the Vette's are heated as well) and multi-multi-adjustable seats (the ZX's, manually; the Vette's driver seat, electrically but for seatback rake). As you can imagine, neither car lacked for creature comforts, with the Vette perhaps getting the apparent nod on paper, but the ZX more than holding its own in actual fact.

A Corvette has been traditionally upmarket of a Z-car in price, and this is still very much the case, especially when one starts fooling with the options list. Our 300-ZX Turbo's base price is $18,699 and, indeed, she goes for this as-tested, what

with all the items cited being standard equipment. By contrast, the Corvette's base of $23,360 rises to $26,210 as-tested, once one opts for the trick Delco-GM/Bose sound system ($895), transparent roof panel ($595), leather-faced seats ($400), electrical adjustment for the driver's seat ($210) and so on, down the list. Its suspension options deserve amplification as well: The Goodyear Eagle VR50 tires on their directionally finned wheels used to be a $561 option, but these are now standard on all Corvettes. Also, at prototype time, the Z51 suspension was slated to have the Bilsteins; early production Z51s didn't because the supply pipeline hadn't been established; and, at any rate, the latest plan is to separate the two: The Z51's stiffer springs and bars go for $51; the Bilsteins, an added $189. Did you follow all that?

Continuing this trend of the Corvette having more of things, including dollars invested, we can observe it has two more cylinders, three more forward speeds, 4.9 in. more wheelbase, 5.8 in. more overall length, 3.1 in. more width, 160 lb more curb weight and 2773 cc more displacement. This is getting silly. Invoke a 1.5 turbo equivalence and the displacement difference shrinks to 1293 cc; but, more to the point, the Corvette's 5.7-liter ohv V-8 produces 205 bhp and 290 lb-ft of torque whereas the 300-ZX's 3.0-liter turbocharged sohc V-6 is rated at 200 bhp and 227 lb-ft. Neither, we shall see, is lacking in oomph.

To confirm this and other relevant truths, four staff members took the cars on a 4-legged loop that gave each of us a bit of freeway, a fair number of desert whoop-de-dos—our Colorado Desert (strangely enough, located in California) is rarely flat, you realize—and also an extremely useful subloop that allowed each driver a direct back-to-back evaluation on precisely the same roads. Other elements of the drive included more than a little hillclimbing and some rather ordinary traffic-limited stuff. It was a Friday afternoon by then; everyone, including us, simply wanted to get home. Our Engineering Editor even passed up a used book store he'd never visited.

Along the way, we did an evaluation of 20 items, everything from engine to interior styling, luggage space and loading to quietness. As is our custom, we rated each of these on a scale of 1 (the pits) to 10 (the winner's circle). Also, after the trip each of us chose a personal favorite in two ways, price-dependent and in the Rich-Uncle mode. An accompanying table collects these subjective data; other tables compare objective matters of general information and performance.

More Power to Us All

THERE'S NO substitute for cubic inches, unless perhaps it's a turbo. "A great rumbling V-8 with gobs of torque," noted one driver. Need you ask which engine he was referring to? We all agreed that the Vette engine's only shortcoming was its relative unhappiness above 4000 rpm. Yet, as another driver noted, "With so much torque, who needs revs?" But we also lauded the excellent driveability, smooth power and exemplary mid-range punch of the 300-ZX. As one driver concluded, "I admire each of these powerplants, but for entirely different reasons."

Discussions of the transmissions generated similar views. We were (almost) unanimous in our appreciation of the Vette's 4+3. Indeed, even the single dissident didn't mind the gearbox—it was the linkage to which he objected. "So stiff and unwieldy," he said, "that it's a blessing some of the shifts are automatic." Others among us recalled how really horrid the typical muscle car shifter used to be, and gave the Vette a pat on the lever for improvement. In general, the more each of us drove the 4+3, the better we liked it. "This is utterly in keeping with the car's character," observed one driver, "because you can hulk that big gearbox around if you like, or just get by on torque if that's your wont."

In a similar vein, the ZX's 3-speed automatic+ OD was also in keeping with its character: smooth, unobtrusive, yet capable. Left in Drive, it shifts rather early, so several of us churned this gearbox around almost as much as we did the Vette's in spirited driving. We liked the OD lockout and, in fact, one driver observed, "This is what the Vette's automatic needs, so it won't hunt around at highway speeds." And with OD engaged, there is a striking similarity between the ZX's kickdown from OD to 3rd and the Vette's 4th OD to 4th direct. Either is admirably suited to highway passing conditions or simply to tug you reassuringly into that seat.

And either powertrain is admirably suited for giving you a quick run through the gears, though our instrumentation recognized that the Vette was just a tad quicker. It beat the ZX off the line, got to 60 in 7.1 seconds versus the ZX's 7.4, reached the quarter mile in 15.6 sec traveling 88.5 mph vs the ZX's 15.7 at 86.0 and continued to pull away, right up to its 136-mph top speed vs the ZX's 133. We'll make three observations about these figures: First, this particular 4+3 Vette is a bit slower than the previous automatic Vettes we've tested; second, the new ZX Turbo is uniformly quicker than the turbo Z-car it replaces; and, last, you'd have to be greedy indeed to want more straight-line performance than offered by either of these cars.

Getting a Grip on the Situation

Two vivid recollections sum up the differences of ride and handling with this pair. One is playing boy racer with the Vette, reaching absolutely astonishing limits of grip while it jiggles you to death on any but mirror-smooth roads. The other is playing suspension engineer with the ZX, as you fool with its cockpit-adjustable shock absorbers.

To take each in turn, the Vette's extremely firm suspension and super-wide tires make it benign almost to the point of dullness, provided the road surface is a good one. The car responds admirably to its steering, once you're accustomed to its quickness, but those desiring throttle control of attitude will be disappointed. "You steer this car to its limits," noted one driver "you don't try to horse it around with the throttle." And these limits are high: We recorded a lateral acceleration of 0.880g around our skidpad and a slalom speed of 63.2 mph, the latter especially impressive when you consider the thought of weaving a 71.0-in. wide car through seven 100-ft gates.

Impressive grip on smooth surfaces, however, degrades into a darty feel as the road surface worsens. "This suspension doesn't just talk to me," said one staff member, "It yells." "It doesn't just yell," noted another, "it beats me about the head and shoulders." And this extremely poor ride ultimately affects the Vette's handling, steering feel, body structure quietness and—we can't help conjecturing—long-range durability. There's a distinct feeling that the entire car is destined to

CALCULATED DATA	Chevrolet Corvette	Nissan 300-ZX Turbo
Lb/bhp (test weight)	16.7	16.0
Mph/1000 rpm (top gear)	36.7	26.1
Engine revs/mi (60 mph)	1650	2300
Piston travel, ft/mi	960	1250
R&T steering index	0.80	1.16
Brake swept area, sq in./ton	193	239

become one giant rattle in time.

This characteristic was confirmed another way in our sound measurements. For example, our readings with the Corvette at maximum 1st gear, constant 50 and constant 70 mph were 80, 73 and 77 dBA, respectively. These compare with the rather more plush ZX's 73, 68 and 73, implying, among other things, that the ZX is no louder at 6000 rpm in 1st or at 70 mph than the Vette is at 50. A boisterous V-8 conspired in this, although the Vette's stiff suspension and the resulting road noise were definitely part of the conspiracy as well.

Indeed, based on more than noise level, we concluded that the ZX exhibits a much better compromise of ride and handling. And you've got three such compromises at the flip of a console-mounted switch. Since prototype intro time, Nissan engineers have wisely broadened the spectrum of the ZX's adjustable shock control. Changes from soft to normal to firm now bring about distinctly different rides for different road conditions. For instance, we could trick ourselves into thinking that the soft setting miraculously erased freeway ripples. The firm setting, though a bit on the jiggly side, was still more comfortable than anything we experienced in the Vette. And, in general, subtle updates of the ZX's MacPherson-strut front/semi-trailing-arm rear suspension have lessened its tendency toward ultimate twitchiness. The car is still answerable to throttle, but now it's a virtue rather than a vice.

These subjective impressions were reinforced by our quantitative testing as well. The 300-ZX rounded our skidpad at 0.795g, up from 0.754g for the previous model. What's more, we recorded a slalom speed of 62.8 mph with the car on its firm shock setting, an impressive 4.2 mph quicker than the previous ZX's twitchy tour around the cones. Even on its soft setting, exhibiting a bit of the earlier car's nervousness, the new one could still maintain 60.3 mph.

These figures, you'll note, are inferior to the Corvette's. And, in fact, the smoother the road, the easier it was for our Vette pilot

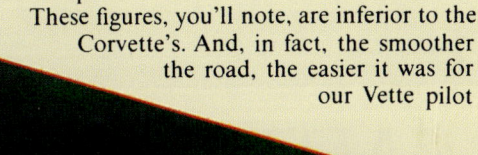

GENERAL DATA	Chevrolet Corvette	Nissan 300-ZX Turbo
Base price	$23,360	$18,699
Price as tested[1]	$26,210	$18,699
Layout	front engine/rwd	front engine/rwd
Engine type	ohv V-8	turbo sohc V-6
Bore x stroke, mm	101.6 x 88.4	87.0 x 83.0
Displacement, cc	5733	2960
Compression ratio	9.0:1	7.8:1
Bhp @ rpm, SAE net	205 @ 4300	200 @ 5200
Torque @ rpm, lb-ft	290 @ 2800	227 @ 3600
Fuel injection	GM Throttle Body	Bosch L-Jetronic
Transmission	4-sp manual + 3-sp overdrive	3-sp automatic + overdrive
Gear ratios, :1	2.88	2.46
	1.91 (1.28)[2]	1.46
	1.33 (0.89)	1.00
	1.00 (0.67)	0.69
Final drive ratio, :1	3.07	3.70
Steering type	rack & pinion, power assisted	rack & pinion, power assisted
Brake system, f/r	11.5-in. vented discs, f & r	10.8-in. vented discs/ 11.4-in. discs
Wheels	cast alloy, 16 x 8½ f, 16 x 9½ r	cast alloy, 15 x 6½JJ
Tires	Goodyear Eagle VR50, P255/50VR-16	Goodyear Eagle GT, P215/60R-15
Suspension, f/r	unequal-length A-arms, transverse fiberglass leaf spring, tube shocks, anti-roll bar/ upper & lower trailing arms, tie rods, halfshafts, transverse fiberglass leaf spring, tube shocks, anti-roll bar	MacPherson struts, lower lateral arms, compliance struts, coil springs, tube shocks, anti-roll bar/ semi-trailing arms, coil springs, tube shocks, anti-roll bar

[1]Price as tested includes: For the Chevrolet Corvette, std equip (air conditioning, elect. window lifts, elect. adj mirrors, sport wheels & Eagle VR50 tires, adj steering wheel), Delco-GM/Bose AM/FM stereo/cassette ($895), transparent removable roof panel ($595), leather seating ($400), elect. adj driver seat ($210), Bilstein shocks ($189), cruise control ($185), central locking ($165), rear-window & mirror heat ($160), Z51 sus ($51); for the Nissan 300-ZX Turbo, std equip (air conditioning, elect. window lifts, elect. adj mirrors, AM/FM stereo/cassette, cruise control, remote-adj shocks, central locking).

[2]For the Chevrolet Corvette, gear ratios are direct (overdrive).

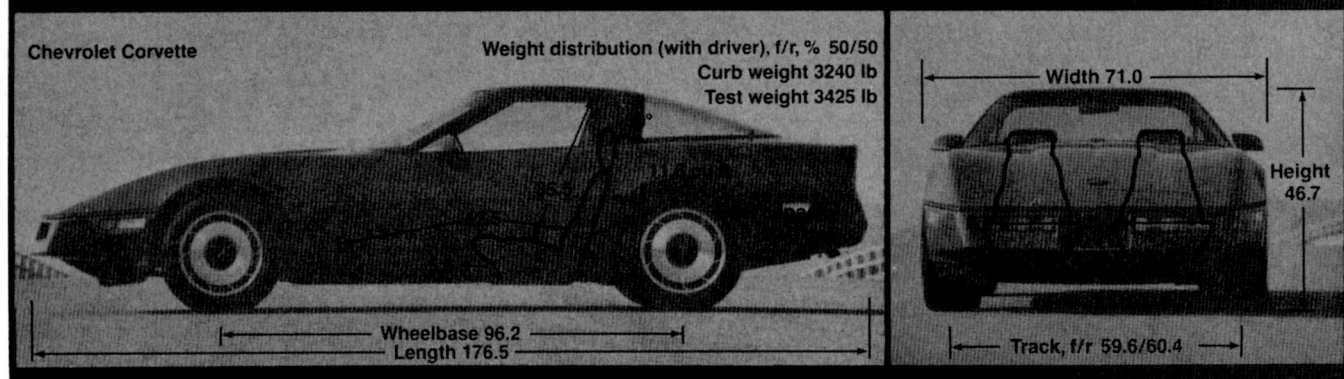

Chevrolet Corvette

Weight distribution (with driver), f/r, % 50/50
Curb weight 3240 lb
Test weight 3425 lb

Width 71.0

Height 46.7

Wheelbase 96.2
Length 176.5

Track, f/r 59.6/60.4

of the hour to pull away from the ZX. On questionable surfaces, though, he bounced around while doing so, got less artful in his line and probably didn't enjoy himself very much. Though distinctly different in their behavior, these two cars aren't that far apart in usable grip and realizable manueverability when mixing it up in a less than perfectly paved world.

Braking behavior of both cars bordered on the phenomenal, though again, with meaningful contrast. In our panic stop evaluations, the Vette posted distances of 144 and 250 ft from 60 and 80 mph, respectively. The ZX bettered these, though insignificantly, with 141 and 249 ft. Both cars had exemplary fore/aft balance; nor did either display any fade to speak of in our 6-stops-from-60 routine. The differences came in how these two responded to heavy braking. The Corvette's firm suspension exhibited next to no brake dive; its pedal felt somewhat on the hard side and not especially amenable to modulation. By con-

trast, the ZX was softer overall; in pedal feel, in longitudinal pitch and even laterally. Its brake pedal had a spongy, longish travel that nonetheless proved extremely easy to modulate. Even with the firm shock setting, though, you'd think twice about heavy braking in a corner, for example.

Now Relax and Drive

YOU SIT low in a Corvette and, for that matter, in a ZX as well. Neither offers the unobstructed outward vision of an especially tall greenhouse; nor is either claustrophobic in any sense. Both cars feel bulky, however, no doubt because of their low seating and commensurately high cockpit sides.

In one sense, we've gotten used to the Corvette's vast array of digital and digital/analog hybrid graphics. Everyone appreciated the wealth of information that can be gleaned from the 3-mode display of coolant temperature/voltmeter, oil temperature/pres-

A GEARBOX SMARTER THAN YOUR AVERAGE DRIVER

WE WERE TANTALIZED by the Corvette's 4+3 Overdrive gearbox at the press introduction, and now we've had opportunity to put quite a few miles on a production Vette equipped with this innovative hardware.

As you may recall, it's a 4-speed manual gearbox combined with a Doug Nash-designed planetary gearset that applies a computer-controlled OD ratio of 0.67:1 to 2nd, 3rd and 4th cogs. Also, there has been a significant modification since the prototype intro; to wit, an OD lockout switch originally scheduled for Europe only has become a part of our setup as well.

How well does it work? To help you form an opinion, locate your handy calculator, examine the accompanying table of gear data and come along for an imaginary drive.

Gear	Direct, mph/1000 rpm	Overdrive, mph/1000 rpm
1st	8.6	none
2nd	13.0	19.5
3rd	18.4	27.6
4th	24.5	36.7

First, if you don't feel like learning anything just yet, then set the OD rocker switch to its off position. It's to your right on the center console, near the electric window and mirror controls. You're now driving a conventional 4-speed, though one with ratios that are unfashionably short these days—especially for a 350-cu-in. engine that's hardly rev-happy to begin with.

Ready to try the OD? Fine, flip the switch. Nothing happens? Not to worry,

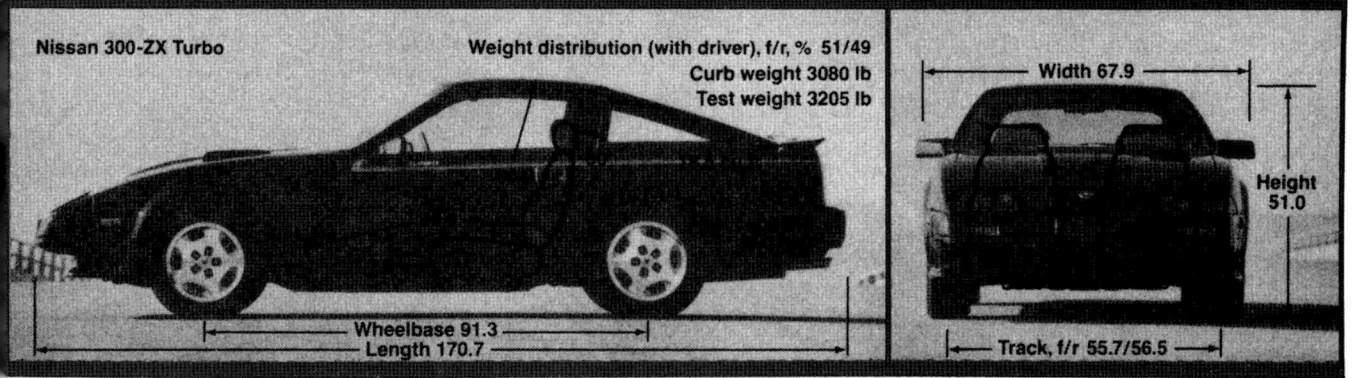

Nissan 300-ZX Turbo

Weight distribution (with driver), f/r, % 51/49
Curb weight 3080 lb
Test weight 3205 lb

Width 67.9

Height 51.0

Wheelbase 91.3
Length 170.7

Track, f/r 55.7/56.5

sure, instantaneous/average mpg and trip odometer/range (the third mode in each case being "off"). In fact, a couple of us brushed up on our English/SI knowledge by flipping yet another switch back and forth on the freeway stretches of our trip. But we'd still like to see blessedly conventional displays of mph and rpm. Two other points: Despite our general dislike of pure digital readouts for mph and rpm, we found ourselves glancing at these rather than the Corvette's adjacent hybrids, probably because of the latter's relatively tight scales. Also, though it wasn't in our test ZX, Nissan's optional digital/hybrid display is even worse: Not only is it difficult to read; it's ugly.

What we really prefer is the ZX's standard instrumentation: large, legible, round gauges. Its only shortcoming is placement of the oil pressure/temperature and boost gauge up on the center console, though these are canted toward the driver to help matters. Below the main cluster is a diagnostic display, warning of

everything from lamp failures to door or hatch ajar, and also a pair of trip odometers (one for tank-to-tank and another for complete trip mileage?). Also, a pleasant-sounding lady in there somewhere warned us whenever a door was ajar. As a rather more useful feature, there's even a little warning light on the air conditioning control panel that signals low Freon level.

Down on the center console are the transmission's OD lockout control and the one for setting shock firmness. We used each of these actively in spirited driving, and came away wishing we could locate them less haphazardly. Put the OD lockout atop the shift lever, we thought; and while you're about it, convince Chevrolet to do the same with its control.

Moving to the rear of the redesigned ZX, we found useful luggage space that was more convenient than with the Vette. The latter's high, long liftover weighed against it; its two lockable compartments were appreciated, however.

it's just that the computer knows more about the powertrain's requirements than you do. It won't invoke OD until the engine reaches full operating temperature. So let the coolant get up to 185 degrees Fahrenheit and try again.

There's no reason for 1st OD, so the computer ignores this overkill. Indeed, 1st gear is good for 43 mph if you insist on revving to 5000 rpm and, in fact, if your 1st-2nd upshift comes at anything beyond 40 mph, 2500 rpm or half-throttle—any one of these suffices—then the computer figures you're intent on having some fun. It then gives you 2nd direct and stays in direct as long as you're in 2nd or 3rd: Upshift, downshift, light on the throttle, heavy on it; the computer doesn't want to upset your enthusiastic driving with any unexpected shifting.

We conjecture that Corvette folks put this enthusiast-motoring idea in the computer's head before the on/off switch got its U.S. clean bill of health. Now that we can disengage it so automatic upshifts into 2nd or 3rd OD won't hamper our fun, we'd be interested in trying a 4+3 that allowed them when we ease up on the throttle.

In any event, now try an easy upshift from 1st to 2nd. The computer gives you 2nd OD and, if you're a nostalgic sort,

you're reminded of what it must have been like driving one of those aero-engine Edwardian cars geared for three thumps per telly pole. For instance, a 1st-gear upshift at 2000 rpm and 17 mph gives you 2nd OD at 900 rpm. Thump, thump, thump. If you're not into Edwardian motoring, perhaps you'd best leave the OD disengaged in slow city traffic.

Then again, suppose you are a latent Edwardian. Another gentle upshift finds you at 35 mph in 3rd OD, with the engine turning a lazy 1250 rpm. A hole opens in the traffic and you'd like to fill it. Time for a downshift? Yes, but let the computer show its stuff: Punch the throttle (anything more than half) and there's an automatic downshift into 3rd direct. Engine revs jump from 1250 to around 1900, and you're off with what feels precisely like an automatic transmission's kickdown—as well it should, because the mechanisms involved are essentially identical. Once you fill that hole, you can upshift gently into top and the computer snags 4th OD automatically. You're going perhaps 45 mph by now, back in the Edwardian mode at 1250 rpm.

Get up to highway speeds now, say 60 mph. In 4th OD at this speed, engine revs are a leisurely 1650. And if you'd

care to switch the Vette's fuel-economy gauge to its instantaneous mode, you'll see around 26 mpg with a steady throttle foot (or cruise control) on a level road. Switch off the OD, the revs rise to 2450 in 4th direct and mpg drops to around 18. Humm. What can we learn from this?

One thing we did learn was that 4+3 fuel economy, even with all this wizardry, is little different from that with the automatic. We recorded 15.0 mpg, versus 15.5 for the car with the Turbo Hydra-matic, and that sounds like a wash.

Now, continue your highway trip in 4th OD and pretend you're driving a car with a conventional automatic transmission. Mash it, and the computer kicks down to 4th direct in exactly the same manner as a conventional automatic; 4th OD returns when you let off the throttle or (heaven forbid) should you be rash enough to reach 110 mph or so with foot to the wood.

It helps, of course, to understand all the nuances of the 4+3's shift strategy so you and it can become good friends. Get to know it and, like us, you may find yourself irritated occasionally when your conventional 5-speed refuses to grab a lower gear when you punch it.

—*Dennis Simanaitis*

PERFORMANCE	Chevrolet Corvette	Nissan 300-ZX Turbo
Acceleration:		
Time to distance, sec:		
0–100 ft	3.1	3.2
0–500 ft	8.3	8.4
0–1320 ft (¼ mi)	15.6	15.7
Speed at end of ¼ mi, mph	88.5	86.0
Time to speed, sec		
0–30 mph	2.4	2.6
0–60 mph	7.1	7.4
0–80 mph	12.6	13.4
0–100 mph	21.4	23.0
Top speed, mph	136	133
Trip fuel economy, mpg	15.0	17.0
Brakes:		
Stopping distance, ft, from:		
60 mph	144	141
80 mph	250	249
Pedal effort for 0.5g stop, lb	20	18
Fade, % increase in effort,		
6 stops from 60 mph @ 0.5g	nil	nil
Overall brake rating	excellent	excellent
Handling:		
Lateral acceleration, g	0.880	0.795
Slalom speed, mph	63.2	62.8
Interior noise, dBA		
Idle in neutral	60	52
Maximum 1st gear	80	73
Constant 30 mph	67	66
50 mph	73	68
70 mph	77	73

Stand Back, Admire and Choose

O N ESTHETIC grounds, the Corvette did quite well for itself. We've come to admire its clean, well developed lines and, by and large, its fit and finish were very good. By contrast, we're not convinced the ZX has clearly profited from its reskinning. "It looks foreshortened," noted one staff member, "as though I'm seeing it through a slightly long lens." "Frumpy," was a more succinct second opinion. The ZX's paint and panels were well executed; there just seemed to be so many of the latter.

Within, the ZX continues this theme of busy detail, though the execution of all its shapes, shades and textures was well done. The Corvette's interior looked positively stark by contrast and a couple of us continue to think its flat plastic surfaces look excessively cheap in a car of this price.

When all the points were totaled, the 300-ZX emerged the winner, 630 to 538. The car amassed a goodly margin of points in those areas reflecting comfort and controls, though it surpassed the Vette in its performance subtotal as well. "So many things are hampered by the Vette's poor ride," summed up one

	Chevrolet Corvette	Nissan 300-ZX Turbo
CUMULATIVE RATINGS—SUBJECTIVE EVALUATIONS		
Performance:		
Engine	32	**36**
Gearbox	28	**36**
Steering	**31**	28
Brakes	**35**	32
Ride	15	**35**
Handling	33	33
Body structure	19	**33**
Subtotals	193	**233**
Comfort/Controls:		
Driving position	30	**32**
Controls	31	**32**
Instrumentation	18	**32**
Outward vision	30	**32**
Quietness	16	**31**
Heat/vent/air conditioning	32	**34**
Ingress/egress	19	**31**
Seats	**30**	29
Luggage space & loading	16	**29**
Subtotals	222	**282**
Design/Styling:		
Exterior styling	**36**	24
Exterior finish	31	31
Interior styling	27	27
Interior finish	29	**33**
Subtotals	**123**	115
Totals	538	**630**
Staff members' preferences:		
Price-independent	5	**7**
Price-dependent	4	**8**

Four staff members' preferences, 1st choice, 2 points; 2nd choice, 1 point.

staff member, "though the 4 + 3 version appeals to me a lot more than the automatics I've driven."

"I agree," noted another staff member, "and I'll go one step further." He went so far as choosing the Corvette as his personal favorite in the cost-no-object mode, though his points margin in favor of the ZX was similar to those of his three colleagues. Clearly such an iconoclastic view called for amplification and, just as surely with our crowd, it followed: "The Corvette 4 + 3 is a boy racer, pure and simple," he said, "and, what's more, it does its boy-racer routine better than any other car I could

name. The ZX," he went on (we always seem to go on, don't we?), "is an extremely well executed sports/GT, but there are others of this genre I prefer." The other three drivers opted for the ZX regardless of who was paying and even our iconoclast admitted it offered more value, especially if comfortable, everyday sporting transportation is your goal.

So what began as a comparison of two apparently similar things concluded on a note of contrasting characters, each exemplary in its own way. Japan's answer to the Vette is alive and well; and so is America's answer to the Z-car.

Viewpoint:
THE RIGHT-STUFFING OF THE 300ZX

Deploy Attenuators and activate Hyper-Drive, Cap'n Buzz! Looks like one bumpy hunk of outer space up ahead!

BY TED WEST

BRIAN BLADES

Nissan Motors is 50 years old. Five decades of building cars and still not a gray hair on the corporate head. Many happy returns, Nissan; may your recalls be few!

"Datsun" has come a long way since it first arrived in significant numbers here in the early Sixties. At that time, the local automotive folk historians in the town where I lived reckoned that this new marque was good for not much more than a belly-laugh or two. There were jokes about teeny little sedans with model names like "Fairlady." There were apocryphal stories about how the name "Datsun" itself was a poor counterfeit of the name "Austin." Surely, this newcomer from Japan would be gone before the week was out.

With the introduction of the Z-car and the original 510, of course, public perception of Datsun began to change fast. These were cars to be taken seriously and nowadays nobody knows it ⟫→

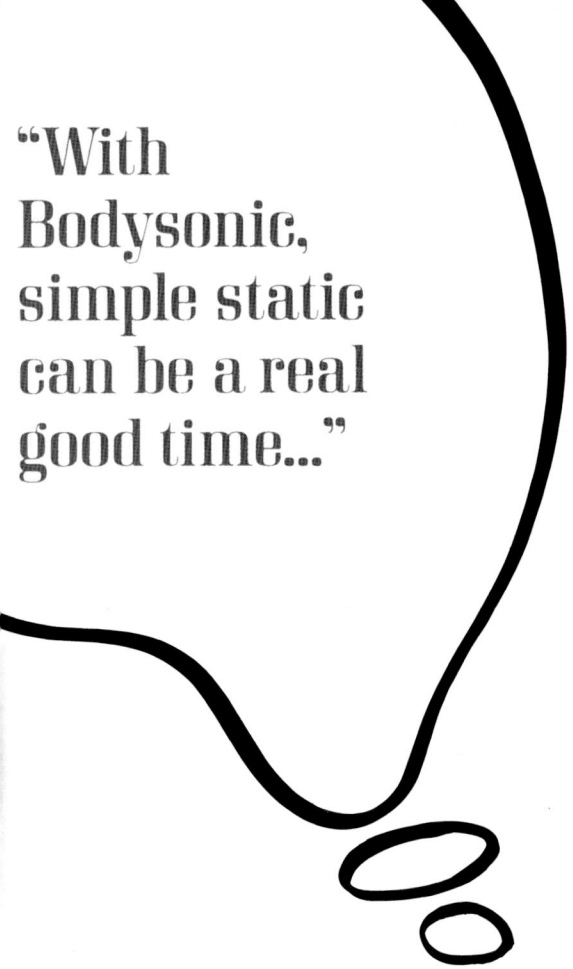

"With Bodysonic, simple static can be a real good time..."

better than the formerly unshakable grandees in Detroit. Nissan has established itself solidly as a respected and influential participant in the domestic automotive market.

In celebration of its 50th, then, Nissan has chosen to mark the occasion with something special, the 50th Anniversary 300ZX Turbo. Far from resorting to mimickry—and least of all, corporate false modesty—this car means to establish Nissan as an industry trailblazer, a peerless innovator busily setting up new standards for the *rest* of the world to mimic. And the 50th Anniversary ZX goes a long way toward making its point. It is a *tour de force*, a dazzling display of high-tech magical mysto-buttonry that'll have even the most steely-eyed and unflappable closet astronaut panting with anticipation.

For once, the phrase isn't mere hyperbole: The 50th Anniversary 300ZX is an embarrassment of riches. At the touch of a gizmo here, a doodad there, it'll do everything for you short of picking your stocks and parting your hair. You think we're being cute? Consider this. Apart from basic automotive controls such as steering wheel, gearshift, pedals, parking brake and ignition switch—and counting a switch with multiple settings or functions as only one control—in the 50th Anniversary ZX we found no less than 89 controls, buttons, toggles, adjusters, attenuators, hyper-space gewgaws. You read right: *89!* And that's just controls you *actively operate*. We didn't bother trying to count the myriad dials, gauges, digital readouts, bar graphs, warning lights and such because, frankly, we're not paid by the hour.

Underneath this plethora of 50th Anniversary features, the basic 300ZX Turbo is still a wonderfully satisfying device, but it's the special packaging that snags your attention here. A goodly number of these features are options on other ZX models, while a few—the most exotic, generally—are the exclusive property of the 50th Anniversary edition. What strikes you immediately, however, is that with this car you get *absolutely everything*. The 50th Anniversary ZX is the last word in what they call on the daytime game shows, "lugg-jury."

From the outside, the 50th Anniversary ZX looks like nothing

so much as a comprehensively Southern-Californiated 300ZX. It bristles with chin spoilers, rear wings, high-performance running boards, speedy-looking graphics. To accommodate wider wheels and tires, its front fenders are flared steel stampings, while the rear flares employ the expedient of add-on ABS/plastic skirts. The handsome vented 16-in. turbine wheels are trimmed in gold to complement the silver, black and gold color scheme, and they mount 6½-in. Pirelli P7 50-Series tires.

The basic 300ZX's styling is reasonably clean and straightforward, but with the 50th Anniversary edition things get busy in a hurry. The silver coachwork is painted black from the shins down, the line of demarcation highlighted by triple gold pinstripes. The rear wing is black and heavy black bordering of the windows, a "reflectorized" T-roof ("Looks sharp!" says the brochure), black beading around the rear fender flare seams, massive black doorhandle bezels and rearview mirror fairings, all standing in stark relief against the bright silver, contribute to an eyeball-juddering impression of interrupted lines and surfaces. The car has all the right "fast" motifs, but placed beside a placid one-tone ZX, your estimate of the 50th's styling will depend entirely on your appetite for "flash."

The car's real flash, however, happens inside the cockpit. The upholstery is gorgeous black leather, with elegant, tastefully small 50th Anniversary logos embossed in the top of the seatbacks, and the driver's seat features a perfectly splendid air-inflated cushion support system with generous lumbar, lateral and thigh adjustments. This flashmobile's seatsmanship doesn't stop there, though. We said that with the 50th Anniversary ZX you get absolutely everything, but we were lying—there wasn't *room* for everything. So Nissan made a choice. In place of electrically adjustable seats (not to be confused with the power *support* system just mentioned), the company installs its unique, all-singing-all-dancing Bodysonic feature—better known hereabouts as Buzz-Buns. This incomparably exotic notion uses eight powerful transducers, four in the seat cushions and four in the backrest, to transmit the stereo's low-frequency rumblings direct to your posterior in the form of, yes, Lord, deep vibration.

Trouble imagining such a thing? Well, if you've ever slipped a quarter into a motel bed Vibra-Fingers unit (no written confessions required here), then you're halfway home. The only important difference is, Vibra-Fingers couldn't carry a tune. Bodysonic can. Oh, yeah.

And truth be told, when used with heavily electronically enhanced music of the green-hair-and-gentlemen's-mascara variety, this system is really rather interesting. You hear—er, feel—resonances you might never have noticed if relying solely on those Stone Age inverted mushrooms stapled to the sides of your skull. For the Libertarians among us, Bodysonic comes with separate seat controls, allowing you and your passenger to individually adjust the vibration level to whatever will set your own *glutei maximi* to hummin' and thrummin'. And for us Republicans, there is provision, as well, for shutting off the entire business and reading a book.

At the core of human nature there exists a certain trenchant contrariness, however, and Bodysonic seems to summon up this quality in copious amounts. We found ourselves experimenting with Bodysonic in every imaginable way, often just for the sheer inappropriateness of it. The results were, may we say, enlightening. It's one thing to feel Brahms in your shoulder blades; another, to have Weather Report massage your lower back. With Bodysonic, simple static can be a real good time, and the sensations available in a violent electrical storm make it well worth setting off late at night in the direction of the nearest fork lightning. The most memorable sensation of all, though, came when we located one of those brief self-help radio spots. Truly, there's nothing on earth to compare with the experience of driving along and feeling Dr Joyce Brothers talking to you through your butt. It lends a new dimension to the phrase "poetic justice."

The 50th Anniversary ZX still isn't finished being startling, though, nossir. Switch on the key, look at the dashboard and

"Digital instruments, for all their initial impact, are the double-knit leisure suit of automotive instrumentation..."

Something nice, we're pleased to say, something extremely nice indeed. With ingenious use of optical ring and LED technology, Nissan has so cleverly miniaturized the necessary circuitry that on the steering wheel hub you will find a complete set of controls for both the audio system and the cruise control. This arrangement is a marvel of convenience and proves its worth the very first time you head out onto the freeway for a drive of more than a few miles. You can dial in cruising speed, slow down, speed up and resume cruise while tuning in Dr Joyce, all without removing your hands from the wheel—thus freeing your feet for other tasks like scratching the back of your neck, peeling bananas, grooming your travel partner. Seriously, the steering-hub control complex is one of the best features of the 50th Anniversary ZX. In combination with the fine Nissan cruise control system, accurate to within about 1 mph, it's one of those rare innovations that basically alters one's automotive perceptions. After you've gotten used to such a convenience, cars without it (i.e., practically everything else on wheels) seem to suffer for its lack.

Beyond these salient features, the Anniversary ZX is crammed with other goodies too numerous to catalog here. Among the nicest is the cockpit-adjustable 3-way electric shock absorber control switch. We found that for normal driving the soft setting was best, while the firm setting stiffened up the ZX well for higher speed running. A very useful item. The ZX's climate control system, though perhaps unnecessarily complex to understand, was also impressive. It automatically monitors seven sensors that read outside ambient temperature, sunload and various cockpit temperature levels, all in an unceasing effort to keep you comfy as Shirley Temple's puppydog. The audio system, too, was excellent—indeed, every system aboard the 50th Anniversary edition is of high quality.

Alas, though, it isn't the level of quality that muddles the waters hereabouts, but rather of functional relevance, or, if you will, sheer clutter. Take the dial on the dashboard, for example, which is sometimes construed as a lateral-g meter, but is in fact only an accelerometer. This unit measures acceleration within a range of 0.5g positive and negative—wizard information to have, surely. And yet, of what real use is it to the driver, beyond perhaps letting him note his approximate negative-g rate as he decelerates through the front bumper of the White Freightliner he didn't see out the windshield?

Of similarly dubious utility is the next instrument to the right, an LCD *compass*! We suffered deep despair one afternoon when we realized our onboard navigational device remained pointed nor-noreast no matter which quadrant of the galaxy the ship was headed, yet all the same, we somehow found our way safely back to the mother-ship that evening, albeit much chastened by this brush with disaster.

Doubtless there will be more than enough buyers to quickly exhaust Nissan's limited supply of Anniversary ZXs, of which only 5000 units will be built, yet there are still many drivers who entertain no private astronaut fantasies, don't secretly wish they were 767 pilots—in fact, don't want to fly at all! For these, pressing buttons and throwing toggle switches and operating remote controls are not the central focus of driving pleasure, and may even distract annoyingly from the basic exercise. Clearly, of course, this ZX's whiz-bang technological filigree does not oblige one to use it all during each and every minute behind the wheel, and, I repeat, the underlying 300ZX Turbo continues to be a superb car. Yet whether said filigree is used constantly or not, its mere presence makes a declarative stylistic statement nonetheless. In short, if flash is what you want, the 50th Anniversary ZX will be worth every penny of its $26,000-ish price tag. If all you require, however, is quickness, fine vehicle dynamics, straightforward controls, a clean windshield and a curvy road ahead, a normal 300ZX Turbo will cost you several thousand bills less and leave you several thousand grins more comfortable. Between these two versions of the 300ZX, the choice just couldn't be more clear-cut.

prepare to be mystified. If you'd been marooned for 10 years on some remote uncivilized island (say, Manhattan) and you just returned this morning, you couldn't feel more totally out-of-touch-with-today than when you first glimpse this ZX instrument panel. It looks like a cross between an arcade computer game and the local utility company's electronic exhibit at the Science Fair depicting energy use during peak- and off-peak periods. Ruffle the ZX's gas pedal and the tachometer's video image, shaped like an LCD ocean wave, begins to build, rising, cresting, crashing mightily upon the shores of the dashboard in a tantrum of over-revved white water. Link together successive bursts of full-throttle acceleration and the tach says it in best southern California fashion: Surf's Up!

Sure, the numbers and displays begin to make sense soon enough. Digital readouts denote tach and speedometer; bar graphs communicate oil pressure, water temperature, fuel level, volts of charge. You get used to the display and it works fine . . . but when all is said and done, dammit, analog instruments *still* tell you more, faster, and with less mental processing, which is precisely why there are no digitals in race car cockpits. Digital instruments, for all their initial impact, are the double-knit leisure suit of automotive instrumentation and they're beginning to look shiny in the seat already.

But wait, there's still more. What is this on the steering wheel hub?

NISSAN 300ZX TURBO

Nothing succeeds like success

PHOTO BY RON WAKEFIELD

BACK IN 1970, Datsun— oops, it's Nissan now— reinvented the medium-price sports car with the sleek, sexy and civilized 240Z. Last year, it reinvented the Z-car concept for the second time in 15 years. But though the 300ZX was hailed as an improvement over the pudgy, plush 280ZX, it disappointed some critics by being too much like its predecessor in appearance and too much like a Cadillac in its level of luxury.

Hardly anyone was disappointed by the third-generation Z's smooth new 60-degree V-6, however. Nor with the advent of a genuine performance rival to the vaunted new Corvette in the form of a 200-bhp Turbo ZX. Not surprisingly in a country that's suffering a relapse of performance fever, the new ZX, especially the Turbo, sold better than ever.

Like most Japanese carmakers, Nissan is wise enough not to tamper with a winner, so the 300ZX is little changed for 1985. The 3-model lineup of turbo and non-turbo 2-seater and normally aspirated 2+2 is back, a standard-equipment T-top roof (featuring lockable panels) being the only discernible difference. The Turbo model gets the full blackout treatment on exterior moldings, plus smoked taillamp lenses. On the option chart, leather interior trim has been divorced from the electronic instrument cluster to which it was previously wedded, a sensible move. Oh—and you won't find a Datsun badge anywhere, a sign that Nissan's tortuous name-change program is almost complete.

The 300ZX is an eminently satisfying driver's car in any form. It has a burly, substantial feel that recalls the Corvette or Porsche 928; yet the ZX seems more athletic somehow, perhaps because of its tighter dimensions and the very fluid action of its shift, clutch and steering. With a forward weight bias and semi-trailing-arm rear suspension, the ZX can be a bit tail-happy, and it could use more roll stiffness. Nevertheless, the car handles with assured alacrity, and there's enough power even with the normally aspirated engine to enable the driver to pick an optimum cornering attitude with ease.

We can't say enough about Nissan's 3.0-liter V-6. It delivers plenty of pull in the intermediate gears, winds smoothly and effortlessly, makes all the right sounds and never tingles your backside with unseemly V-6 vibrations. It's the sort of engine that—as they used to say— makes you want to take the long way home. With 40 extra horsepower and 54 more lb-ft of torque, the turbo version is naturally the more vivid performer. Only mild turbo lag and occasional driveline snatch in fast upshifts mar its otherwise exemplary behavior.

We have more good things to say about the ZX cockpit. The basic driving position is well judged, and it can be tailored via a standard tilt wheel and cozy, comfortable seats with all the necessary adjustments (plus a few not-so-necessary ones on the Turbo model). We're not much fond of electronic instrumentation in any car, and the ZX's is no exception. But you have a choice, and the analog cluster is a model of legibility and layout. And forget what you've read about the dash: sure it looks busy, but the ergonomics are excellent. So is workmanship, from carpet fit to instrument-panel moldings to side-window sealing (though T-top fit could be better).

It all adds up to a refined, well built GT offering a choice of interesting or really interesting performance, plus smooth road manners, high mechanical refinement, a ride that won't beat you to death, and first-cabin appointments. It may not be a revolution like the 240Z, but the 300ZX is a standout in today's market. And given the much fiercer competition, that may be the greater achievement.—*Reid Howard*

SPECIFICATIONS

Curb weight, lb/kg	3080	1397
Wheelbase, in./mm	91.3	2319
Length	170.7	4336
Width	67.9	1725
Height	51.0	1295
Fuel capacity, U.S. gal./liters	19.0	72
Engine type		turbocharged sohc V-6
Displacement, cu in./cc	181	2960
Bhp @ rpm, SAE net/kW		200/149 @ 5200
Torque @ rpm, lb-ft/Nm		227/308 @ 3600
Fuel injection		Bosch L-Jetronic
Transmission		5-sp manual or 4-sp automatic
Layout		front engine/rear drive
Brakes, front/rear		vented disc/disc
Wheels (std equip)		cast alloy, 15 x 6½JJ
Tires		P215/60R-15
Steering		rack & pinion, power assisted
Suspension, front/rear: MacPherson struts, lower lateral arms, compliance struts, coil springs, tube shocks,anti-roll bar/semi-trailing arms, coil springs, tube shocks, anti-roll bar		

PERFORMANCE & ECONOMY

0–60 mph, sec	7.4
Standing ¼ mi, sec @ mph	15.7 @ 86.0
Top speed, mph	133
Stopping distance from 60 mph, ft	141
Lateral accel, 100-ft radius, g	0.795
Interior noise @ 70 mph, dBA	73
EPA fuel economy, mpg, city/highway	17/23

PRICE

List price	$19,699

ROAD & TRACK ROAD TEST

NISSAN 300ZX & 300ZX TURBO

Facelifted, heavier and not as lively as before

NISSAN THE CURRENT, THIRD-GENERATION Datsun/Nissan Z-car, the 300ZX, is now almost 2½ years old. When introduced in fall 1983, it was a thorough but conservative update of the Japanese company's GT coupe, with one not-so-conservative change: a new 3.0-liter sohc V-6 engine that produced 160 bhp in its normally aspirated form and 200 bhp turbocharged. This excellent engine helped move the luxurious, relatively heavy 300ZX closer to the ranks of enthusiast drivers' machines, a concept from which the previous 280ZX had strayed.

AT A GLANCE	Nissan 300ZX Turbo	Chevrolet Corvette	Mazda RX-7 Turbo
Curb weight, lb	3325	3280	est 2830
Engine/drive	inline-6/rwd	V-8/rwd	2-rotor Wankel/rwd
Transmission	5-sp M	4+OD M	5-sp M
0–60 mph, sec	7.2	5.8	6.6
Standing ¼ mi, sec @ mph	15.7@ 89.0	14.4 @ 96.0	15.2 @ 92.5
Stopping distance from 60 mph, ft	145	133	154
Lateral acceleration, g	0.77	0.91	0.85
Slalom speed, mph	na	61.0	63.1
Fuel economy, mpg	17.0[1]	19.0	19.2[1]

	Pro	Con
300ZX Turbo:	smooth V-6 engine, high performance, extensive luxury features, good workmanship	mediocre handling, busy interior and exterior design, turbo lag, lacks ABS
Corvette:	very high performance with reasonable fuel economy, very high cornering power, ABS	bulky for a 2-passenger car, tends to rattle and squeak, awkward operation of 4 + OD transmission
RX-7 Turbo:	smooth, high-revving rotary engine, high performance, comfortable and practical interior	Styling lacks originality, low fuel economy for performance and weight, lacks ABS

In turbo form the 300ZX turned out to be a fairly close challenger to the Chevrolet Corvette, accelerating to 60 mph in 7.4 seconds and the quarter-mile in 15.7 and reaching a maximum of 133 mph. And at $18,699 it was affordable, as high-performance cars go.

But one thing the high-performance car market doesn't do is stand still. In the last two years Nissan's competitors have all introduced new or substantially revised models: the Porsche 944 Turbo, Pontiac Fiero GT, Mazda RX-7, Toyota Supra and a much improved Corvette. For 1986 Nissan has seen fit to leave its engine essentially unchanged (only electronic adjustments for improved drivability and a water-cooled center bearing for the turbo are new) while offering a retuned suspension with new wheel and tire packages and accompanying fender flares.

You certainly couldn't call the body changes cosmetic. Although the fender width is now 67.9 in. (1.4 more than before but equal to the former width at the mirrors), the flares are reasonably subtle. They don't call a lot of attention to the new version, but together with the new front airdam, flared rocker panels and rear spoiler, they are sufficient to identify it to Z enthusiasts. By virtue of improved underhood airflow, the Turbo loses its hood scoop—did Nissan listen to us when we described the scoop as looking tacked-on? The new fenders are nicely contoured and the bump-ers, now body color, are more attractive, but the ZX is still no model of styling expertise. Different wheel styles and sizes come on the non-turbo (15 x 6½ in.) and Turbo (16 x 7); both are good-looking, but the latter's radial vanes aren't very logical. Unlike Corvette's they aren't cast left and right, so the vanes go backward on one side.

With the same P215/60HR-15 tires, the standard 2-seater has increased track dimensions of 57.3/58.1 in. front/rear (versus 55.7/56.5 in 1985), putting the tires about ½ in. closer to the fender width for a slightly more aggressive stance. With wider P225/50VR-16 tires but the same flares, the new Turbo's track dimensions are inset slightly to 56.5/57.3.

We were naturally interested in the improvements the revised stance would produce and tested two cars, a Turbo and a non-turbo, both 5-speed 2-seaters. The answer is: none. Acceleration figures for the Turbo were approximately equal to those of the previous version, for the naturally aspirated model inexplicably slower; in the case of the Turbo, there is little apparent lag, but that's partly because the boost is not exhilarating. The handling was a real disappointment: Cornering forces were distinctly inferior (0.77–0.77g vs 0.80–0.82), braking distances were longer (262–277 ft from 80 mph vs 249–253) and the brake fade in six

successive ½g stops from 60 mph went up from nil to an alarming 54 percent. Wha' hoppen? The only thing we could conclude, other than inferior manufacturing standards, was that an increase in weight—a surprising +250 lb for the 300ZX, +245 lb for the 300 ZX Turbo—has extracted its penalties.

As on the previous version, the steering is both vague (despite slightly higher effort to give the impression of feel) and a little too quick, making accurate placement of the car difficult if learnable. The gear change is on the notchy side; there is no problem getting the right gear but it's not very pleasant. Differences in the soft/normal/firm ride control can be felt—over Botts dots, for instance—but we suspect that the typical ZX owner will use the soft setting most of the time; it gives a better ride, and although the nose bobs a bit under braking, the ZX's overall comportment isn't so wallowy as to be objectionable (as it is on the Maxima SE sedan).

So if better performance has not been achieved, what can the new ZX buyer look for? Both of our test cars had digital instrument displays, not our cup of tea, but fortunately a proper analog panel is available. Interior equipment is lavish and accommodation slightly improved (head room benefits from lower seats). The quality of finish is excellent, and the all-electric seat adjustments, including fore/aft and up/down on the cushion, angle and side sup-

port on the backrest, and 3-point lumbar support, work very well. Steering-wheel-mounted radio and cruise-control buttons in the current fashion aren't really that valuable, but the compass was fun and could be really useful in the boonies at night.

The ventilation system is excellent: strong and easy to control. Not satisfactory were the instrument illumination (some readouts not read-outable in daylight, a common complaint with electronic displays from many makers); the T-top panels, which didn't fit well; and the mediocre sound system quality.

All our comments so far add up to a serious panning of the latest ZXs. We admit that they offer a lot for the price, and that they can be driven quickly, comfortably and conveniently. But as enthusiasts' cars, they're moving away from the kind of direct and businesslike performance that we prefer—just as the 280ZX did from its Z-car forebear. From a marketing viewpoint, Nissan certainly knows its business; but we suggest that the company might try offering *one* truly serious performance version—lighter, tighter, more direct in its controls, with a minimum of gimmicks. It might not generate significant additional income for Nissan, but it would do wonders for the ZX image. Nissan may have created this market originally, but the competition for it is getting more serious.

Perhaps that's where the MID4 comes in.

PRICE

	300ZX	300ZX Turbo
List price, west coast	$17,599	$20,099
Price as tested	$18,619	$22,449

Price as tested includes 300ZX: electronic package ($1120); Turbo: combined electronic & leather package ($2350)

GENERAL

	300ZX	Turbo
Curb weight, lb	3240	3325
Test weight	3395	3455
Weight dist (with driver), f/r, %	51/49	50/50[1]
Wheelbase, in./mm		91.3
Track, f/r	57.3/58.1	56.5/57.3
Length		170.7
Width		67.9
Height		51.0
Trunk space, cu ft		18.5
Fuel capacity, U.S. gal		19.0

ENGINE

	300ZX	Turbo
Type	sohc V-6	
Bore x stroke, mm	3.43 x 3.27/87.0 x 83.0	
Displacement, cc	181/2960	
Compression ratio	9.0:1	7.8:1
Bhp @ rpm, SAE net	160 @ 5200	200 @ 5200
Torque @ rpm, lb-ft	174 @ 4000	227 @ 3600
Fuel delivery	Bosch L-Jetronic	
Fuel requirement	unleaded, 87 pump octane	

[1]Single entry indicates specifications are identical.

DRIVETRAIN

	300ZX	Turbo
Transmission	5-speed manual	
Gear ratios: 5th	(0.76) 2.81:1	(0.80) 2.83:1
4th	(1.00) 3.70:1	(1.00) 3.54:1
3rd	(1.31) 4.85:1	(1.38) 4.89:1
2nd	(1.90) 7.03:1	(2.06) 7.29:1
1st	(3.32) 12.28:1	(3.35) 11.86:1
Final drive ratio	3.70	3.54:1

CHASSIS & BODY

Layout	front engine/rear drive
Body/frame	unit steel
Brake system, f/r	10.8-in. vented discs/11.4-in. vented discs; vacuum assisted
Wheels, f/r	cast alloy, 15 x 6½JJ ... 16 x 7JJ
Tires, f/r	P215/60HR-15 ... P225/50VR-16
Steering type	rack & pinion, power assisted
Turns, lock-to-lock	3.6

Suspension, front/rear: MacPherson struts, lower lateral links, compliance struts, coil springs, tube shocks, anti-roll bar/semi-trailing arms, coil springs, tube shocks, anti-roll bar

CALCULATED DATA

	300ZX	Turbo
Lb/bhp (test weight)	21.2	17.3
Bhp/liter	54.0	67.5
Mph/1000 rpm (5th gear)	25.9	26.9
Engine revs/mi (60 mph)	2320	2230
Brake swept area, sq in/ton	218	222

ROAD TEST RESULTS

ACCELERATION

Time to distance, sec:

	300ZX	Turbo
0-100 ft	3.2	3.2
0-500 ft	9.0	8.5
0-1320 ft (¼ mi)	16.9	15.7
Speed at end of ¼ mi, mph	82.0	89.0

Time to speed, sec:

	300ZX	Turbo
0-30 mph	2.6	2.4
0-50 mph	6.5	5.3
0-60 mph	9.1	7.2
0-70 mph	12.3	9.6
0-80 mph	16.0	12.3
0-100 mph	35.0	21.4

SPEEDS IN GEARS

5th gear (rpm)

	300ZX	Turbo
mph (4950)	128	133
4th (6000)	120	123
3rd (6000)	89	89
2nd (7500)	62	59
1st (7500)	35	35

FUEL ECONOMY

	300ZX	Turbo
Normal driving, mpg[2]	18.0	17.0

[2]trip fuel economy

BRAKES

Minimum stopping distances, ft:

	300ZX	Turbo
From 60 mph	148	145
From 80 mph	277	262
Control in panic stop	very good	
Pedal effort for 0.5g stop, lb	13	13

Fade: percent increase in pedal effort to maintain 0.5g deceleration in 6 stops from 60 mph ... 54 ... 54

Overall brake rating ... fair ... fair

HANDLING

Lateral acceleration,
100-ft radius, g ... 0.77 ... 0.77
Speed through 700-ft slalom, mph ... na ... na

INTERIOR NOISE

	300ZX	Turbo
Constant 30 mph, dBA	60	63
50 mph	65	67
70 mph	70	71

SPEEDOMETER ERROR

	300ZX	Turbo
30 mph ind. is actually	30.0	30.0
60 mph	60.0	60.0

ACCELERATION

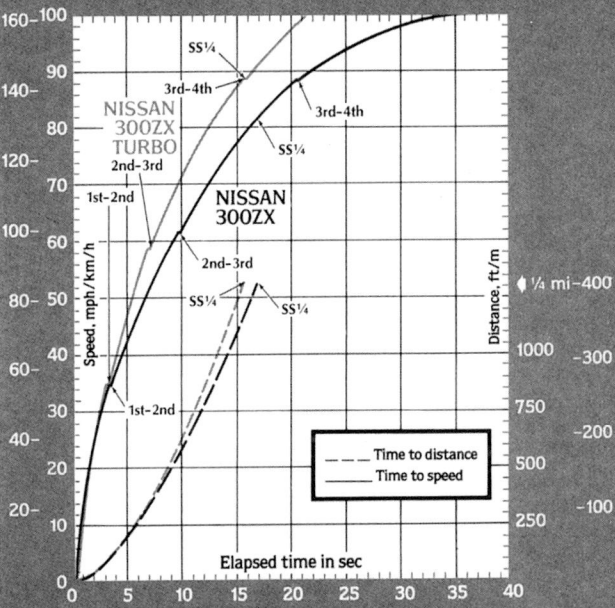

NISSAN 300ZX & TURBO

A study in the perils of noble lineage

PHOTOS BY RON PERRY

NISSAN LIFE CERTAINLY AIN'T easy for a boy named Sue, but in many ways it's even tougher for the offspring of a legendary parent. Just ask Bronco Nagurski, Jr. Or Marvis Frazier. Or Geoff Brabham. Or Kyle Petty.

No matter how good you are or how much better the game may have become, there's always that bigger-than-life figure looming out of the past, acquiring more and more stature as it recedes further and further from recent (accurate) memory.

Which brings us, more or less, to the 1987 Nissan 300ZX. Here's this perfectly civilized, thoroughly attractive GT car, propelled by one of the best powerplants wrought by man and what do we say, year in, year out? We say, "Pretty good, kiddo.

Stick with it and someday you might just be as good as your old man."

The old 240Z stuck out from its surrounding landscape in a way no sports or GT machine has managed since, and it's likely, given the sophistication of today's GT game, that none will ever do so again. Small wonder that we tend to remember cars like the original Z with our hearts, as well as our heads.

When the original Z-car gave way to the "awesome" ZX series back in 1978, there was no question that something was lost in the transition—a tigerish spirit, the sense of instant race car that goes with no-nonsense roll stiffness and spring rates.

As far as that goes, something was also gained—a wealth of electronic gadgetry

and, more important, weight.

For 1987, though, it appears that several years of concerted carping about the avoirdupois issue has finally hit home in Nissan design circles. In the course of its first facelift since the current series was introduced in 1983, the new Z-cars have actually managed to shed a little weight. It's not really enough to get excited about—101 lb for the normally aspirated car and 60 lb for the Turbo—but any move down the scale is a move we applaud.

Exciting may also be a bit too much of a descriptor for the exterior revisions, but there's no denying the enhanced cosmetic appeal of the new car. At the front, the major component in the facelift is an integrated one-piece bumper/air dam, with faired-in quartz-halogen fog lamps. The lamps have been relocated below the bumper, and the entire end cap has been executed in body color.

The same approach has been employed at the rear of the car, where bumper and license plate box have all been combined in one body-colored end cap. The rear light panel has been expanded into a straight section that sweeps across the back of the car. Wheels have also undergone cosmetic revision, appearing for 1987 in brush-finish alloy on the normally aspirated and 2 + 2 editions (15 in.), while the Turbos (base price $21,399) get a new charcoal-finish turbine-vane design (16 in.). As before, the vaned wheels have nothing to do with brake cooling; the castings are not specific to one side of the car or the other, which means one side runs backward and the other frontward. You can decide which is which for yourself.

Generally speaking, these are all subtle changes, the kind that must be considered in a side-by-side comparison with the previous model to really assess or, for that matter, even notice. However, when we did just that we were ready to call the changes a positive step forward. We're not sure whether the revised 300ZX does in fact live up to its billing as a "lower, more aggressive look." But it is definitely cleaner and more cohesive.

The list of revisions isn't confined to what you can see, and here too Nissan seems to be showing concern for the Z-car's gone-to-fat image. Front spring rates have been bumped, firmer bushings installed, the power assist steering pump recalibrated and the rear anti-roll bar diameter increased (to 24 mm).

Nissan's 3-way cockpit-adjustable shock absorbers (Turbo only) are also back for 1987, and some attention has been devoted to making more distinction between the settings.

All these tweaks have been made in the name of better handling response and feel, and our 300ZX test car (at press time the revised Turbo was just entering production) did have a generally tauter feeling than its predecessor, but the result may not quite match the investment in overall effectiveness. On-center steering feel is still on the numb side, increased effort notwithstanding, and substantial understeer continues to be the dominating characteristic in hard cornering. The rapid transition to oversteer in dropped-throttle situations does seem to be improved, but herding a ZX back and forth in rapid transitions continues to be a job for skilled hands and careful attention to timing.

However, for all its concessions to comfort and occupant pampering, we don't want to imply that the 300ZX can't satisfy the enthusiast who is familiar with exploring the limits of adhesion. This is no paper tiger. One proof of the car's capabilities is its performance in the 1986 Firestone Firehawk endurance races for street-stock cars. With Max Jones and 19-year-old Tommy Kendall sharing the driving, a 300ZX Turbo dominated the series (against Firebirds, Camaros, Porsche 944s and Mustangs) and won the championship. Street stock as delivered and street-stock racing, of course, are not exactly the same thing, but there's no question that there's more to the current ZX series than swoopy good looks and a great engine.

As for the latter, it comes to the new model year unchanged, save for a modifi-

cation to the turbocharger designed to reduce friction and spool-up time. Horsepower (200 at 5200 rpm) and torque (227 lb-ft at 3600) for the Turbo are the same. Although the advent of the turbocharged Toyota Supra has put the ZX at a disadvantage in the Japanese GT power derby, Nissan's 60-degree V-6 has more than enough muscle to get the job done and is a thoroughly pleasant engine to live with—smooth, strong and willing.

There's plenty of development potential in the V-6, of course. A 230-bhp 24-valve twincam turbo version already exists in Japan. However, Nissan has the high-output edition of the V-6 ticketed for use in its new mid-engine 2-seat sports car, the Mid4, which should hit the U.S. market as a 1988 model.

One final area of the performance hardware inventory that's had some attention for 1987 is braking. Nissan installed vented discs on all four wheels last year, and this year the assembly includes larger cali-

pers. The objective here is to add improved fade resistance to the ZX's already strong overall braking power. However, with anti-lock braking systems trickling more and more into the realm of affordability, ABS looms as the standard by which all systems will be measured, so the ZX rates as not quite state of the art.

The redesign found its way inside the ZX, but only as far as the instrument panel, which has had both its analog and digital instrumentation reworked to improve legibility. Our test car was equipped with the analog equipment, which is the standard setup and, in our view, the preferable one as well. Digitals are an option.

As before, the ZX continues to be a garden of electronic delights, with an impressive array of equipment standard. The electronic equipment option package ($1300) adds cruise control, power adjustments for the driver's seat, 80-watt AM/FM stereo/cassette, automatic climate control and steering-wheel-mounted con-

	PERFORMANCE
Base price................................$18,499	**PERFORMANCE**
Price as tested..........................$20,949	Acceleration
Price as tested includes: std equip. (air cond, AM/FM stereo/cassette), elect. equip. pkg ($1300), leather pkg ($1150)	Time to distance, sec:
	0–1320 ft (¼ mi) 16.9
	Speed at end of ¼ mi, mph...........................82.0
GENERAL DATA	Time to speed, sec:
Curb weight, lb 3140	0–30 mph...................................2.6
Length, in. 170.7	0–60 mph...................................9.1
Suspension, f/r ....MacPherson struts, lower lateral links/semi-trailing arms	0–80 mph...................................16.0
	Braking
Brake system, f/r ....10.8-in. vented discs/11.1-in. vented discs	Minimum stopping distances, ft:
	From 60 mph 148
Wheels................................cast alloy, 15 x 6½	From 80 mph 277
Tires.......................................215/60VR-15	Control in panic stop ....very good
Steering type ....rack & pinion, power asst	Handling
Engine type ....sohc V-6	Lateral accel, 100-ft radius, g 0.77
Displacement, cc 2960	Speed thru 700-ft slalom, mph ....na
Bhp @ rpm, SAE net ....160 @ 5200	Interior noise
Torque @ rpm, lb-ft............................174 @ 4000	Maximum, 1st gear................................na
Transmission..............................5-sp manual	Constant 70 mph 70
	Fuel economy, mpg ....est 18.0
	na means information not available

trols for cruise and stereo.

Basic seating is long on comfort and adjustability—there's an optimal driving position for just about anyone—and the overall level of fit and finish is first-rate. Nissan continues to make leather upholstery available as a ZX option ($1150), and if this sumptuous cockpit seems to be one of the factors that keeps the current Z-car from measuring up to the ghost of its hallowed ancestor, well, Nissan has learned that plenty of potential customers out there think the late-Eighties' incarnation is just fine.

And if there are those who think otherwise, hard-liners waiting for a return to the style of the original Z, we have to say don't hold your breath. Even though Nissan is on record regarding its aim to bring the ZX back a little toward the sporting side of the GT mainstream, the personal luxury portion of the market is where the action is today. Combine that factor with the imminent arrival of the Mid4 and you have a climate of diminished motivation. Why change a successful program?

The legend is safe.—*Tony Swan*

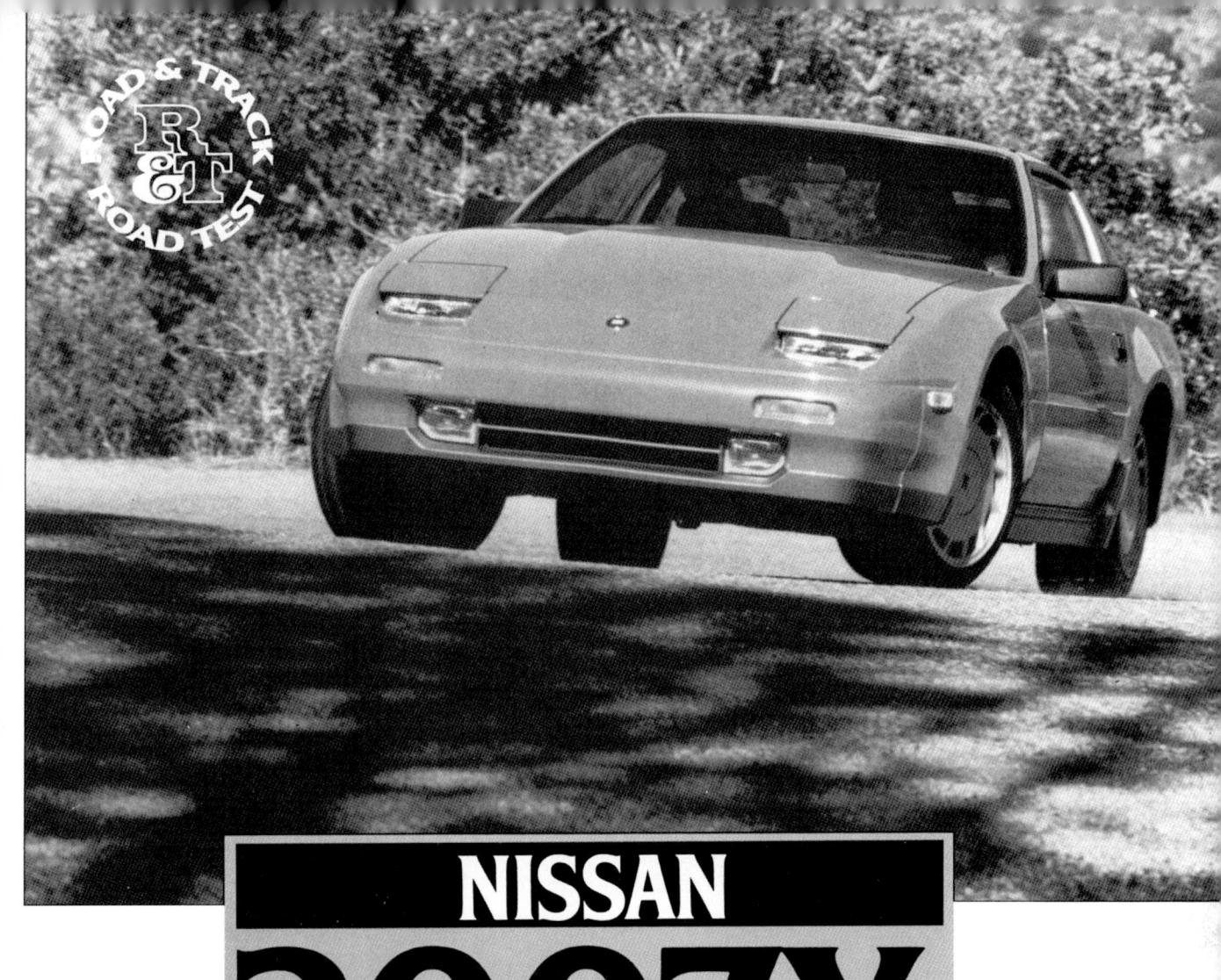

NISSAN
300ZX TURBO

Chasing the elusive

PHOTOS BY RON PERRY

HITTING A MOVING target, as skeet shooters will tell you, is not the same as plinking away at a row of tin cans. It takes concentration to pop those clay pigeons; miss, and they hit the ground with a thud. Automotive marketing is like that.

Nissan has been out there on the GT-car shooting range for a lot of years now, racking up a pretty good score in the process. Almost everyone liked the Datsun 240Z; for proof, just look around and count the number of 240s that have survived. Or, for more concrete evidence, consider that Nissan has continued to churn out succes-sors, and obviously has put a lot of effort into doing so. The 300ZX, in normally aspirated GS, 2+2 GS and Turbo (our test subject) versions, is the current iteration of what promises to be a continuing line.

But chasing moving targets means you're going to miss once in a while. What we have here is a miss. A "near-hit," it's true, but "close" doesn't count for much in this game.

Obviously, a lot of people think the latest Z in the line—now Nissan instead of Datsun, and 300ZX instead of 240Z—*is* a hit, and far be it from us to say they're wrong. They wouldn't believe it, anyway. Needs, usage and expectations vary; that's why we're not all driving Datsun Bluebirds.

Tradition plays an important role in the makeup of the 300ZX. From the outside, 240Z influence is perceptible, even if the early car's lean and hungry look has been exchanged for something a little more massive. Taken as a whole, it's a handsome design, with fender detailing and profile view being particularly appealing.

Last year's restyling, allegedly done to draw attention away from Toyota's new-generation Supra, has done the ZX a power of no good, adding mass where it wasn't needed. The new rear-lamp treatment, in particular, fattens up the Nissan's tail, which doesn't need more bulk. Still, it's the execution and not the basic ideas that lets the car down.

Having six cylinders under the hood is another part of the Z-car tradition.

Nissan chose to go with a vee configuration for the 300ZX, with a single cam per bank and two valves per cylinder. Revisions for the 1988 model include a raised compression ratio (now 8.3:1) for better off-boost response and a "high-flow" turbocharger; the net result is five extra horsepower for the 3.0-liter ZX turbo engine (now 205 at 5200 rpm).

Trouble is, the engine doesn't want to wind up that high. Beyond 4500 rpm, it feels sluggish and emits an annoying subharmonic growl that isn't easy to tolerate for any length of time. Worse, at steady speeds a small but noticeable shake—felt like a fouled sparkplug but was more likely the result of the engine's 90-degree "uneven-fire" layout—did intrude. Turbo lag is no problem, though given the relatively low boost and short piping runs (no intercooler, here), one would not expect much delay in response.

All the right chassis pieces are in place too, yet they perform better on paper than in the real world. Despite the independent suspension—struts in front, semi-trailing arms in the rear—and the 225/50VR-16 Goodyear tires, the ZX is happier when kept away from challenging roads. Under pressure, the chassis is indecisive and slow to respond, taking too much of the driver's attention away from the road ahead. Time is lost waiting for the suspension bushings to take a set, and the numb steering makes it difficult to avoid overcorrecting when the car's weight finally does stop redistributing itself. Apply throttle and the ZX wants to plow; lift off and the tail lurches outward.

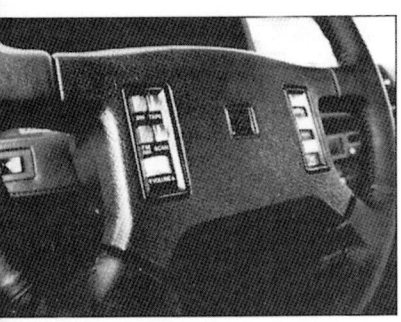

Push harder and the ZX will do better, but it's getting to be too much like work at that stage.

Put the cockpit-adjustable shock absorbers in the "gimmick" column. Though the three positions on the switch do produce readily apparent changes in shock response, none of them is quite right. Set the switch to S(oft) and the ZX wallows; N(ormal) is close to the ideal but a little stiffer than necessary; F(irm) is too bouncy to be tolerable for long.

Braking is another Nissan short suit. ABS is not included within the ZX's 4-wheel vented-disc system, and its omission is unfortunate. Hard application in a straight line will lock the front wheels; used as heavily in a turn—not recommended because of the chassis response anyway—the inside rear will lock up. In daily use, however, they're just fine.

In fact, in daily use, the whole ZX is just fine. For the kind of driving that makes up 95 percent of almost everybody's time behind the wheel, Nissan has produced a competent package. Trips to the store, highway travel and even inching through traffic are situations when the 300ZX's finer points can be appreciated.

One of those plus-points is the interior layout. Almost everything a GT customer might want is in there somewhere, from full instrumentation—the usual speedometer, tach, fuel-level, coolant-temperature and turbo-boost gauges, plus a much-appreciated combination dial showing oil pressure *and* temperature—to a pair of comfy seats and a nicely sized 3-spoke steering wheel. In true Z-car tradition, turbo boost and oil gauges are placed in the center of the dashboard and angled toward the driver. There's even a reasonable amount of package space, thanks in part to the ZX's 2-seat configuration; buyers who require kiddie/puppy/kitten seats in back must look to the stretched 2+2 and be prepared to give up the turbocharged engine.

Good as it is, the interior still drew its share of brickbats. Reading that array of instruments at night isn't as easy as it would be if Nissan had chosen something other than orange lighting, or if the designers hadn't thrown in excessively busy markings (2.5-mph and 100-rpm increments for speedometer and rev counter, respectively) on the major dial faces. And, as is becoming all too common, the ventilation and radio panels are a difficult-to-use maze of pushbuttons and hieroglyphics. Nissan (and other) stylists need to learn that big, easy-to-use knobs don't have to be unattractive, and that they are much easier to operate.

Everything we've criticized on the 300ZX Turbo is the result of age. This is an elderly design, and its wrinkles can be covered up but not erased by applying the automotive equivalent of pancake makeup. It's time for Nissan to send the car in for a facelift and then pack it off to the gym to get those muscles toned up.

Include the 300ZX Turbo in a comparison test with other GT cars of similar price, and it's going to come in last. Not worst, understand, because there are no "worsts" in the bunch. Just last. Not all the opposition comes from newer designs, either; two that immediately come to mind were intro-duced in current (though as-yet unrefined) form when Nissans were still Datsuns. That they have improved while the 300ZX has not is just due to the others using more efficient Band-aids, and maybe because the companies have better understood what goes on the list of GT car requisites.

Unsatisfied? Let's compare the 300ZX with the original 240Z. That one had a good-looking and well detailed body, willing inline 6-cylinder engine and fairly simple specifica-tions. Against it were a cheapish interi-or, 4-speed transmission (What do you want? That was 1971!) and rear-drum brakes that locked up.

Seventeen years later, the 300ZX Turbo has a good-looking but less well detailed body, a not-so-willing V-6, a beautifully finished interior, 5-speed transmission, incredible complexity, and rear disc brakes that lock up.

The new Z-car is faster in a straight line (125 mph top, 7.4 seconds 0–60 mph), probably goes around corners faster if not as enthusiastically, is qui-eter, and needs 14 feet less distance to stop from 80 mph. The new car costs a lot more, too, as does everything else.

Faced with intense competition from outside, and the pull of tradition within, Nissan has created a car that is much less than it could be. Students of history will theorize—correctly, we think—that the 300ZX's replacement will come much closer to hitting the always-moving GT-car bull's-eye.

At the moment, however, the elu-sive clay pigeons Nissan is shooting at are too often hitting the ground un-touched.—*Ray Thursby*

PRICE

List price, all POE	$23,149
Price as tested	$26,124

Price as tested includes std equip.: (cruise control, air cond, elect. window lifts, central locking, alarm sys, tilt steering wheel), pkg of special radio w/graphic equalizer, 8-way adj driver's seat, heated mirrors ($1300), leather trim ($1000), digital instruments ($675)

GENERAL

Curb weight, lb	3265
Test weight	3415
Weight distribution (with driver), f/r, %	51/49
Wheelbase, in.	91.3
Track, f/r	56.5/57.3
Length	173.4
Width	67.9
Height	49.7
Trunk space, cu ft	23.0
Fuel capacity, U.S. gal.	19.0

ENGINE

Type	turbo sohc V-6
Bore x stroke, mm	87.0 x 83.0
Displacement, cc	2960
Compression ratio	8.3:1
Bhp @ rpm, SAE net	205 @ 5200
Torque @ rpm, lb-ft	227 @ 3600
Fuel injection	Nissan multiport
Fuel requirement	unleaded, 87 pump oct

DRIVETRAIN

Transmission	5-sp manual
Gear ratios: 5th (0.71)	2.63:1
4th (1.00)	3.70:1
3rd (1.36)	5.03:1
2nd (2.08)	7.69:1
1st (3.24)	12.30:1
Final-drive ratio	3.70:1

CHASSIS & BODY

Layout	front engine/rear drive
Body/frame	unit steel
Brake system, f/r	10.9-in.vented discs/ 11.0-in. vented discs, vacuum assist
Wheels	cast alloy, 16 x 7JJ
Tires	Goodyear Eagle VR, 225/50VR-16
Steering type	rack & pinion, power assist
Turns, lock to lock	2.8
Turning circle, ft	32.2

Suspension, f/r: MacPherson struts, lower lateral arms, compliance struts, coil springs, tube shocks, anti-roll bar/semi-trailing arms, coil springs, tube shocks, anti-roll bar

CALCULATED DATA

Lb/bhp (test weight)	16.7
Bhp/liter	69.3
Engine revs @ 60 mph in 5th gear	2200
R&T steering index	0.90

ROAD TEST RESULTS

ACCELERATION

Time to distance, sec:

0–100 ft	3.2
0–500 ft	8.4
0–1320 ft (¼ mi)	.4
Speed at end of ¼ mi, mph	91.5

Time to speed, sec:

0–30 mph	2.5
0–40 mph	3.8
0–50 mph	5.2
0–60 mph	7.4
0–70 mph	9.3
0–80 mph	11.7
0–90 mph	14.5

SPEEDS IN GEARS

Maximum engine rpm	6100
5th gear (rpm) mph	(4500) 125
4th (6100)	120
3rd (6100)	89
2nd (6100)	58
1st (6100)	36

FUEL ECONOMY

Normal driving, mpg	21.0

BRAKES

Minimum stopping distances, ft:

From 60 mph	159
From 80 mph	268
Control in panic stop	good
Overall brake rating	fair

HANDLING

Lateral accel, 100-ft radius, g	0.85
Speed thru 700-ft slalom, mph	62.4

INTERIOR NOISE

Idle in neutral, dBA	50
Maximum, 1st gear	79
Constant 70 mph	70

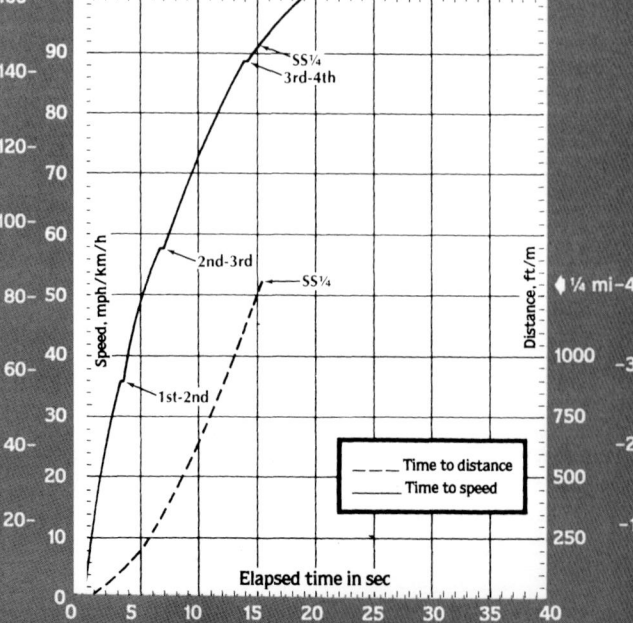

ACCELERATION

SS¼ 3rd-4th

2nd-3rd

SS¼

1st-2nd

- - - Time to distance
— Time to speed

Elapsed time in sec

IT GOES ALMOST without saying that few sports cars have enjoyed the kind of success run up by Nissan's Z-car series. But if you're interested in buying your own chapter of that story, you'd better hurry, because the Z-car as we've known it in the last few years—specifically, the ZX—is marching toward history, with an all-new replacement due in mid-1989. While the new car is, at this writing, still shrouded in secrecy, most indications point toward a substantial change from the current car, as distinct from an evolutionary update. So if the current shape tickles your fancy, you have only a few more months before it disappears.

With the end of production so near, it's not surprising that Nissan hasn't invested much in making a distinction between the 1988 ZX and the 1989. A couple new pearlescent colors have been added to the palette, along with some almost-subliminal trim changes.

However, the 1989 ZX and ZX Turbo continue to excel at the qualities that have made them so popular for so long—competent, stable high-speed touring capability wrapped in a seductive, sumptuously appointed package. Although there has been ongoing debate as to whether anything this hedonistic can be called a sports car, remember that the original 240Z revolutionized the definition of what a sports car could and could not be by introducing the novel idea of comfort to the concept.

Besides the obvious seductions of design and furnishings, one of the most appealing features of the ZX series has been its 3.0-liter V-6 engine, an old smoothie that's going to outlive the current car. Nissan bumped output and response in both the normally aspirated and turbocharged versions last year by 5 bhp each, helping the Z-cars keep pace with their numerous competitors,

particularly in midrange response.

The independent suspension, including Nissan's adjustable shock absorbers, also is carried over without change, although the Z-car team did dial in more roll stiffness recently, in response to suggestions that the ZX was getting a little soft. Normally aspirated editions continue to get 215/60R-15 tires, while the turbos wear 225/50VR-16s, and 4-wheel-disc brakes, with vented front rotors, are standard on all cars.

When it comes to creature comforts, Nissan understands not only what you need, but also what you want. Electric power for windows, central locking, mirrors and seat adjusters; automatic climate control, super stereo system, cruise control, wheel hub-mounted sound system controls—there's plenty in the way of standard equipment, and plenty more in the option package groups. Just check the appropriate boxes on the order form. But hurry.

SPECIFICATIONS

Base price, base model $22,299	Fuel capacity, U.S. gal. 19.0	Transmission 5M*, 4A
Country of origin .... Japan	Fuel economy (EPA city), mpg 17	Final-drive ratio............................ 3.70:1
Body/seats .... 3D/2*, 2+2	Warranty, years/miles 3/36,000,	Suspension, f/r .... ind/ind
Layout .... F/R	3/unlimited rust-through	Brakes, f/r.................................. disc/disc
Wheelbase, in. 91.3	Engine .... 165-bhp sohc V-6	Tires 225/50VR-16
Track, f/r 56.5/57.3	Optional .... turbo sohc V-6*	Steering type..................... rack & pinion (p)
Length 173.4	Bore x stroke, mm .... 87.0 x 83.0	Turning circle, ft 32.2
Width 67.9	Displacement, cc........................... 2970	Turns, lock-to-lock 3.6
Height 49.7	Compression ratio 8.3:1	
Curb weight, lb 3255	Bhp @ rpm, net .... 205 @ 5200	
Luggage/cargo capacity, cu ft 23.0	Torque @ rpm, lb-ft .... 227 @ 3600	

*indicates model described in specifications

THE BOULEVARDIER STOPS HERE

**It's all-new. It's exciting.
And . . . it's now a real sports car.**

BY DENNIS SIMANAITIS

PHOTOS BY JOHN LAMM

I'VE JUST DRIVEN one of the best sports cars in the world; one that's refreshing in style, balanced in feel and exhilarating in performance. And, curiously enough, this sports car has the same name as a handsome boulevardier of note, the Nissan 300ZX.

A little history may put things in perspective. Way back in 1970 there was another sports car from the same company, then known as Datsun. The 240Z was a milestone design showing the world that sports cars didn't have to be stark, open, impractical or, for that matter, even British. Its next iteration in 1974, the 260Z, was essentially one of engine displacement. But then softening of the arteries set in, as the 280ZX went sporty-car in 1978 and the 300ZX became positively boulevardier in 1983. A very nice boulevardier, mind: Diluted though the 300ZX had become, for a while there it attracted customers at a rate of 5000/ month, far and away the best selling Z of the lot. It was not, however, the sort of machine to stir the souls of hard-core sports car enthusiasts.

Even, for example, enthusiasts within Nissan. And, as you may have noticed, these enthusiasts have been busy of late infusing new excitement into that corporate giant. Witness the 240SX, the Maxima and the car described in this very magazine. This one, here, now.

Examine the new 300ZX and you will see some Z-car heritage, but only hints of it. Compared with the previous Z, the car is shorter (by 3.9 in.) and wider (by 2.6 in.). Yet its wheelbase is 5.1 in. longer, with the result being less overhang and increased chunkiness. What's more, there's a new proportion of nose to rear deck with the cockpit farther forward, giving a suggestion of mid-engine potency to the car's front-engine/rear-drive nature.

And along with this styling analysis there's a story to tell, one that shows just how responsive Japanese automakers can be. In the first draft of this article, I wrote, "Less successful to my eye is the front end, dominated visually by that overly large emblem in the panel between the headlights. I'd have swapped it, corporate pride withstanding, for something more subtle . . ." Well, you can see the emblem in our accompanying photos, but you won't see it when cars go on sale. Even as this article was being prepared, Nissan called to let me know that two suggestions from journalists had already been adopted: A seatback release lacking on the prototypes had been added, and that emblem had been removed. Huzzah for the power of the press—and for Nissan's responsiveness.

Now, where was I? Ah, yes, the car's rear three-quarter view is particularly attractive, the way the taillights are crisply ensconced in their blacked-out panel. And I really love that side

window, an arc of decreasing radius that suggests a classic car shape yet is still so fresh.

These are elements of pure form, but there is excellent engineering here as well. The headlamps, for instance, use new optical technology allowing the lenses to be raked at a 60-degree angle to vertical. A lot of Cray super-computer time went into CAFV, computer-aided flow visualization, of the car's front end, a critical region defining not only air penetration but also engine cooling and ground clearance. The wheels are set flush with the bodywork for reduced drag. Overall, the car's C_X works out to 0.31, quite respectable in light of its lift characteristics being superior to the Porsche 944 Turbo's or Chevrolet Corvette's, two of its evident targets.

There's another interesting aspect of the bodywork; this one, characterized by what's not there. The rear bumper panel is abbreviated, all the better to give enticing little glimpses of virile exhaust system, suspension components and differential.

The unibody structure, completely new, is 35 percent stiffer in bending mode and 20 percent stronger in torsional respects than the one it replaces. Continuous arc welding of some pieces, reinforcement of other panels with thermosetting resins and use of high-strength steel all enter into this. One payoff is rigidity equivalent to that of a closed coupe, despite

the T-roof configuration of all 300ZXs destined for our market. (Alas, no full convertible is envisioned.)

Crashworthiness and repair also profit from clean-sheet (or is it now blank-screen?) design. Modular replacement, for instance, reduces the costs of collision damage and, one would assume, of insurance. And, even as fender-benders are prudently avoided, the 300ZX's corrosion resistance is enhanced by widespread use of a new 2-side-zinc/nickel-coated steel.

The extreme stiffness of chassis gives suspension engineers a stable platform on which to mount their hardware. Though not really active in the pure sense (and not 4-wheel steer—more on this anon), this suspension fits the term "reactive" to a T. That is, in reacting to loads of cornering, accelerating and braking, it adjusts itself optimally to give enhanced stability, maneuverability and driver feel.

At each front corner, a lateral link and tension rod define the kingpin's lower pivot point. Its upper pivot depends on another 2-piece

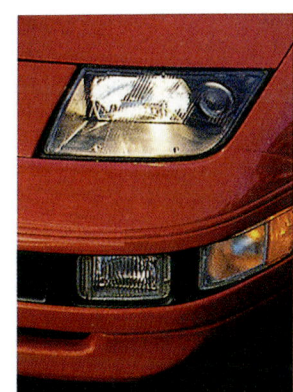

■ Technology blends with esthetics: the 60-degree rake of the headlights, the V-6's artful plumbing, bodywork offering glimpses of differential and suspension, and brake calipers peeking out through wheel spokes.

■ The ZX cockpit is set up with well-defined areas of function. Pods flanking oversize analog gauges are within fingertip reach from the steering wheel. Use of color and texture reflects Nissan's newly evolving design esthetic.

linkage, one that is rather unconventional: First, there's an upper arm angled forward, outward and upward from a relatively high chassis pickup point. Second, an intermediate link curves downward and inward connecting this upper arm with the kingpin. The point of all this is to separate optimization of the many constraints typically tangled up in a more conventional layout, things like camber, caster, anti-dive, anti-squat and steering offset. The coil spring, shock absorber and anti-roll bar act off the intermediate link, giving them an efficient 1:1 ratio of control.

As an example of the elegant engineering embodied in this front end, let's look at one implication of the angled upper arm: its effect on camber control.

Ideally, for maximum stability and grip, the tire should stay at a right angle to the road under all conditions. Traveling in a straight line over bumps and dips, you'd like as little camber change as possible in response to suspension travel. And, if this were the only constraint, you'd choose an upper arm of roughly the same length as the lower arm; this, to approximate a parallelogram action of zero camber change.

Alas, but you'd like to go around corners too, wouldn't you? And in cornering, you *want* camber change so that orientation of the tire, particularly the heavily loaded outside one, will account for body roll and remain more or less upright. For this, you'd like the upper arm to be *shorter* than the lower one.

What's a suspension engineer to do?

If he's at Nissan, he devises that upper link angled forward from its chassis pickup. Then the arm's effective (albeit sometimes imaginary) length is determined by where its axis of swing intersects the wheel's centerline. So, when its wheel is pointed straight ahead, the

link's lateral image can be as long as required for straight-line stability. Yet, when leaned on in a corner, the arm's shorter length gives the desired amount of negative camber, thus helping to keep its wheel upright as the body rolls. Notice that this cornering argument works only in favor of the outside wheel, but not to worry. The inside wheel, essentially unloaded, has the easy job anyway. Neat, eh?

The rear suspension of the 300ZX uses a multilink layout similar to the Nissan 240SX's. Each hub is located by a lower A-arm, another lateral link angled farther back and a pair of upper links that just miss forming an A of their own. As with the front suspension, this multiplicity of links frees the design of entangling compromises.

The lower A-arm's chassis pickup points are angled with regard to the car's centerline and, what's more, they reside in bushings that are supple axially but stiff in the vertical direction. When loads of cornering or braking are applied, this compliance causes the entire A-arm to shift backward and inward slightly, and the lateral link likewise rotates to the rear. The result is toe-in of the rear wheels, just enough to enhance stability under these conditions.

The twin upper links characterize an imaginary kingpin axis that angles inward from top to bottom. This inward slant produces the same degree of toe-in in response to either form of braking, be it driver-induced (which acts at the tire contact patch) or the engine-induced kind (which acts at the wheel centerline).

Collectively, these links and arms define planes, arcs and axes going every which way, each with carefully calculated purpose and each the product of a great deal of computer-aided design. Viewed from the side, for instance, rear-wheel travel defines an arc that's centered just barely rearward of the ideal point of zero-squat/zero-lift. That's to say, any tendencies of excessive lift or squat have been engineered out of the ZX's suspension.

Its steering has had any bad habits excised as well. The 300ZX has rack-and-pinion, but what makes it special is a novel twin-orifice road-speed-sensitive power assist, developed to counter what Nissan engineers saw as inherent tradeoffs of previous speed-sensitive units.

First, some background: One approach to speed-sensitive assist is to vary the steering pump's flow rate inversely with road speed: The faster you drive, the less flow through the pump, the less flow through the system's control valve, or orifice, and the less assist. This works fine until you give a quick stab of the wheel at high speed, an emergency maneuver, for instance. Then it's all too possible for a flow-rate system to "catch," that is, to find itself momentarily low on fluid through the orifice and, thus, low on boost.

Another approach is called hydraulic reaction control. As its name implies, this one varies hydraulic pressure at the control orifice to augment the system's mechanical resistance, its steering feel, typically provided by a built-in torsion spring. At low speed, only a little hydraulic resistance is added, and the driver experiences full assist. As speed increases, fluid at higher pressure provides additional resistance, generating added feel. This approach is more amenable to fine-tuning than is its flow-rate counterpart. However, it has tradeoffs too: complexity and, what's worse, a tendency toward jerky response, especially just off center.

Nissan's solution, an entirely new one, is to have two separate control orifices in the system. At low speed, the flow is routed through both orifices, which together are sized to produce the desired full assist. Then, as speed increases, a drain valve gradually diverts flow from one of the orifices, ultimately leaving only the other orifice to control the assist. And this latter one is sized to provide optimal assist for high speed.

To say the brakes are conventional is only in contrast to the 300ZX's suspension and steering. They too are high in technological content, with 4-wheel vented discs, opposed-piston calipers of aluminum for reduced unsprung weight and ABS as standard equipment. The wheels of the ZX have an open spoke pattern; this, for at least two reasons: assuring maximum airflow for cooling the discs—and as styling statements, giving tantalizing views of the discs and caliper assemblies. This is a car that's proud of its mechanical nature.

But what about under its hood? Here, the only holdover from the previous ZX is the numerical designation representing its almost 3.0-liter displacement, 2960 cc, to be exact. Cylinder heads and block, valve gear, crankshaft, intake and exhaust are all new for this quad-cam 24-valve 60-degree 222-bhp V-6.

Downstream of its centrally mounted air cleaner and airflow meter, for example, are separate intake and exhaust tracts for each bank with tuned intake runners, aerodynamically tapered ports and dual exhaust. Each cylinder has its own separate ignition as well, in a system similar to those pioneered by Saab and Buick. Connected directly to each sparkplug is a compact coil that gets its trigger signal from the engine-management computer. Another refinement owing its origins to another automaker, this time Alfa Romeo, appears in the valve gear. NVTC, Nissan Valve Timing Control, uses hydraulic means to rotate a helical gear connecting the camshaft and its drive pulley. Basic timing is tuned for high-speed efficiency, but at low to medium rpm and light load, orientation of the camshaft and its drive pulley is shifted causing the intake valves to

SPECIFICATIONS

Curb weight	3220 lb
Wheelbase	96.5 in.
Track, f/r	58.9 in./60.4 in.
Length	169.5 in.
Width	70.5 in.
Height	49.4 in.
Fuel capacity	19.0 gal.

ENGINE & DRIVETRAIN

Type	4-valve dohc **V-6**
Bore x stroke	87.0 x 83.0 mm
Displacement	**2960 cc**
Compression ratio	10.5:1
Horsepower (SAE net)	**222 bhp @ 6400 rpm**
Torque	**198 lb-ft @ 4800 rpm**
Fuel delivery	electronic fuel injection
Transmission	**5-sp manual**

CHASSIS & BODY

Layout	**front engine/rear drive**
Brake system, f/r	**vented disc/vented disc; ABS**
Wheels	cast alloy; 16 x 7½
Tires	**P225/50R-16 91V**
Steering type	**rack & pinion, variable power asst**

Suspension, f/r: **upper angled arms** with intermediate links, lower lateral arms, tension rods, coil springs, tube shocks, anti-roll bar/**lower angled A-arms,** lower angled lateral links, twin upper links, coil springs, tube shocks, anti-roll bar open and (more critically) to close sooner. This effectively shifts the 198-lb-ft torque peak to lower rpm and lessens the tradeoffs inherent in valve timing of the fixed variety.

And isn't it refreshing when an automaker takes concepts of another manufacturer and refines them. So often, a Not Invented Here syndrome prevails, where folks waste considerable time and effort dodging around someone else's good idea, only to come up with something truly mediocre.

Even the 5-speed gearbox admitted some redesign. Analyses of many transmissions, for instance, showed that shifts into 2nd or 3rd tended to require increased effort, the result being an unbalanced feel. Nissan's response with the 300ZX is to fit new double-cone synchronizers for these gears. Shift-lever orientation was another area of study, with short stroke of an upright lever deemed optimal. So engineers devised a floor-mounted shifter remote from the transmission whose short actuation is enhanced by a support rod connecting the point of pivot with the transmission housing.

Other controls in the 300ZX cockpit show similar care in development. There's a unity of form and function that's evident to anyone familiar with Nissan's Arc-X concept car, its new Maxima or the 240SX. Soft contours, interesting textures and free-flowing panels predominate. The driver's environment is centered on an instrument cluster, thankfully large, readable and analog, rimmed by control pods. To the driver's right are controls for heat/vent/air conditioning and wipers. To the left are lights, cruise-control master switch and rear-window heat. And each of these controls is Honda-esque in execution (high praise). There's well nigh perfect engineering of feel, just the right actuation effort, stroke and response feedback.

To some eyes, though, there's an esthetic tradeoff: The dashboard is perhaps not quite as smoothly integrated as that of the 240SX. But a design goal with the 300ZX was to have all the important controls within driver's reach without having to take one's hands off the steering wheel, and the dual pod layout certainly accomplishes this.

Well, we've examined the new 300ZX from front to rear, from top to bottom. But enough of examination already. What's it like to drive?

As I noted at the beginning, it's one of the best sports cars in the world. I realize this may sound more than a little premature, based as it is on admittedly brief experience—and all at Nissan's Tochigi test facility. But I believe the opinions of my colleagues and, even more telling, of future customers will bear me out.

For instance, Tochigi's Country Road circuit is a twisty two-lane, with an off-camber here, a decreasing radius there, and more than a few bumps designed to upset a car's composure; the

sort of place where "oops" is a bad word.

Around there, the new 300ZX could be driven with a level of confidence bordering on bravado, even before you remind yourself which way the road goes. Pushed to *your* comfortable limit, the car still has some reserve. And this word applies in two distinct senses, "reserve" as in having some untapped performance remaining, and also in the sense of being generally benign. The new 300ZX is a car that simply never snaps back.

Its steering communicates very well, with nary a kickback but plenty of information about grip at the front tires. At the car's evidently high limits, however, this steering seems to spend a good deal of its time communicating a single word—understeer. On the other hand, trading comments with Nissan folks, I sensed that this is precisely what they want: suspension tuning that gives predictable handling, more than a good dose of forgiveness—and absolutely no unpleasant surprises.

The brakes, ABS-invoked or otherwise, work just fine, with the sort of pedal that makes trail-braking artful.

Straight-line performance is in keeping with a car of this character, 0–60 mph in the low 7-second range, I'd guess. And around Tochigi's high-banked oval I settled in for a drama-free tour at an indicated 130 mph. Even had the T-roof panels out for a while there, with plenty of wind noise but surprisingly little buffeting.

And if you're a particularly patient sort, let me tell you about another new 300ZX I drove, the Turbo. It has *twin* turbos and *twin* intercoolers and *300* bhp. And its suspension adds a new HICAS variation, Nissan's latest production iteration of 4-wheel steer with just a twitch of counter-steer to enhance yaw response at turn-in. Responsive though the normally aspirated car is, the Turbo makes it feel positively tame. Expect the Turbo to reach 60 in the mid-5s. (I recorded a hand-held low-6 sec without lots of ordeal.) Expect it to give a wonderfully GTP-like whooop-whoooop-whooop from its wastegate as you run up through the gears. And, alas, expect it to be October or so before you can buy one.

By contrast, the normally aspirated 300ZX had its world introduction at the Chicago Auto Show in early February. It's expected to be on sale by April, with a 2+2 version following in three months or so. If I could pin down prices, I'd be able to make regular killings on all the international monetary markets. But we can bet Nippon-logical competitive pricing will obtain, perhaps $25,000, say, for a normally aspirated 2-seater. Whatever happens to the dollar/yen relationship, I'd aim these new ZXs at other real sports cars of the Stuttgart/Bowling Green variety. And isn't *that* a funny geographical linkage?

NISSAN 300ZX

The class of its class
PHOTOS BY JOHN LAMM

PREDICTION: THE ALL-NEW Nissan 300ZX will set standards for sports cars in the $25,000 to $30,000 price range that will have every other maker of sporting equipment scrambling triple time to catch up. In every conceivable area of importance to an enthusiast—handling, ride, steering, braking, styling, structure, ergonomics, engine, transmission, you-name-it—it is better than or, at worst, the equal of every other sports car on the road today. Including several costing considerably more. It is a car that will influence sports-car design for years to come—not unlike the impact the original 240Z had when it was introduced to the United States in late 1969.

If you think we had run out of superlatives in our introductory article on the 300ZX a short two months ago, think again. We've had our Webster's working overtime keeping up with our feelings about the new Z. Since that story with driving impressions based upon some rather limited stick time on Nissan's Tochigi proving grounds. we've had an opportunity to spend considerable time in the car on our home turf. Driving that also included extensive back-to-back impressions of a 1989 Porsche 944 Turbo and a 1989 Chevrolet Corvette convertible hardtop equipped with the Z52 suspension package. That suspension package, by the way, is not the take-no-prisoners Z51 handling option, but rather a suspension designed for ride comfort as well as world-class handling.

Rather than repeat ourselves, we'll refer you to our earlier story in the March 1989 issue for background on the development of the new 300ZX. But very briefly, for those who came in late, here are a few vital statistics. The new car is built on a 5.1-in. longer wheelbase than the previous ZX, but it's nearly 4 in. shorter. It's wider, too, by more than 2 in. Lots of Cray Supercomputer time went into optimizing the aerodynamics, the structural characteristics and the suspension design.

Initially, only the 2-place model with standard T-roof will be offered. A few months later a 2+2 will be introduced, and around October a 300-bhp twin-turbo version will hit the road with back tires spinning. But enough of specs. Let's get back to the road . . . and the track.

"State of the art" is an overworked descriptive term these days, but it certainly is appropriate for the 300ZX's V-6. This much-modified 3.0-liter, 24-valve, twincam engine cranks out an impressive 222 bhp at 6400 rpm and 198 lb.-ft. of torque at 4800. Crank-fired ignition with a coil for each sparkplug and variable valve timing are just two of the engine's so-

phisticated features. Basic timing is tuned for high-speed running, but thanks to that variable timing, every one of the V-6's 7000 available revs is usable. At low revs the intake valves open and close sooner, effectively shifting the torque curve to lower rpm, resulting in an enormously broad and flexible power band.

Light the tires from rest and keep your right foot down (except during upshifts), and the ZX will click off consistent 0–60-mph times in just a tick or two over 7 seconds. You'll reach 100 mph in less than 20 sec. The quarter mile is only 15.5 sec. into your future, and you'll be traveling 90.5 mph as you cross the 1320-ft. stripe. What impresses most while all this is taking place is the ease with which it happens. It's like asking a marathoner to run around the block. That's not even enough distance to work up a sweat. From idle to maximum revs, the ZX's engine is smooth, relaxed and quiet. That's not to imply that it doesn't make sports-car sounds. It does—lovely, melodious tones that speak as much of refinement as they do of performance.

High-speed running is also a ZX forte. How does 120 mph suit you? Not enough? Well, then, move up to 140. Around the high-banked oval at Nissan's Arizona Test Center, we saw those numbers and higher . . . all the

way to the car's 148-mph top speed. All was calm, secure and stable. Even in 30–40-mph crosswinds the ZX was totally unperturbed.

That feeling of absolute security at high speeds is a reflection of the efforts that went into the 300's suspension design. We all know how the previous ZX's ride and handling had taken on the character of a boulevard GT. The new car isn't a home run in these departments; it's a grand slam. We started our suspension evaluations with some 55–65-mph cruising just to get a feel for the car at normal U.S. speeds. The first thing you notice is how compliant the ride is over Botts dots and tar strips. So we adjourned to an absolutely horrible road that runs right in front of the ATC. Horrible because of the condition of the pavement: broken, pot-holed, rippled, bumpy. But perfect for ride evaluations. We tried it at 60 mph, we tried it at 80 mph. Finally we tried it at 100 mph in an effort to unlock the Nissan's ride secrets.

If there is a secret, it's called structural rigidity. The new car is superior to the old car in every way—bending, torsion, rigidity. Hard as we tried, we couldn't get the 300 to misbehave. It soaks up bumps, dips and every other pavement irregularity like the proverbial sponge. You feel the wheels working via feedback

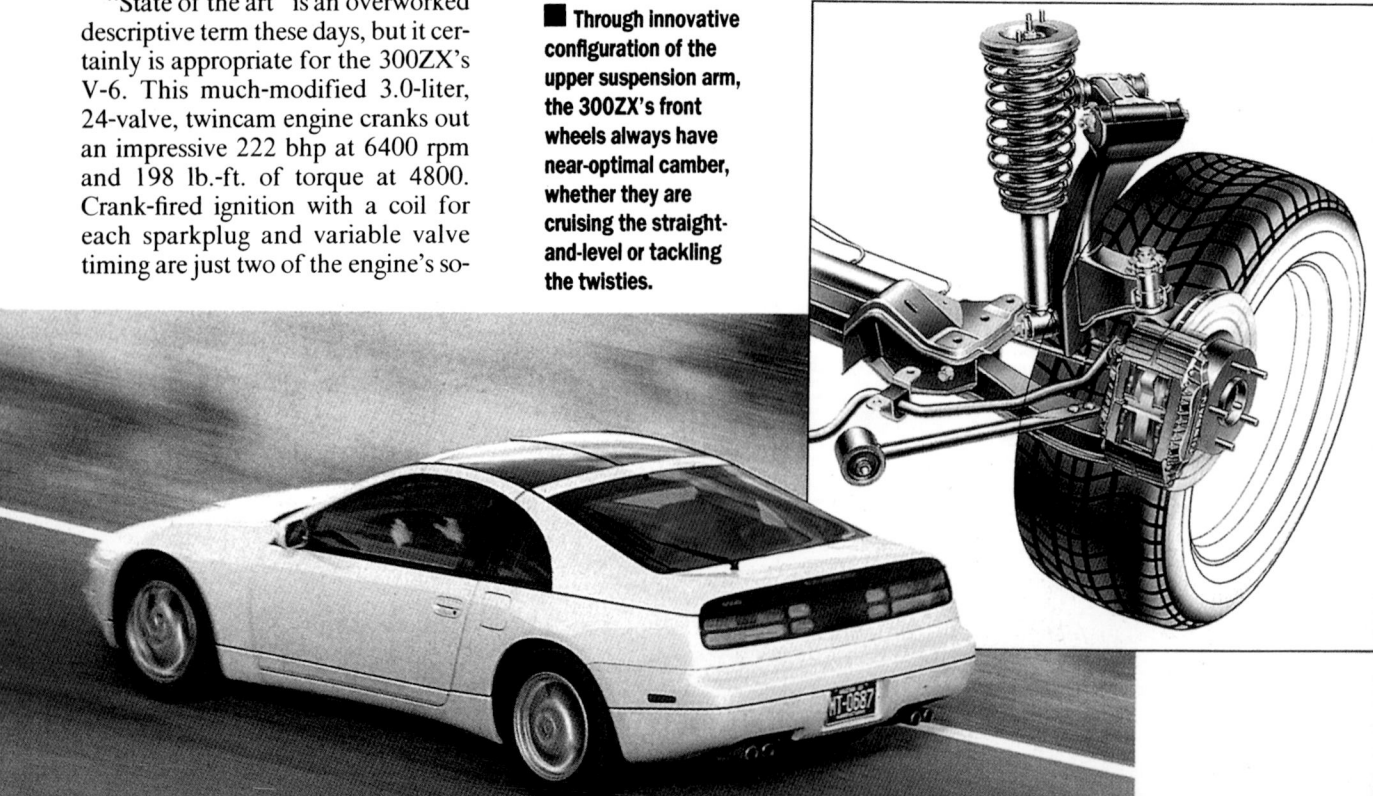

■ Through innovative configuration of the upper suspension arm, the 300ZX's front wheels always have near-optimal camber, whether they are cruising the straight-and-level or tackling the twisties.

NISSAN 300ZX

PRICE

List price, all POE .... **est $27,500**
Price as tested .... **est $27,500**

Price as tested includes std equip. (air cond, AM/FM stereo/cassette, elect. window lifts, T-bar sunroof, elect. adj mirrors, cruise control, central locking).

IMPORTER

Nissan Motor Corp, PO Box 191, Gardena, Calif. 90247

0–60 mph .... 7.1 sec
0–¼ mi .... 15.5 sec
Top speed .... 148 mph
Skidpad 0.88g
Slalom .... 65.6 mph
Brake rating ....excellent

DRAWING BY BILL DOBSON

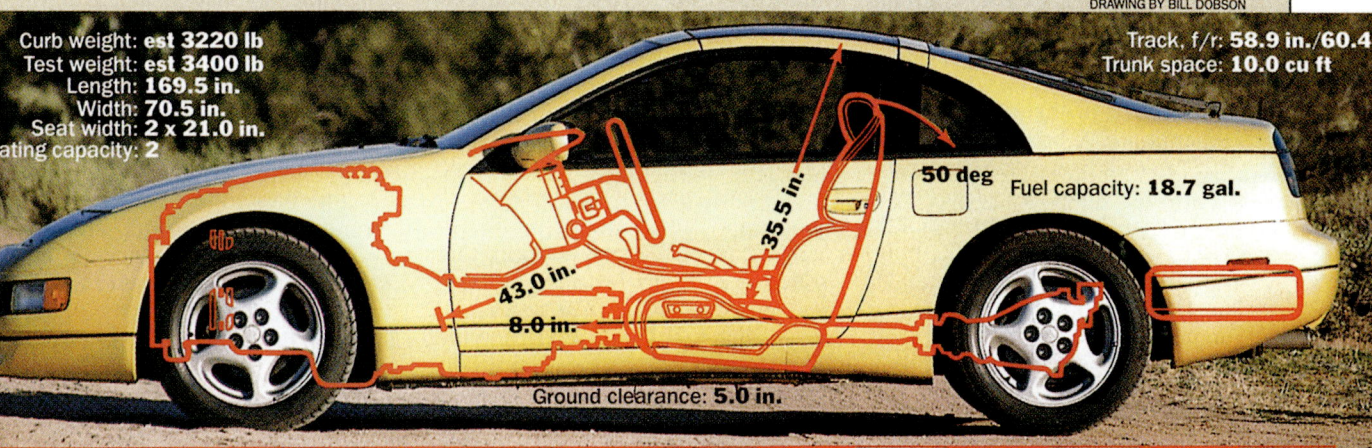

Curb weight: **est 3220 lb**
Test weight: **est 3400 lb**
Length: **169.5 in.**
Width: **70.5 in.**
Seat width: **2 x 21.0 in.**
Seating capacity: **2**

Track, f/r: **58.9 in./60.4**
Trunk space: **10.0 cu ft**

35.5 in.
50 deg
Fuel capacity: **18.7 gal.**

43.0 in.
8.0 in.
Ground clearance: **5.0 in.**

Wheelbase: **96.5 in.**
Weight dist (with driver), f/r, %: **55/45**

ENGINE

Type ....iron block, alloy head, **V-6**
Valvetrain .... variable timing, dohc, 4-valve/cyl
Displacement ....181 cu in./2960 cc
Bore x stroke ....3.43 x 3.27 in./ 87.0 x 83.0 mm
Compression ratio 10.1:1
Horsepower
 (SAE) ..... **222 bhp @ 6400 rpm**
Bhp/liter 75.0
Torque ..... **198 lb-ft @ 4800 rpm**
Maximum engine speed....7000 rpm
Fuel injection ......Nissan ECCS port
Fuel ....prem unleaded, 91 pump oct

CHASSIS & BODY

Layout .... **front engine/rear drive**
Body/frame .... unit steel
Brakes
 Front ....**11.0-in. vented discs**
 Rear ....**11.7-in. vented discs**
 Assist type .... vacuum, ABS
 Total swept area ....304 sq in.
 Swept area/ton ....179 sq in.
Wheels..........cast alloy, **16 x 7½**
Tires ......Dunlop SP Sport D40 M2, **225/50VR-16**
Steering ...rack & pinion, pwr assist
 Overall ratio 16.8:1
 Turns, lock to lock 2.8
 Turning circle .... 34.1 ft
Suspension
 Front........**angled upper arms, lower A-arms,** "3rd links," coil springs, tube shocks, anti-roll bar
 Rear..**multimember** (upper lateral links, angled upper links, mid-lateral links, lower angled A-arms), coil springs, tube shocks, anti-roll bar

DRIVETRAIN

Transmission ....**5-sp manual**

Gear	Ratio	Overall ratio	(Rpm) Mph
1st	3.21:1	13.12:1	37
2nd	1.93:1	7.86:1	62
3rd	1.30:1	5.32:1	92
4th	1.00:1	4.08:1	124
5th	0.75:1	3.07:1	(6400) 148

Final drive ratio 4.08:1
Engine rpm @ 60 mph in 5th 2600

INTERIOR NOISE

Idle in neutral .... 46 dBA
Maximum in 1st gear......... 74 dBA
Constant 50 mph .... 65 dBA
70 mph .... 70 dBA

INSTRUMENTATION

160-mph speedometer, 9000-rpm tach, oil press., coolant temp, fuel level

FUEL ECONOMY

Normal driving..........est 23.5 mpg
EPA city/highway ..... est 17/25 mpg
Cruise range ....est 415 miles
Fuel capacity ....18.7 gal.

MAINTENANCE

Oil/filter change ....7500 mi/na
Tuneup ....na
Basic warranty .... 36 mo/36,000 mi

ACCELERATION

Time to speed	Seconds
0–30 mph	2.3
0–40 mph	3.8
0–50 mph	5.4
0–60 mph	7.1
0–70 mph	9.5
0–80 mph	12.2
0–90 mph	15.2
0–100 mph	19.1
Time to distance	
0–100 ft	3.1
0–500 ft	8.4
0–1320 ft (¼ mi):15.5 @ 90.5 mph	

BRAKING

Minimum stopping distance
 From 60 mph ....134 ft
 From 80 mph ....233 ft
Control ....excellent
Pedal effort for 0.5g stop........ 15 lb
Fade, effort after six 0.5g stops from
 60 mph ....20 lb
Brake feel ....very good
Overall brake rating ....excellent

HANDLING

Lateral accel (200-ft skidpad) ..0.88g
 Balance .... mild understeer
Speed thru 700-ft slalom ..65.6 mph
 Balance ....neutral
Lateral seat support ....very good

Subjective ratings consist of excellent, very good, good, average, poor; na means information is not available.

through the wheel. But kickback? Perish the thought.

So you think, "If it's this good in ride, it's gotta be too soft to handle well." So you make a few quick lane changes to test the transient response. The front end seems to anticipate your every move. Almost instinctively the ZX tracks where you place it. The steering is wonderfully precise, direct and positive. There's none of that vague artificial feel that we've come to associate with Japanese power-assisted steering. Feedback and road feel are superb. Ditto the effort, regardless of road speed or quickness of input.

But how about low-speed cornering? Does the 300 plow? And what about its high-speed handling characteristics? Does it tend toward trailing-throttle oversteer? Does the rear end get twitchy if you stay on the power? There are only two words that aptly describe the ZX's behavior: "total balance." If there are vices to the 300's handling, we have yet to uncover them. The ZX's interactive suspension works with the driver in every driving situation. There are always plenty of options for the driver to choose. In tight 1st- and 2nd-gear cornering, you can apply power and get the rear wheels to spin. Or you can lift off the throttle and achieve mild tuck-in. And it's all totally benign and predictable.

Brakes? What do you think with an anti-lock system standard? Panic stops from 60 and 80 mph require only 134 and 233 ft., respectively. Locking, twitching or other control problems? With ABS you can eliminate those words from your braking vocabulary.

Someone who understands the definition of the word "ergonomics" designed the ZX's interior. Gauges and major and minor controls are all logically located and close at hand. The seats, particularly those with manual as opposed to power adjustments, offer a range of positions that relegate a tilt or telescoping steering wheel to the category of redundancy—which is probably the reason the ZX doesn't offer one. The attention to detail extends to the leather-wrapped wheel. There are no stitches on the horizontal spokes to dig into thumbs that are rested there. The materials used and the fit and finish are all first-cabin. There are a lot of sports cars that offer driver-friendly environments, but the ZX's is more likely to evoke an ear-to-ear grin.

So what we have in the new 300ZX is the perfect sports car, right? Not quite. A few nits need to be picked. We don't like the passive safety belts. Worse, they add an awkward design element. When the doors are open and the window is down, an ugly B-post protrudes from the rear of each door. It's there for structural considerations—those darn passive belts. It had us wishing that Nissan could have incorporated a device that would retract the posts when the doors were opened with the windows rolled down, a la the door design on the BMW Z1.

The all-new manual gearbox is a delight—efforts are light and precise, and the linkage has a Rock of Gibraltar feel to it. But we were a little disappointed with the notchiness of the 4–5 shift in our test car.

If the new Nissan lacks the bottom-end grunt of a Corvette and the top speed of a 944 Turbo, it has superior flexibility, smoothness and rev-ability. It handles as well as the Corvette and better than the 944 Turbo, with high-speed stability that even the *Autobahn*-developed Porsche can't match. The ride is superior to either of these other world-class sports cars.

The impact of the all-new 300ZX will be felt in sports-car circles for years to come. After a day's driving, the Editor-in-Chief came back to enthuse, "This is the car that I believe will move the naturally aspirated 944 to second place on Jackie Stewart's list of the best-balanced automobiles in the world."

■ Look and feel of interior are consistent with the 300ZX's high-performance chassis. Digital temperature control is an option.

PHOTOS BY DEAN SIRACUSA

STRAMAN 300ZX CONVERTIBLE

Z top goes down!

BY ANDREW BORNHOP

IF THE OWNER of a 1990 Nissan 300ZX were a fly on the wall in the R. Straman Company's shop, he might cringe and think twice if he saw his car in the initial stages of convertible conversion. Stripped of its interior, the car is decapitated by a skilled craftsman with a good ole Milwaukee power saw. As precise as the lop job is, the metal shavings and aroma of burnt steel make it seem too harsh a treatment for such a sleek car. But what other method is there? Remember, the first step toward a Martin guitar is the swing of an ax.

In either turbo or non-turbo form, Straman gives the 300ZX a refreshing gust of air. The Costa Mesa, California-based coachbuilder's workmanship is top-notch, even keeping most of the original seals in place. No fiberglass is used, and the 2-arm top looks and operates as if it were factory-spec.

With the top up, the formerly arched hatchback takes on a flattop notchback look, sporting a legitimate trunk with a lengthened rear decklid made of steel. And with the top down, the car has an aggressive appearance dominated by the swooping beltline.

And hallelujah, the chassis feels tight, as a brief drive in the car brought to light little evidence of cowl shake. The interior noise level is a touch higher than that of the coupe, but that's expected.

The secret to its stiffness lies in Straman's chassis reinforcements. Rectangular tubes of mild steel run beneath each rocker panel and connect the rear subframe to the front subframe at box-section braces just aft of the front wheel wells. From that point, upright braces extend to the base of the A-pillars.

Most evident, though, is the structure bar between the B-pillars. Esthetically questionable, it aids torsional rigidity. Its presence is also justified, however, by the B-pillars, which had to be retained as anchor points for the seatbelts.

Actuation for the top is by electric control of two hydraulic pumps: one to raise the top over the structure bar, and the other to pull the roof back into an area just ahead of the new trunk. The driver has to get out of his seat only if he wants to snap the fabric boot into place. Raising the roof is simple: Push a button, then clasp the latches at the windshield header.

Cost for the conversion? Richard Straman pegs the three-week process at $8500. Not bad for a car capable of giving a Porsche 944 S2 Cabrio a run for its money, at a considerably lower price.

About three Convertibles are made each week, with most of the orders coming in from dealers. "We're going to make it a limited-edition car," quips Straman, "limited to the number of people who want it." ◪

■ Factory seals, spring-loaded tensioners behind the B-pillars, and clasps taken from Mazda's RX-7 Convertible give Straman's soft-top a finished look that should prove to be weathertight.

NISSAN 300ZX TURBO

A world-class sports car responds to its pressure points

L IKE INDIANS SWARMING around a circle of Conestoga wagons, people at the filling station hummed and buzzed around the Nissan 300ZX. Bright red and voluptuous, it drew several customers away from their gas pumps for a closer look. "Looks like a new Porsche," effused one. "Is that a new Ferrari?" questioned another. One person simply asked, "What is it?"

The general public's difficulty in identifying it as a Z-car is a credit to both Nissan and the new 300ZX. Its shape is evocative of the best Zuffenhausen and Maranello have to offer, but to compare it to these other designs is to deny the car its own identity. Gone is the somewhat chunky, chiseled appearance of the previous 300ZX, replaced with a lithe, poised-to-spring look. The wheelbase has been lengthened and the overhangs and overall length have been reduced; now, one curve blends smoothly into the next. And there are the lovely details that keep your eyes playing over its surface for more—the recessed antenna, the flying-buttress rear pillar flowing forward in an uninterrupted arc to become the A-pillar, and 5-spoke

PHOTOS BY SCOTT DAHLQUIST

wheels with quasi-elliptical openings large enough to show off the massive aluminum brake calipers.

A peek under the aluminum hood reveals the compact 60-degree 3.0-liter V-6 that has evolved into a much more exotic species since its debut in the 1984-model Z-car. Now it's capped off with dohc heads with four valves per cylinder and has variable camshaft timing, separate intake tracts for each bank, and a distributorless ignition system with tiny coils perched atop each sparkplug. That's a lot of hardware to stuff beneath the Z-car's severely tapered nose, but Nissan's engineers managed it with only the slightest hint of a hood bulge.

It's all the more amazing that two turbochargers, two intercoolers and all their requisite plumbing (not to mention the hydraulic actuator for the rear-wheel steering) were shoehorned in place without modifying the hood. The intercoolers are placed low in the nose and inhale through horizontal slots below the turn-signal/foglight clusters. Their location requires labyrinthine ductwork to reach the turbos and makes the engine compartment one of the most crowded in all of automobiledom. But it's also one of the most powerful engines in production, cranking out a rousing 300 bhp (yes, that's 100 bhp/liter) at 6400 rpm and 283 lb.-ft. of torque at a low 3600 rpm (automatic-transmission versions have the same torque, but 20 fewer bhp because of a fuel-management curve and camshaft profiles better suited to that gearbox).

To allow the engine to live at these power levels, the compression ratio was dropped from 10.5:1 to 8.5:1. The Turbo's aluminum-alloy pistons have internal channels cast near their crowns, allowing oil sprayed there through an opening on the piston's underside to absorb more heat. An external oil cooler is fitted. Connecting-rod bearings are changed to a high-strength copper/lead alloy called Kelmet, and aircraft-grade steel exhaust valves are substituted to sustain the higher thermal loads.

The turbochargers themselves are hybrid Garrett units developed exclusively for the 300ZX, using T25 compressor housings and T2 turbines for what Nissan's engineers deemed the smoothest delivery

of power throughout the engine's operating range. Following the latest practice, they're cooled by both oil and water, the latter automatically circulated until the turbos are below the coolant's heat of vaporization.

The power produced by this engine needs an extraordinary suspension system to put it all to the ground, and the 300ZX's complex multilink system is nearly up to the task right out of the box (see "The Boulevardier Stops Here," March 1989, for more detail).

To this, the company adds its Super HICAS (High-Capacity Actively Controlled Suspension), a rear-wheel-steering system offered on the Japanese market since 1985. Super HICAS doesn't provide low-speed countersteer, like Honda's mechanical system, in search of a tight turning circle. Rather, it provides same-phase steering at higher speeds preceded by just a flick of countersteer that "pitches" the chassis, providing the driver with the correct cornering sensations. Front-end steering also is revised, with a quicker ratio (14.8:1 versus 16.8:1).

Other areas are fortified as well. Front wheel and tire sizes remain the

same, but rear-wheel width is increased 1.0 in. (to 8½ in.); rear-tire width grows as well (to 245/45ZR-16), and the speed rating is increased to Z all around. The clutch plate has 38 percent more capacity and now has vacuum assist, the driveshaft's universal joints are larger, and the 2nd and 5th gearsets in the manual transmission are strengthened. Front brakes are also improved, the vented rotors 0.2 in. wider for better heat dissipation.

Our first chance to drive Nissan's 300ZX Turbo came at the Shannonville Motorsports Park in Belleville, Ontario, Canada on one of its two short circuits used primarily by high-performance driving schools. The engine's throttle response is quite good considering the length of the plumbing, and the addition of the turbos does nothing to change the precise low-vibration feel of the V-6.

There's some deadness just off idle, then boost comes on with an uncanny lack of melodrama and is felt as a strong, continuous push through redline. Those accustomed to the thumb-twiddle/hold-on-for-dear-life thrill ride provided by the Porsche 911 Turbo will be disap-

■ Underhood, there's a potpourri of technology in groups of four (as in valves per cylinder and camshafts) and two (as in turbochargers and intercoolers). Enough power is produced (300 bhp) to spin the speedometer's needle to a governed maximum of 155 mph.

pointed; but those whose idea of a good time is tractable, predictable gobs of power will be pleased. We clocked a 0–60 time of 6.5 seconds and sailed through the quarter mile in 15.0 sec. at 96.0 mph, despite some annoying tire patter off the line. Those are numbers that will secure the Turbo a place in the upper echelon of modern performance cars.

At 0.91g around the skidpad, the Nissan is not too far off the standard-bearer Corvette ZR-1's posting of 0.94g. At Shannonville, the Turbo's suspension drew mixed reviews. Some preferred the normally aspirated 300ZX provided for comparison, feeling that the Super HICAS-equipped Turbo surrendered a bit of chassis feedback. That sentiment was mirrored by our Road Test Editor who said, "At times clumsy, but quick," after setting a near-record speed of 66.4 mph through our 700-ft. slalom (the ZR-1 did 65.7 mph, incidentally).

If anything has been lost in feedback, it has been more than made up for in the Turbo's absolutely confidence-inspiring handling. Although it's impossible to separate the contributions of the Super HICAS system from the Turbo's wider tires and different suspension calibrations, we found it easier to push the Turbo through the fast sections of the track and found its drop-throttle behavior much more forgiving.

Nissan has made strides with this car (and with the rest of its revamped model line) worthy of the highest praise. Five years ago, if you said the 300ZX was among the world's best-handling cars, you'd have been met with polite laughter. Say it now and you're simply stating a fact. ◆

NISSAN 300ZX TURBO

0–60 mph	6.5 sec
0–¼ mi	15.0 sec
Top speed	est 155 mph
Skidpad	0.91g
Slalom	66.4 mph
Brake rating	excellent

PRICE

List price, all POE ....$33,000 Price as tested $33,900

Price as tested includes std equip. (air cond, AM/FM stereo/cassette, removable T-top, elect. window lifts, elect. adj mirrors, central locking, foglights, anti-theft system), electronics package of auto. temp control, elect. adj driver's seat, heated mirrors ($900).

ENGINE

Type	turbo 4-valve dohc **V-6**
Displacement	181 cu in./2960 cc
Bore x stroke	3.43 x 3.27 in./ 87.0 x 83.0 mm
Compression ratio	8.5:1
Horsepower (SAE):	**300 bhp @ 6400 rpm**
Torque	**283 lb-ft @ 3600 rpm**
Maximum engine speed	7000 rpm
Fuel injection	Nissan ECCS port
Fuel	prem unleaded, 91 pump oct

GENERAL DATA

Curb weight	**est 3480 lb**
Test weight	**est 3630 lb**
Weight dist, f/r, %	**est 55/45**
Wheelbase	96.5 in.
Track, f/r	58.9 in./61.2 in.
Length	169.5 in.
Width	70.5 in.
Height	49.2 in.
Trunk space	10.0 cu ft

DRIVETRAIN

Transmission ....**5-sp manual**

Gear	Ratio	Overall ratio	(Rpm) Mph
1st	3.21:1	11.84:1	40
2nd	1.93:1	7.12:1	67
3rd	1.30:1	4.80:1	99
4th	1.00:1	3.69:1	129
5th	0.75:1	2.77:1	est (6325) 155

Final drive ratio 3.69:1
Engine rpm @ 60 mph in 5th 2450

CHASSIS & BODY

Layout	**front engine/rear drive**
Body/frame	unit steel, aluminum hood
Brakes, f/r	**11.0-in. vented discs/ 11.7-in. discs**; vacuum assist, ABS
Wheels	cast alloy; **16 x 7½J f, 16 x 8½J r**
Tires	Michelin MXX; **225/50ZR-16 f, 245/45ZR-16 r**
Steering	**rack & pinion,** power assist
Turns, lock to lock	2.4
Suspension, f/r:	**angled upper arms, lower A-arms, "3rd links,"** coil springs, tube shocks, anti-roll bar/**multimember** (upper lateral links, angled upper links, mid lateral links, lower angled A-arms), coil springs, tube shocks, anti-roll bar

FUEL ECONOMY

Normal driving	est 18.5 mpg
EPA city/highway	18/24 mpg
Fuel capacity	18.7 gal.

INTERIOR NOISE

Idle in neutral	47 dBA
Constant 70 mph	72 dBA

ACCELERATION

Time to speed	Seconds
0–30 mph	2.5
0–60 mph	6.5
0–80 mph	11.0
0–100 mph	16.5
Time to distance	
0–100 ft	3.2
0–500 ft	8.2
0–1320 ft (¼ mi)	15.0 @ 96.0 mph

BRAKING

Minimum stopping distance	
From 60 mph	132 ft
From 80 mph	231 ft
Control	excellent
Pedal effort for 0.5g stop	18 lb
Fade, effort after six 0.5g stops from 60 mph	22 lb
Brake feel	excellent
Overall brake rating	excellent

HANDLING

Lateral accel (200-ft skidpad)	0.91g
Balance	moderate understeer
Speed thru 700-ft slalom	66.4 mph
Balance	neutral

Subjective ratings consist of excellent, very good, good, average, poor.

Test Notes . . .

■ The longest lingering impression after a day at the track is that this Turbo is one of the finest all-round sports-car packages available today. Acceleration, braking, handling—it does it all, and with uncommon finesse.

■ The 300ZX Turbo's HICAS rear-wheel steering substantially enhances transient stability; combining it with 0.91g of lateral grip, the Turbo posted the second-fastest speed we've recorded through our slalom.

Long-Term Update

June 1970

Nissan 300ZX Turbo

WHAT NISSAN HAS done with the new 300ZX is an inspiration to us all, taking what was a sports car barely worthy of that appellation and transforming it into a world-class machine, as coordinated as a circus juggler and as refined as white sugar. More inspiring yet is the Turbo version, our choice as the latest steed in our livery of long-term cars. Twin turbos and intercoolers bump output of the 3.0-liter V-6 from 222 bhp to 300, peak torque from 198 lb.-ft. to 283, developed at a low 3600 rpm. Flexible power is the engine's forte, with such an even onset of boost it feels almost like a normally aspirated engine of much larger displacement. Its smoothness, ability to really rev and a delicious little hiss from the wastegates say otherwise, though.

The shift lever is precise and has short throws, though the 4th–5th shift requires more concentration than other gear changes. Compared with other 1990 300ZXs we have driven, our long-term car's gearbox seems a little stiffer and scratchier; perhaps it's due to newness (just over 1500 miles). Other peeves are its poor rearward views because of thick "hidden" B-pillars (one driver's solution: "If you're worried that someone's there, simply nail the throttle and you're out of harm's way") and an automatic temperature-control system that chooses where it wants to direct airflow. Bothersome, but they're just a tiny helping of sour grapes from an impressive cornucopia of a car.

SPECIFICS	
Total miles (first report)	1506
Average mpg to date	16.8
Best mpg (avg of 3)	na
Worst mpg (avg of 3)	na
Repair costs to date	0
Maintenance costs to date	0
List price	$35,175

na means information is not available as yet.

December 1970

Nissan 300ZX Turbo

EVERY PICTURE TELLS a story: Some scoundrel made off with our silver Z's wheels and tires late one August evening. Fortunately, it happened just *before* we replaced the original-equipment Michelin MXXs, badly worn at 14,000 miles. Could Nissan have sent the Turbo out its maiden season on the DOT equivalent of F1 qualifying rubber? Possibly. The compound provides good grip, yet a life span that's a fraction of what most modern radials supply.

In fairness, the front wear can be partially attributed to a problem with toe-in. At the rear, our editors' heavy right feet may have been the culprits; it certainly is easy to spin the rear tires.

Nissan graciously supplied us with replacement rims, which would have cost more than $1000 from the dealer. Mounted and balanced new tires, though, set us back $1257.

The last 15,000 miles have seen praises come on with the intensity of the 300ZX on full boost. Whether the comments are about handling ("The car slices through traffic like a silver ribbon"), power ("When you hit 5000 rpm, you'd better be pointed in the right direction") or the car in general ("Corvette engineers must be losing sleep over this car"), they all point to a car that is pure in design and performance.

SPECIFICS	
Total miles	17,399
Miles since last report	15,893
Average mpg to date	17.9
Best mpg since last report (avg of 3)	24.2
Worst mpg since last report (avg of 3)	11.2
Repair costs to date	0
Maintenance costs to date	$1524
List price	$35,175

NISSAN 300ZX TURBO

A year of 300 horsepower on tap, and 18 mpg to boot

BARELY A MONTH after the 300ZX Turbo arrived at R&T's office last year, my brother Rodney and I had the pleasure of using its near-silent 300 bhp for a Saturday night run to Phoenix for the 1990 U.S. Grand Prix. Arriving late and without reservations, we spent the night in the car. Sleep was sporadic, at best, because the seats don't fully recline and the steering wheel wouldn't get out of my lap. Fortunately, our wake-up call—the wail of a Formula 1 car piercing the morning air—got our blood flowing better than a cup of coffee. And as race day faded and weariness set in, a simple twist of the Z's titanium ignition key fired us up again.

The Z has that kind of effect, and the trip home brought to light the many qualities our staff has admired over these 31,297 miles: the excellent rush of power when the audible twin turbos kick in, the superbly balanced handling with its precise steering and excellent traction, and the overall high level of fit and finish throughout.

Despite this visceral performance and a spotless reliability record, there were a few bothers. The ride, for one, with its rocker-switch-controlled damping, was far too stiff. In either Sport or Tour mode, trips down freeways made of sectional concrete found us tightening our stomach muscles to counter the incessant bumps. And when we wanted to change lanes, the thick C-pillars made the driver dependent on the large, well-placed side mirrors. Also, many thought the climate-control system should have more than a two-speed fan.

By 18,000 miles, the Z's vacuum-assisted clutch had grown harder to depress, and the 5-speed transmission was exhibiting signs of wear. From the beginning, shifts to 3rd and 5th gear felt a bit scratchy, and 2nd gear recently joined that list. Cold mornings highlighted the problem, which the dealer said wasn't there. After the car was returned, however, Nissan did replace the clutch. A technician noted it had been "thoroughly used, not abused."

Tire wear also concerned us because the original rubber lasted only 14,000 miles, and the replacements cost a healthy $1257. Strangely, but to our pleasure, the new set has lasted much longer, sporting plenty of tread when we returned the car. Like the first set, the Michelins worked well—their sticky compound often shooting gravel into the Z's tinny fenderwells—but they transmitted lots of road noise into the cabin.

At the Z's extensive 30,000-mile service, all fluids—save battery acid and gasoline—were changed. While $607 may sound costly, it is typical for cars in the Z's price range.

With the U.S. Grand Prix upon us again, that initial trip to Phoenix in the Z comes to mind. Without reservation, I'd do it again. Well, not without *hotel* reservations. ⬡

1990 NISSAN 300ZX TURBO

Delivered price	$35,175
Resale value at end of test (est wholesale from *Kelley Blue Book*)	$25,725
Total miles covered in test	31,297
Miles since last report	13,898
Average miles per gal.	18.0

COSTS, OVERALL & PER MILE

Depreciation	$13,309
Gasoline	1740 gal. @ $2413
Oil	1 additional qt @ $2
Routine maintenance	$966
Repairs and replacements not covered under warranty	$1257
Overall cost for 31,297 miles	$17,947
Cost per mile	57¢

REPAIRS & REPLACEMENTS

Front-end alignment, tires, front brake pads

PHOTO BY DREW MOTTA

Steve Millen Sports Cars GTZ

SUPER Z

When racing is in your blood, it's in your road car too

BY JOE RUSZ
PHOTOS BY JEFFREY R. ZWART

*P*ERHAPS YOU'VE SEEN him on television driving a Porsche 944 Turbo
(the one that pops out of a tunnel, does
a 180-degree turn and stops in the road
facing the camera), piloting one of two
Nissan 240SX coupes in a motorized
pas de deux (to the tune of "Me and My Shad-
ow"), gunning a 300ZX around ATC's high
banking or testing the Sentra that "I would
build if I owned a car company."

If you were fortunate enough to attend Le
Mans in 1990, you may have seen him at the
wheel of a Nissan R90CK Group C car, setting
a race lap record that earned him rookie-of-the-
race honors.

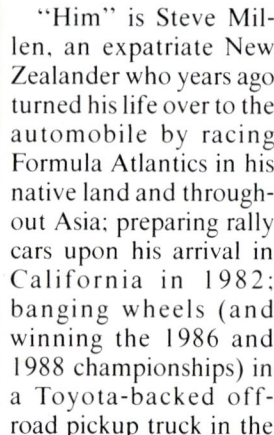

"Him" is Steve Mil-
len, an expatriate New
Zealander who years ago
turned his life over to the
automobile by racing
Formula Atlantics in his
native land and through-
out Asia; preparing rally
cars upon his arrival in
California in 1982;
banging wheels (and
winning the 1986 and
1988 championships) in
a Toyota-backed off-
road pickup truck in the
Mickey Thompson Entertainment Group sta-
dium racing series; and driving in car commercials, print advertisements and, sometimes, for
Road & Track covers and road test features.

"I love cars," says Millen. "I like to fiddle
with them, modify them. I'm not a guy who
can go to the beach on Sunday." Unless, of
course, that beach is Daytona, West Palm, Miami or Long, where you'll find Steve behind
the wheel of an IMSA GTO car, the Nissan
Performance Technology Incorporated 300ZX
Turbo. A contract driver for NPTI, Millen had
a respectable 1990 season, winning at Miami,
Mosport and Road America and finishing 4th
in the championship—in spite of four DNFs
caused mostly by fluke mechanical problems.

"Racing is number 1 with me," says the 37-
year-old Kiwi. So what sort of road car suits
someone who has gone 230 mph on the Mul-
sanne Straight? "I think the ZX is neat," says
Millen. But he didn't mean just any ZX. Given
Steve's penchant for tinkering, it wasn't long
before he began to massage his new 300ZX
Turbo. Cosmetic stuff came first: front air dam
and rear lip spoiler, 17-in. Momo wheels with
Yokohama AVS tires. Serious modifications

came later. "I thought it would be neat to give the ZX extra power. But then it needed brakes. And suspension."

Like Topsy, the project began to grow. While poring over parts catalogs, searching for the right components, Steve was buttonholed by a local Nissan dealer who suggested that Millen Sports Cars build an all-out, limited-edition 300ZX Turbo. Something that would not only go fast, but also look the part. And that, in a nutshell, is how the GTZ was born. Distinctive or outlandish, depending on your mind set, this super Z delivers impressive numbers. From a standstill, 60 mph is just 5.0 seconds away; the quarter mile, 13.5 sec. In a broken field run through the slalom, the GTZ averages 67.3 mph, a new R&T record.

Yet, the car is equally at home tootling through traffic because it retains most of what the factory put into it. "The engine has never been opened up," claims Millen, who explains that with the exception of a couple of body pieces, all of the components that make up the GTZ bolt on. Of course, they're available to the public, through Steve Millen Sports Cars of Santa Ana, California, a company co-owned by Millen and Dave Schollum, a fellow Kiwi who backed Millen in his early racing endeavors.

Our guided tour of the GTZ begins on the outside with the body, which has a vented front air dam and a louvered air intake that fits between the headlights and increases airflow to the twin turbos. A Ferrari F40-style rear wing is complemented by a molded lower bumper surround. Steel-framed vents with perforated metal backing are incorporated into front and rear fenders. Strictly cosmetic on the prototype, they are meant to direct air to the auxiliary transmission and rear differential coolers.

Three-spoke wheels, built to Millen's specifications by Elite, use billet aluminum centers welded to spun aluminum rims. Seventeen inches tall, the 9½-in.-wide rims are shod with Z-rated Yokohama A008R tires and tinted

a titanium hue to complement the color of the bodywork.

For art's sake, the GTZ is painted a golden orange. The various Sikkens lacquers, blended and applied by Maurice Alvarez and Don Penny of Autotrends in Santa Ana, include 12 base coats of orange, three coats of gold pearlescent and four coats of clear urethane. Although it's not exactly the color one would choose for a stealth bomber (or a stealth car), it's perfectly appropriate for a showpiece—and a cover car.

Our tour continues with the suspension: progressive-rate springs, adjustable shocks (Koni up front, Tokico at the rear), adjustable anti-roll bars (28 mm front, 21 mm rear). A complete non-Turbo 300ZX rear subframe with differential replaces the Turbo's Super HICAS setup, saving some weight and improving performance by reducing the final drive ratio from 3.69:1 to 4.08:1. The subframe is held in place by Delrin hard plastic bushings that keep everything glued in place when the driver buries his boot in the firewall and unleashes those 430 lb.-ft. of torque.

▓ **Every nook of the GTZ holds a new surprise. From top right, a glovebox full of exhaust pyrometers and boost control; drilled pedals; and a differential oil cooler. Engine appears deceptively stock.**

The brakes are extra large with 11.6-in. rotors that are cross-drilled and vented axially. They're Nissan factory parts borrowed from the Skyline Group A racing cars that compete in Japan and Australia and used in concert with carbon-metallic brake pads that are the same as those used on NPTI's GTO racer.

The next-to-last stop on our tour of the Millen GTZ brings us to the engine. Stock on the inside, it's fitted with high-flow fuel injectors, larger-than-stock Garrett turbochargers and 50-percent larger intercoolers. There's a low-restriction air filter that's part of an HKS package containing a Vein Pressure Converter and modified air-mass sensor. The idea here is to increase airflow to those hefty compressors.

Their output is handled by an HKS Electronic Valve Controller (EVC) that regulates the operation of the turbocharger wastegates, which are fitted with HKS electronic control

The Other Office

When he's not driving cars in television commercials or building super Zs or selling performance parts, Steve Millen can be found at his "day job," driving Nissan's 300ZX Turbo in the Exxon Supreme Series, the International Motor Sports Association's championship for production-based sports cars and coupes.

Commonly known as GTO (and GTU) cars—for Grand Touring Over (and Under) 3.0 liters—they share company name and model assignation with their road-going counterparts. But not much more. Although the roof, windshield, cylinder heads and engine design are stock, in accordance with IMSA regulations, everything else is purpose-built—often of exotic materials not found in the average production car.

Take the Nissan-backed 300ZX Turbo, Millen's workplace on 15 IMSA race weekends. Built from the ground up by Clayton Cunningham and company in El Segundo, California, the car uses a chrome-moly steel tubular chassis that serves as the foundation for myriad mechanical components. Inner panels and bulkheads of sheet aluminum (also used for the floor) are complemented by a carbon-fiber outer skin, contoured to loosely resemble that of the road car.

For convenience, the bodywork consists of four major pieces (nose, tail section and two doors) that can be removed (and replaced, if need be) simply by loosening several Dzus fasteners. For localized access to the engine, it's possible to remove only the hood, which is a subassembly of the one-piece nose.

The stock steel 300ZX roof is permanently attached to the rollhoops, which, along with numerous cross- and diagonal members, make up the car's birdcage-like chassis. The structure is extremely stiff, just the way Trevor Harris, chassis and suspension designer of the Nissan GTO car and the Nissan Performance Technology Incorporated GTP racer, likes it. By the way, the car shown here is a second-generation chassis and is based on the 300ZX 2+2, which has a longer wheelbase. Seems that the original cars, built in 1989 by T-Mag, were only as long as the normal Z. Cunningham stretched them in mid-1990 and markedly improved their handling.

Harris' other contribution to the 300ZX Turbo-racer, the car's suspension, is pretty straightforward. Although there are a few mystery bits that the team would rather not discuss, it's a time-proven design: upper and lower A-arms with coil springs over shock absorbers (front and rear). And, of course, a cockpit-adjustable rear anti-roll bar.

Although there's nothing unusual about the Nissan's extra-large, vented brake discs, the calipers are worth a mention. A Clayton Cunningham idea, they feature internal water-cooling for endurance. None of this is visible without removing the car's 18.0 x 14.0-in. front and 18.0 x 15.0-in. rear BBS modular wheels—shod with Yokohama racing tires, rather than the ubiquitous you-know-whats.

At the rear of the chassis, behind the rear cockpit bulkhead, is a heavy-duty differential. Custom-built by Electramotive Engineering (now NPTI), it uses a Frankland case and ring and pinion; change gears and Salisbury-type limited-slip differential from a Hewland VGC racing transaxle; and numerous handcrafted bits. Our test car, built to last year's rules, was required to have its 5-speed transmission in the stock location, behind the engine. But the new Nissan GTO car, which makes its debut this spring, will be allowed to use a Hewland transaxle located at the rear.

A fuel cell with dry-break filler, oil reservoir and battery attach to the aft end of the chassis. Coolers for the transmission, differential and water-cooled brakes are located in front of, and behind, the rear wheels. The placement of these components is designed to offset the weight of the twin valves. Hot stuff, which explains the engine oil cooler that's part of the modification.

A special exhaust system designed by Millen Sports Cars bolts on behind the catalytic converter and feeds the spent mixture into a pair of Flowmaster mufflers.

To ensure that the twin-turbo V-6's 460 bhp makes it to the gearbox, there's a Centerforce clutch with a special dual friction disc that uses a bronzelike coating on the engine side and a

more conventional, fiberlike covering on the other surface.

Last stop: the GTZ's interior. Note the Momo Panther steering wheel and leather shift knob. Steel pedal pads (a Millen product) fit atop the stock rubber ones and keep your feet from sliding off. Open the glovebox and observe the command post that controls the engine's output and monitors its performance: an HKS boost control unit (for the EVC) with

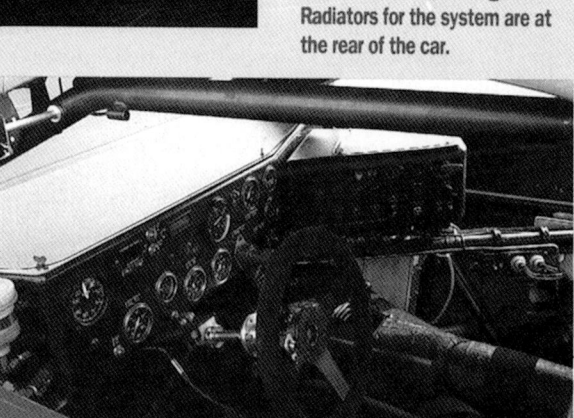

turbochargers, intercoolers and radiator, plus the engine cooler, that are crammed into the front of the car. And of the engine, currently a racing variant of the Nissan sohc 12-valve V-6 (the new car gets the 24-valver).

With its specially cast aluminum block (patterned after the production block), the engine is the handiwork of NPTI craftsmen and is built at the company's facilities in Vista, California. Almost all of its pieces are made to order (by NPTI or vendors) and rather than enumerate them, let's just say that only the aluminum cylinder heads (ported and polished, of course) are stock.

At most races, the car is fitted with the 2750-cc version of the Nissan V-6, because this bore and stroke combination makes good power, is reliable and allows a favorable weight (2650 lb.). And while a 3000-cc variant with Phase 3 camshafts works quite well (with the car ballasted to 2700 lb.), the team would like to use a 2500-cc powerplant that permits the car to weigh 2600 lb.

In the midst of all of this paraphernalia sits Steve Millen,

PHOTOS BY THE AUTHOR

The vented and cross-drilled brake rotors are cooled conventionally with ducted air; their massive calipers, however, use water as the cooling medium. Radiators for the system are at the rear of the car.

strapped into a carbon-fiber driving seat, facing an array of gauges that monitor boost, air inlet temperature, oil and fuel pressure, fuel usage, engine, gearbox and differential oil temperatures, plus brake and coolant temperatures. And if that's not enough, there's the requisite tachometer redlined at 7800 rpm.

Knobs controlling brake bias and rear anti-roll bar stiffness are also set into the carbon-fiber dashboard. Switches that activate the fuel, oil and water pumps—plus electrical circuit breakers, fuel mixture control and starter button—are mounted on an aluminum pod to the driver's right.

There's no cellular phone; Steve's "business calls" come via two-way radio from the crew chief. There's also no telemetry gear, although an onboard computer keeps tabs on engine operation and spews its information into a trackside monitor during pitstops.

Proof that this is one formidable Z-car (driven by an equally formidable driver) can be found in the IMSA record book. It shows that in 1990, the Nissan GTO, competing in 11 races, sat on the pole five times and won three races.

Anxious to learn more about what makes Steve and the Nissan GTO run, we invited Millen and the Clayton Cunningham Racing crew to Carlsbad Raceway.

A few exploratory acceleration runs showed that 4th and 5th gear were too short: Steve was running out of revs long before the end of the quarter mile. The crew went to

work, and about an hour later, the car was ready for another shot. This time, the gearing was perfect and times dropped. But the car couldn't get off the line well, so the gang softened the rear springs. This time when Steve unleashed the engine's 700-plus horsepower, the car launched like a Sidewinder missile.

Zero to 60 mph took a mere 3.0 seconds; the quarter mile, an electrifying 10.7 sec. at which time the GTO was nearly topped out at 135 mph.

Don't be deceived by its modest speed. Geared for racing, the Nissan is capable of 220-plus mph, opines Millen. "In testing at Sebring in 1989, I followed Geoff Brabham's Nissan GTP through a turn, then tucked in behind it. Geoff was just blown away when I passed him on the straight."

Steve explains that although the GTO car doesn't have the incredible downforce of the GTP racer, it has about the same horsepower.

Reversing the process (stopping), we learned that the Nissan GTO decelerates at an eyeball-popping rate. Unfortunately, this simply can't be measured properly at less than racing conditions (80 mph, our highest braking speed, doesn't even get the brakes warmed up). You simply have to experience it yourself.

Better yet, ask Steve Millen. He'll be in the office—a red, white and blue Nissan 300ZX Turbo—at an IMSA/Exxon Supreme Series GTO race, appearing at a road course or street circuit near you.

—Joe Rusz

buttons that call up boost settings of 50 and 100 percent over stock (12.0 and 16.0 vs. 8.0 lb.) and a knob that dials up as much as a 200-percent gain in boost pressure; a 20-psi boost gauge with recording telltale; two telltale-equipped exhaust temperature gauges (one per turbo) to keep tabs on fuel mixture and ignition timing; control panel for the HKS Vein Pressure Converter.

Tour complete, it's time to take the GTZ to Carlsbad Raceway where we find that by opening the glovebox and turning the HKS control module's knurled knob almost fully clockwise

Once Over Lightly

Being chosen as one of *Road & Track's* "10 Best Cars in the World" says volumes about the Nissan 300ZX Turbo. Both it and the normally aspirated versions captured honors in their respective price categories (R&T, December 1990), a testimonial to a car and a car company that have made a remarkable comeback from a period of stagnation. And yet, sensational as the stock Z is, there's a certain sameness about any production automobile that becomes apparent right about the time the payments kick in.

No one is more aware of this than Steve Millen, whose company, Steve Millen Sports Cars, offers a complete line of components for the 300ZX. In addition to bits that are merely marketed by Millen, there's a whole repertoire of Z things manufactured by Stillen (a contraction of Steve Millen). Included in the inventory are all

the body pieces needed to turn your Turbo into a GTZ, or just a few items to set it off from the rest of the Z-car crowd.

Steve's red 2+2 road car, pictured here, showcases the most popular bolt-ons: Stillen front air dam and wraparound rear spoiler; 17 x 7½-in. Momo 5-spoke wheels sporting 235/45ZR-17 Yokohama AVS rubber; Momo leather shift knob; and Momo Ghibli 3 steering wheel with integral cruise control switches (built into the hub).

That's enough to make the Z-car distinctive. To make it exclusive, take another trip to the Millen Sports Cars well.

—*Joe Rusz*

PHOTO BY RICHARD M. BARON

(to 5 o'clock), we crank in 17.0 lb. of boost, the most Millen recommends with 92 RON unleaded pump gasoline. For test purposes, Steve has filled the tank with 102 octane. Tweak goes the boost knob, nearly to the stop (kids, do not try this at home). He makes a run and finds the telltale frozen at 19 psi.

Dozens of runs—carefully monitored by the IMSA GTO racing crew—show us that the GTZ likes its high-energy diet. The quickest pass with tires alight produces a quarter-mile time of 13.5 sec. at 109.5 mph.

These are impressive figures, but not nearly as remarkable as the speeds the GTZ reaches in the slalom. With R&T ace pylon-shaver Kim Reynolds at the wheel, the super Z notches up a personal best of 67.3 mph. On the skidpad, the show is almost as good—0.93g—second highest for a production-based automobile. Credit for this goes to the suspension and those extra-sticky Yokohama A008Rs keeping all four wheels locked onto their trajectory.

But what good's a supercar if you can't drive it on the road, right?

So we did. And found that the GTZ attracts attention (it's difficult not to notice that orange paint job and treetop-tall rear wing). Knowing this, we drove discreetly. Okay, maybe not all the time because it's an absolute carnival ride to tip into the throttle, hear those twin turbos spool up and hang on as the Millen reels in the horizon.

Unlike the stock 300ZX Twin Turbo, the GTZ *feels* turbocharged. Even at the low (50 percent) setting response is immediate. At 100 percent (high), it's not only immediate, it's breathtaking. Wheelspin can occur easily in lower gears until those sticky Yokohamas take hold. Then the power builds, to the redline and beyond—to about 7500 rpm when the limiter kicks in. Fun it is. Play it's not. At 100 percent or more, a tip of the throttle delivers the automotive equivalent of rapture of the deep. Not what you want when the road surface is less than ideal.

As expected, handling is superb. The GTZ is like a radio-controlled ballistic missile that zeroes in on a target. Response is superb, and roll nonexistent. Braking is exceptional (there's more braking than any road car will ever need). But the competition pads are *squeaky*, making it difficult if not impossible to be unobtrusive.

Here's a surprise: In spite of shorter, stiffer springs, the GTZ's ride isn't much harsher than the stock 300ZX Turbo's. And (can you believe it?), the car does not scrape its spoiler at every driveway and speed bump.

A tractable, smooth road car that performs, handles and feels like a race car: That's the GTZ. See what happens when you let an automobile enthusiast and successful race driver build a road car?

STEVE MILLEN SPORTS CARS GTZ

MANUFACTURER

Nissan Motor Corp, PO Box 191, Gardena, Calif. 90247/Steve Millen Sports Cars, 1627 S. Boyd St., Santa Ana, Calif. 92705

PRICE

List price, FOB factory	$34,570
Price as tested	$52,015

Price as tested includes std equip. (air cond, AM/FM stereo/cassette, T-top roof, elect. window lifts, elect. adj mirrors, cruise control, central locking). Millen modifications include: larger Garrett T25G turbos, larger intercoolers, engine oil cooler, high-flow fuel injectors, revised engine-management computer ($6178); Centerforce dual-friction clutch ($600); differential bushings & oil cooler ($500); larger brakes ($2000); Stillen exhaust system ($700); modified springs, adjustable shocks & anti-roll bars ($1100); Stillen design wheels ($1900); Yokohama A-008R tires ($700); Stillen GTZ body trim ($2267); interior trim ($1500).

0–60 mph	5.0 sec
0–¼ mi	13.5 sec
Skidpad	0.93g
Slalom	67.3 mph
Brake rating	excellent

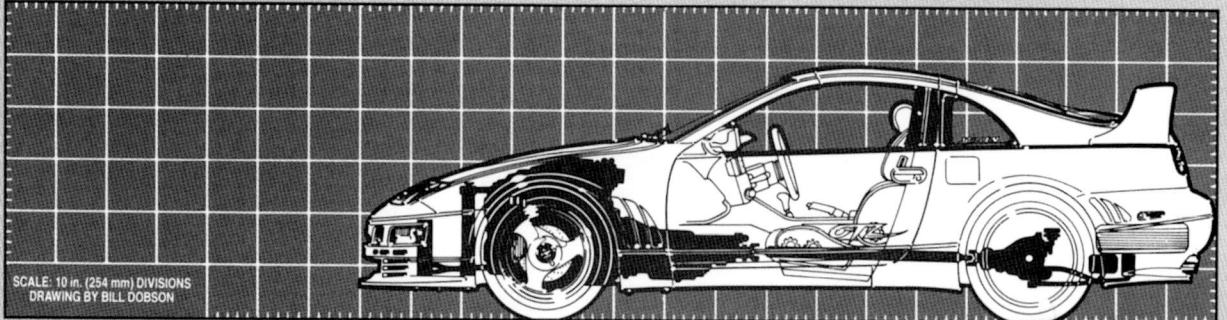

SCALE: 10 in. (254 mm) DIVISIONS
DRAWING BY BILL DOBSON

ENGINE

Type .... twin turbo, iron block & aluminum head, **V-6**
Valvetrain .... dohc, 4-valve/cyl
Displacement ... 181 cu in./2960 cc
Bore x stroke ....3.43 x 3.27 in./ 87.0 x 83.0 mm
Compression ratio 10.1:1
Horsepower
  (SAE) ..... **460 bhp @ 6500 rpm**
Bhp/liter 155.4
Torque ......**430 lb-ft @ 4750 rpm**
Maximum engine speed....7000 rpm
Fuel injection ....Nissan ECCS port
Fuel requirement ... premium unleaded, 92 pump oct

CHASSIS & BODY

Layout .... **front engine/rear drive**
Body/frame .... unit steel
Brakes
  Front.......**11.6-in. vented discs**
  Rear ....**11.6-in. vented discs**
  Assist type................. vacuum
  Total swept area ....430 sq in.
  Swept area/ton.........245 sq in.
Wheels ....modular alloy, **17 x 9½**
Tires .... Yokohama A-008R, **275/40ZR-17**
Steering .... **rack & pinion,** pwr asst
  Overall ratio 16.8:1
  Turns, lock to lock 2.8
  Turning circle .... 34.1 ft
Suspension
  Front.........**angled upper arms, lower A-arms,** "3rd links," coil springs, tube shocks, adj anti-roll bar
  Rear .... **multimember** (upper lateral links, angled upper links, mid-lateral links, lower angled A-arms), coil springs, tube shocks, adj anti-roll bar

DRIVETRAIN

Transmission ....**5-sp manual**

Gear	Ratio	Overall ratio	(Rpm) Mph
1st	3.21:1	13.12:1	39
2nd	1.93:1	7.86:1	65
3rd	1.30:1	5.32:1	96
4th	1.00:1	4.08:1	125
5th	0.75:1	3.07:1	est (7000) 166

Final drive ratio 4.08:1
Engine rpm @ 60 mph in 5th 2530

GENERAL DATA

Curb weight	**3490 lb**
Test weight	3600 lb
Weight dist (with driver), f/r, %	55/45
Wheelbase	96.5 in.
Track, f/r	58.9 in./60.4 in.
Length	**169.5 in.**
Width	**70.5 in.**
Height	**49.4 in.**
Ground clearance	5.0 in.
Trunk space	10.0 cu ft

INTERIOR NOISE

Idle in neutral	62 dBA
Maximum in 1st gear	81 dBA
Constant 50 mph	76 dBA
70 mph	82 dBA

ACCOMMODATIONS

Seating capacity	2
Head room	35.5 in.
Seat width	2 x 21.0
Leg room	43.0 in.
Seatback adjustment	50 deg
Seat travel	8.0 in.

INSTRUMENTATION

160-mph speedometer, 9000-rpm tach, oil press., coolant temp, boost press., fuel level

MAINTENANCE

Oil/filter change	3500 mi/3500 mi
Tuneup	15,000 mi
Basic warranty	na

ACCELERATION

Time to speed	Seconds
0–30 mph	2.4
0–40 mph	3.3
0–50 mph	4.0
0–60 mph	5.0
0–70 mph	6.0
0–80 mph	7.2
0–90 mph	9.1
0–100 mph	11.1

Time to distance
0–100 ft	3.0
0–500 ft	7.5
0–1320 ft (¼ mi): 13.5 @ 109.5 mph	

BRAKING

Minimum stopping distance
From 60 mph	128 ft
From 80 mph	215 ft
Control	very good
Pedal effort for 0.5g stop	13 lb
Fade, effort after six 0.5g stops from 60 mph	13 lb
Brake feel	excellent
Overall brake rating	excellent

HANDLING

Lateral accel (200-ft skidpad)	0.93g
Balance	mild understeer
Speed thru 700-ft slalom	67.3 mph
Balance	mild understeer
Lateral seat support	very good

FUEL ECONOMY

Normal driving	est 16.0 mpg
EPA city/highway	na
Cruise range	285 miles
Fuel capacity	18.7 gal.

Subjective ratings consist of excellent, very good, good, average, poor; na means information is not available.

Test Notes . . .

■ The power of the Millen GTZ feels like a twin-turbo 300ZX's with the boost turned way up. That is, it feels both powerful and mechanically refined, but without the extra lag bigger turbos would suggest.

■ The GTZ's Yokohama A-008Rs are amazingly sticky; they demand very hard driving to break them loose through the slalom. And yet their response is also well matched to the 300ZX's normal steering feel.

■ With all of the GTZ's power at your disposal, it's also nice to know that it can be reduced—with the push of a button—to stock levels if road conditions deteriorate.

NISSAN

300ZX
TWIN TURBO

Part living room, part rocketship

PHOTOS BY RICK GRAVES

All-conquering flagships like the 300ZX Twin Turbo aren't designed to fit into the normal realm of automotive experiences. Instead they are supposed to transport you somewhere else with deceptive ease, sheltering you from harsh reality on one hand while warping space and time on the other. Such capabilities don't come cheaply or often, because the equation is so difficult to solve satisfactorily. But Nissan has definitely given a correct answer to the definitive GT question with its high-caliber ZX, building in equal parts living room and rocketship.

While it's easy to be mesmerized by the liquid oxygen tank, reaction motor,

steerable nozzles and other thrust equipment, the real world the 300ZX turbo whisks you through probably puts more demands on the recliner chairs, wall-to-wall carpeting and table lamps. After all, the most difficult task the 300-bhp 300ZX is normally asked to perform is to idle in traffic with the air conditioning on. To ensure comfort, Nissan engineers started with an exceptionally well laid-out cockpit design, then gave a little in the weight department, adding the insulation and power-assisted comforts of home.

From first glance the 300ZX's interior is a pleaser. The immediate impression is of the carpeting running up the console, around the doors and halfway up the dash. The feeling is integration

70

Showing a lot of 928 influence, the interior provides many comforts.

the ZX swells up atop a rounded, fast-moving wave of torque, then rips ahead as the wave breaks into 7000 rpm of white water.

This power delivery is exhilarating and safe, when probing the limit on back roads. Combined with the sophisticated chassis, the power is both impressive, yet unintimidating. Believe me, the 300ZX is fast, faster than the dragstrip numbers suggest because of initial turbo lag, yet even the relatively inexperienced can use almost all of it.

"Sophisticated chassis" is an understatement the same way calling a Cray supercomputer's circuitry "advanced" is. As the specifications show, there are enough bars, links, bushings and struts under the 300ZX to cage Barnum & Bailey's cat show. Toss in Nissan's Super HICAS electronically controlled rear suspension, which steers both in and out of phase with the front wheels, variable steering assist and a host of other details, and you've got a car that practically talks. The 300ZX turns in like a tiddlywink and has the high-speed stability of an anvil. Try to make it oversteer and it will, but as soon as you're about to spin into the mulberries, it pulls itself back in shape with a load of understeer. It doesn't hurt that the 4-wheel-disc brakes have more grip than a mad tabby clinging to a shag rug, either. Any way you drive it, the 300ZX performs as though it were reading the road in front of it.

Exceptional as the 300ZX's handling is, it is not without room for debate. For one thing, the ZX is a GT, not a sports car, and there's a weight penalty to pay. At times the big Nissan feels like, well, a big car. It is never ponderous, but like the massive, powerful machine it is, it can build inertia that takes conscious effort to overcome. Fast, yes. Flickable, no.

The variable-boost steering and second-guessing suspension are helping friends, but they are also another layer between driver and pavement, and often the sensations are modified beyond what previous experience has taught. Perhaps this new breed of supercar requires the most adaptive driver to take it to its very limit. Certainly up to a notch or two below the limit the ZX makes heroes out of sedan drivers, and in that real-world context the 300ZX is a big step forward.

Ah, there I go again, making my living room act like a rocketship. In the

without the annoying flashiness of a show car's interior where the seats, door panels, console and instrument panel have been blended into a seamless torus. Getting in and out of the 300ZX is easy after adjusting to the low ride height, and once behind the wheel there's a coziness without feeling cramped—unless you exceed 6 ft. The 300ZX's bubbled roofline is low, so taller or long-waisted drivers find the roof close. Should this be too confin-ing, the standard T-top panels unlatch for unfettered vertical room. Otherwise, the sloping dash and expansive, steeply raked windshield make the interior seem more spacious than it really is. Large people may wish for a tad more foot room, especially those wearing cowboy boots who can foul their toes above the pedalwork, but this is a minor inconvenience. Only rear three-quarter vision over the driver's left shoulder could use improvement. The small quarter window makes lane-changes to the left a glance-in-the-mirror and pray proposition.

Then again, the twin turbo piloto has little need to see what's behind him. Just as the space shuttle sets you back in your seat at takeoff, Nissan's prime mover has power to burn. Like any turbo engine, the 3.0-liter V-6 takes a moment to spool up. From a complete rest at intersections this can take an annoying pause as the heavy coupe walks into the face of traffic off the cams and without boost. Then the tach hints at 3000 rpm and the gush of power surges through the driveline and the ZX is off and sprinting. Thankfully, the turbos feed in gradually, so instead of a power hit, as dirt bikers say, real world good handling means you can see the front fenders when parking, and that is no problem in the ZX. In fact, living with the 300ZX is really compromised only by factors inherent to the car's job description. There's not a large amount of luggage room, but certainly enough for two to enjoy a week's touring. Underhood it looks like someone sandcast the mechanicals in place, using the inner fenders as the mold. Drop a tool atop the V-6 and there's no fear of losing it; nothing short of a liquid or gas can penetrate more than a few inches into the maze. In short, the engine compartment is tightly packed.

As for idling in traffic, the ZX does it without a whimper. Climate control is up to expectations, as is the sound system. The only comfort related items worth mentioning are the ride and road noise. The 300ZX is equipped with 2-way adjustable shocks: touring and sport. I found the softer touring selection gave a surprisingly choppy ride along with excellent handling for the "default" mode. Flipping over to sport was just too much; I flipped back to touring immediately and left it there, even for the darty back road stuff. After a day or two behind the wheel the ride faded from mind. Although it can't be called plush, it certainly is never harsh, and is simply a tradeoff for flat handling.

Road noise was louder than other 300ZXs I've driven, and possibly reflects the pebbly road textures encountered during the test period. On the other hand, the 300ZX occupants ride just forward of the rear wheelhouses, so some road noise is sure to pass through. Again, this is a relatively minor point, and considering the sound system is usually drowning out the road rumble, one that doesn't bear much listening to, so to speak. At no time was there any vibration of consequence, which is not surprising as the 300ZX uses a rubber-isolated suspension.

A comment on the subtle yet exciting styling is important. For a near-exotic, the Twin Turbo barely stands out against its tamer, normally aspirated brother. About the only way to tell them apart is to look for the discreet "Twin Turbo" on the rear decklid, the slotted vents at the front corners or the tasteful rear spoiler. Yet for all its undercover ways, the ZX draws crowds and favorable comments at almost ev-

ery stop. Some see the badge, spy the massive brake calipers behind the open spoke wheels or note the sloping windshield or wide track and peg the Nissan for the rocketship it is. Others take in the leather upholstery, miles of low-nap carpeting, digital climate control and stylish, yet functional switch work

around the instrument cluster. They see the *Ranch & Coast* living room and approve. Amazingly, both are right, and if they choose to live with the ZX, will come to enjoy the rounded styling as it subtly changes with the light. I doubt many rockets are as beautiful or as comfortable.—*Tom Wilson*

PRICE

List price, all POE .... $33,500   Price as tested...................... $34,500
Price as tested includes std equip. (T-top, fog lights, tinted windows, elect. adj mirrors, elect. window lifts, central locking, cruise control, air cond, AM/FM stereo/cassette, rear window heat, rear window wiper, anti-theft system), leather pkg ($1000)

ENGINE		GENERAL	
Type .... turbo dohc 4-valve V-6		Curb weight ....3475 lb	
Displacement .... 2960 cc		Test weight .... est 3630 lb	
Bore x stroke ....87.0 mm x 83.0 mm		Weight dist, f/r, % 55/45	
Compression ratio 8.5:1		Wheelbase .... 96.5 in.	
Horsepower, (SAE) .... 300 bhp @ 6400 rpm		Track, f/r...............58.9 in./61.2 in.	
Torque .... 283 lb-ft @ 3600 rpm		Length .... 169.5 in.	
Maximum engine speed .... 7000 rpm		Width................................... 70.5 in.	
Fuel injection.................... electronic port		Height .... 49.2 in.	
Fuel requirement ..... unleaded, 91 pump oct		Trunk space .... 23.7 cu ft	

DRIVETRAIN

Transmission..5-sp manual			
Gear	Ratio	Overall ratio	(Rpm) Mph
1st....................	3.21:1	11.84:1	40
2nd....................	1.93:1	7.12:1	67
3rd....................	1.30:1	4.80:1	99
4th....................	1.00:1	3.69:1	est 129
5th....................	0.75:1	2.77:1	est 155
Final drive ratio 3.69:1			
Engine rpm @ 60 mph in 5th .... 2450 rpm			

CHASSIS & BODY

Layout ....front engine/rear drive
Body/frame .... unit steel
Brakes, f/r............. 11.0-in. vented discs/
11.7-in. vented discs, vacuum assist, ABS
Wheels..... cast alloy, 16 x 7½J f, 16 x 8½J r
Tires........... Michelin MXX, 225/50ZR-16 f,
245/45ZR-16 r
Steering ....rack & pinion, power assist
Turns, lock to lock 2.4
Suspension, f/r: angled upper control arms, lower A-arms, third links, coil springs, tube shocks, anti-roll bar/upper lateral links, angled upper links, mid-lateral links, lower angled A-arms, coil springs, tube shocks, anti-roll bar

BRAKING

Minimum stopping distance	
From 60 mph .... 132 ft	
From 80 mph .... 231 ft	
Control.................................excellent	
Overall brake rating ....excellent	

na means information is not available.

Subjective ratings consist of excellent, very good, good, average and poor.

ACCELERATION

Time to speed	Seconds
0–30 mph 2.5
0–40 mph 3.6
0–50 mph 5.0
0–60 mph 6.5
0–70 mph 8.8
0–80 mph 11.0
0–90 mph 13.4
0–100 mph 16.5
Time to distance	
0–100 ft 3.2
0–500 ft 8.2
0–1320 ft (¼ mi) .....15.0 sec @ 96.0 mph

FUEL ECONOMY

Normal driving .... 19.6 mpg
EPA city/highway.............18 mpg/24 mpg
Fuel capacity.........................18.7 gal.

HANDLING

Lateral accel (200-ft skidpad) 0.91g
Balance................. moderate understeer
Speed thru 700-ft slalom............ 66.4 mph
Balance.................................... neutral

PHOTOS BY BRIAN BLADES

Nissan 300ZX and 240SX Convertibles
Top-down twosome
BY RICHARD HOMAN

NO ONE IS ever going to accuse Nissan of not giving the people what they want. Back when the 200SX was at the end of its road, and insurance companies were having a field day with premiums on 4-valve-per-cylinder, 2-seat sports coupes, Nissan obliged the public's desire for fun with the 12-valve, 4-cylinder, 2+2 240SX. And when the old 300ZX got fat and GT-sassy, the Z-car folks burned the old mold and created the current-generation 300, a true sports car by anyone's definition.

Now the legislative nation that had it all and lost it wants it all again: Convertibles are back in vogue. And here comes Nissan, aiming to please with roadster versions of its front-engine/rear-drive fleet, the 300ZX and 240SX SE.

From a structural point of view, the task of creating an open-air 300ZX was a relatively simple one. Additional bracing,

beefier crossmembers and thicker sheet metal stiffen the car's midsection. Its A-pillar and rear crossmember also get fortified.

The most crucial element of rigidity on the ragtop 300ZX is also its most esthetically controversial: Nissan decided to retain a structural bar between the B-pillars. This bar lets the seatbelt anchors remain in the pillar and,

more important, vastly improves the integrity of the framework, making the fresh-air-conditioned 300ZX feel as solid as its enclosed counterpart.

The drop-top 240SX, on the other hand, goes through two series of extensive head-to-toe fortifications, the first by Nissan in Japan, the second by ASC in the U.S. Indeed, an accounting of the new and modified pieces

on the SX makes it appear as though just about every bracket, brace and body panel has either been replaced or reinforced. Nevertheless, the 240 could still take a few lessons in torsional rigidity from its big brother. The 321 lb. the SE gains in the conversion, is given up in acceleration, a situation further aggravated by the car's 155-bhp 16-valve 2.4-liter twin-cam four being coupled to a 4-speed automatic transmission. (Take it or leave it: No manual box is offered.)

The soft-shell 300ZX hardly seems to notice its 210 lb. of additional mass—weighing in at 3430 lb. versus 3220 for the T-top—thanks in large part to its wonderful 222-bhp 24-valve normally aspirated 3.0-liter V-6 engine (alas, the 300-bhp turbo-charged six isn't offered here) combined with its exemplary 5-speed manual transmission.

Surprisingly, the two Nissans appear to share very little in

■ **The 300ZX loses its top, gains an unsightly structural bar.**

their convertible mechanisms. Even more unusual, the $21,995 240SX gets the motorized top while the close-to-$40,000 300ZX has a do-it-all-by-hand version.

The 300ZX system requires undoing the header clamps and then releasing the hard-plastic boot directly behind the seats. The top then folds neatly into the boot, which closes flush with the trunk. (The boot contains a small wind deflector to further pacify any hint of wind buffeting.) The whole process takes a half-minute or so, with practice.

On the 240SX side of things, you also begin by releasing two header clamps, but the folding of the top is then taken over by a motorized hydraulic pump actuated by the touch of a button on the dash. This top collapses into a space behind the rear seats and in front of the small, but usable trunk. This process also takes about 30 seconds, without practice. To fit the soft tonneau cover takes a bit longer.

It seems almost a crime to disturb the pleasing lines of the 300 and 240, and, truth be told, Nissan is guilty. Neither car gets a visual boost from its conversion—top up or down—although each possesses the quality of sacrificing its best face for a virtuous cause.

With their tops raised, both cars are best driven with liberal use of the sideview mirrors when changing lanes. This pre-caution is inspired by blockage of the rearward view because of the design of the tops. Head room is not compromised in either Nissan.

Drawing a page from the 300ZX's conversion, Nissan mounted a post on each door of the 240SX to anchor the safety belts for the driver and front-seat passenger. Not the most elegant solution to the seatbelt-mounting problem, but infinitely preferable to the low, perpetually slack and hard-to-reach doorframe-mounted belts found on many aftermarket convertibles.

At speed, the top-down maelstrom in the cockpit of the 240SX is accompanied by a fairly significant level of noise, with very little relief afforded by rolling up the windows. But then, if you aren't willing to throw both caution and coiffure to the wind, you don't deserve a convertible. With the top up, life goes back to normal and the driving compartment becomes a quiet, sedate capsule with only a hissing touch of wind noise noticeable at speeds above 70 mph.

The open-air interior of the 300ZX Convertible is a placid environment, relatively free from gusts. Even your unadventurous friends who claim that life can be lived fully without open-air motoring will be sure to remark favorably about this car's quietude.

Both cars are blessed by long lists of standard features. And blessedly short lists of options. The 240SX SE Convertible boasts electric window lifts, central locking, an AM/FM stereo/cassette system and leather-wrapped steering wheel; air conditioning and a Sony compact disc player are the sole options. If you've dreamed of it, the standard 300ZX Convertible probably has it, a 4-speed automatic and Sony CD player being the complete choice of options.

In last month's cover story, R&T hailed the return of the convertible as a means of personal expression and enjoyment. Nissan heard the call. Now, with the 300ZX and 240SX SE convertibles, Nissan can add its support to the movement.

■ The additional weight of the electrically actuated top and a mandated 4-speed automatic take the edge off the convertible 240SX's acceleration, but its precise, predictable handling can now be enjoyed alfresco.

300ZX TWIN TURBO

Much more than the sum of its parts

PHOTOS BY DEAN SIRACUSA

When Nissan's engineers set out to build "the world's best sports car," they literally broke the venture down into its component parts. The design teams set out to build the world's best sports car, one piece at a time. Engine, transmission, brakes, suspension, even instrument panel and shift feel all came under scrutiny. To those purists who wax endlessly eloquent about soul, or character, or the personal vision of a single-minded designer, the approach seemed almost laughably simplistic, a naive attempt to build a world-class automobile based on an assemblage of computer printouts and CAD displays.

It also worked. If you measured the world's best by the numbers, the 300ZX Turbo stood at the top of the heap. The standard ZX, with its twin-cam, 24-valve V-6 spinning out 222 bhp, was competent enough, but the turbocharged version was a stunner. With its engine thoroughly hyperventilated via twin intercooled turbos, the 3.0-liter V-6's output jumped to a nice, round 300 bhp. The computer-designed multi-link front and rear suspension kept both ends firmly planted, while its Super-HICAS 4-wheel steering meant the Turbo turned like a slot car. It was fast, it handled, and with its 4-wheel vented discs only a brick wall would stop you faster.

If you preferred more subjective criteria, the 300ZX also set standards for comfort, as well as interior and exterior styling. What's more, in day-to-day living the Nissan was no more demanding than a goldfish. Successful was a bit of an understatement; knockout was closer to the mark.

But that was three years ago, and the marketplace isn't kind to those at the top. Since then, the Mitsubishi 3000GT and Corvette ZR-1 have both stolen some of the ZX's thunder in terms of raw performance, and the new Porsche 968 and Corvette LT1 both threaten to erode its position even further. The Turbo's 300 bhp, fully independent suspension, 4-wheel disc brakes and ABS are no longer class-leading, but merely expected ante for the class.

Such thinking, however, ignores the 300ZX's real forte. It was not just a world-class sports car, it was also a helluva nice *car.* And that remains something the others can't take away. With everything from fully automatic climate control to power windows, door locks and seats, the ZX provides the kinds of conveniences expected of a luxury performance car. A pair of finely sculpted seats coddle driver and passenger, and—new this year—ultrasuede trim enhances the interior and a driver's side airbag adds another level of safety. In fact, the only options remaining on the 1992 300ZX Turbo are a leather seating package and an electronic, 4-speed automatic.

Its performance has only dimmed in comparison with others of its class, and even there falls behind only on the specs charts. It will still scoot from 0 to 60 in under 7 sec, and cover a quarter-mile in 15 sec flat. It can stuff your elbows into the door panels to the tune of 0.91 g, and come to a halt in 132 ft from 60 mph. Those might not be class-leading figures, but they're nothing to be trifled with, either.

More important, however, is the sheer competence with which the ZX can untie a knotted stretch of two-lane.

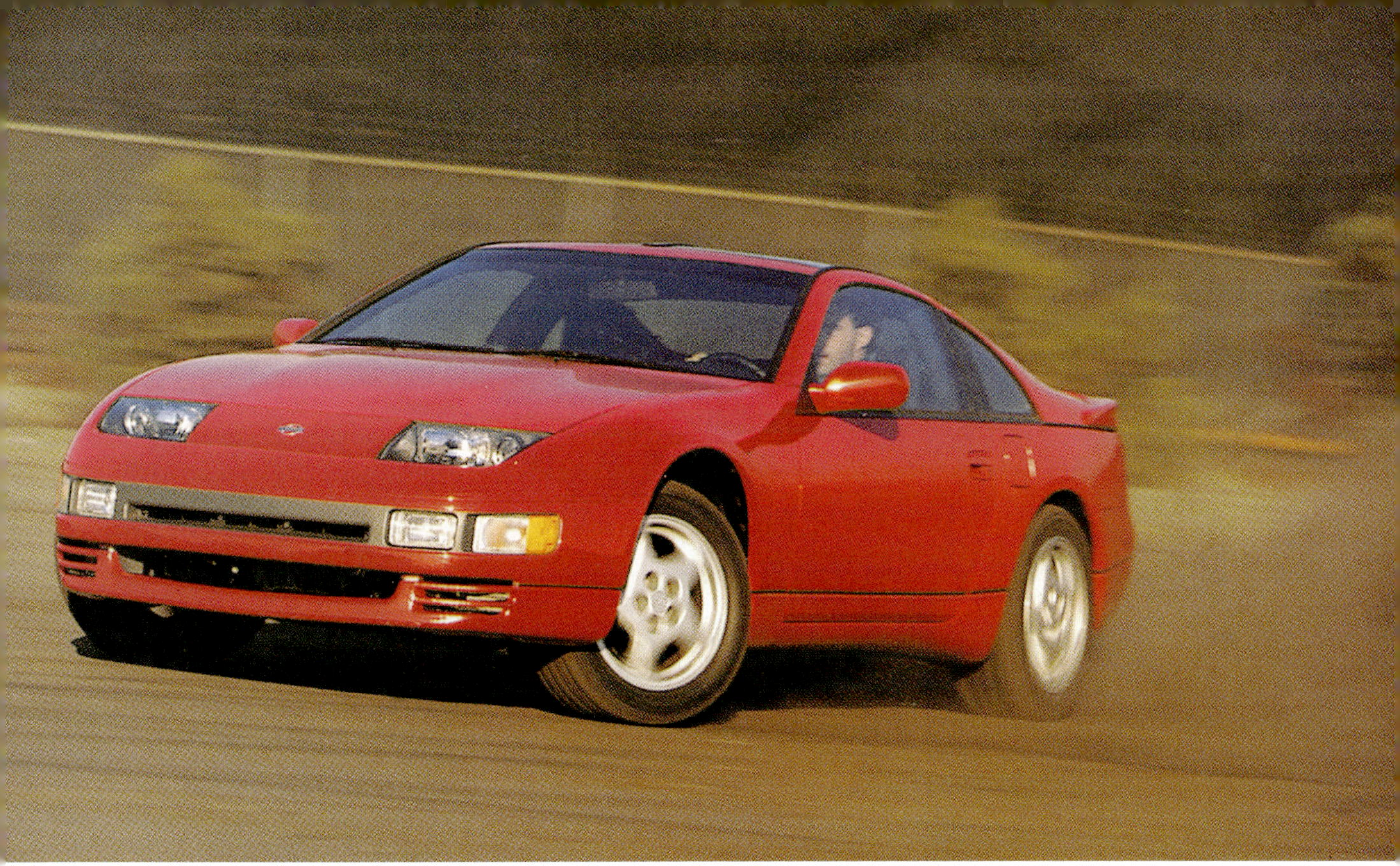

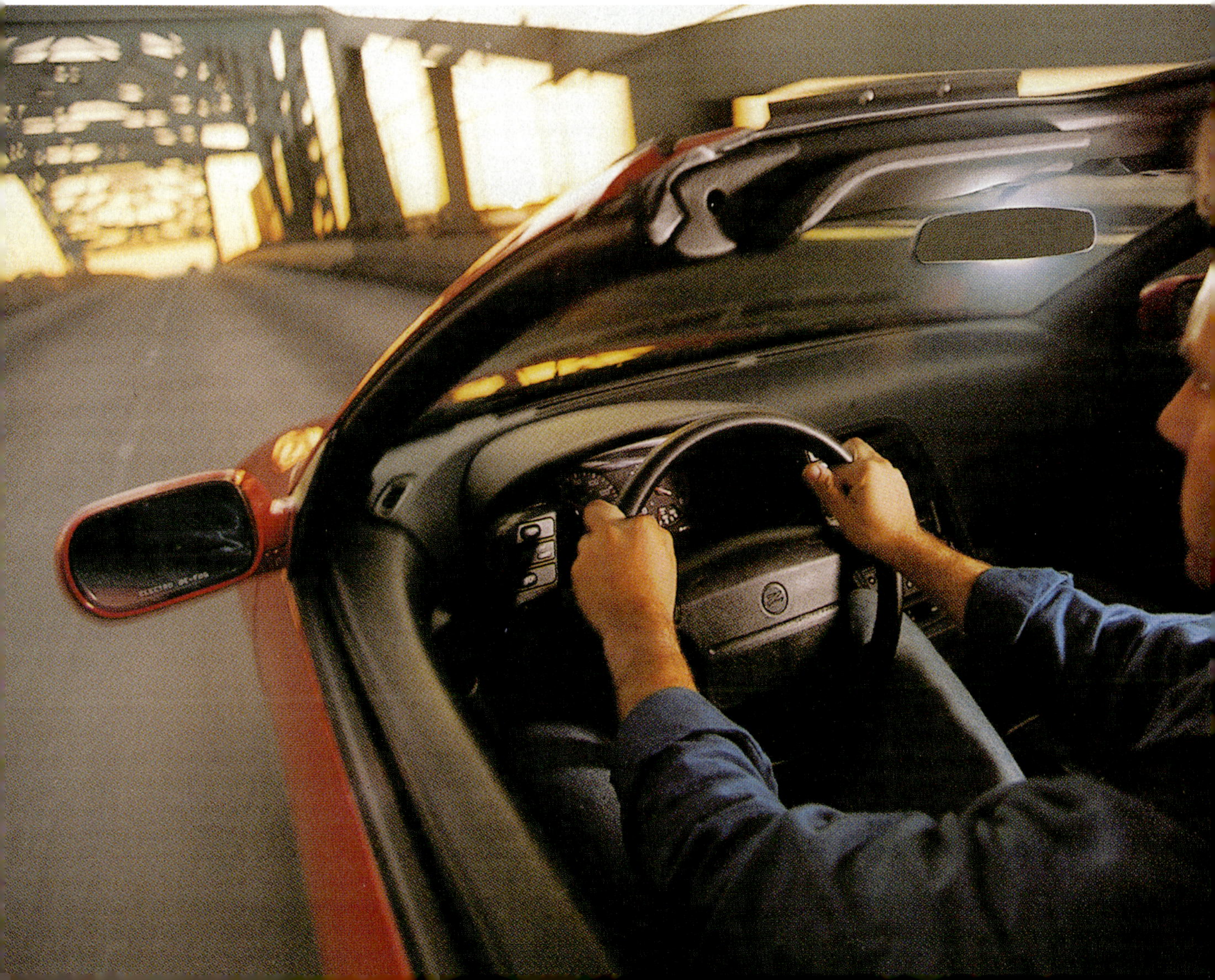

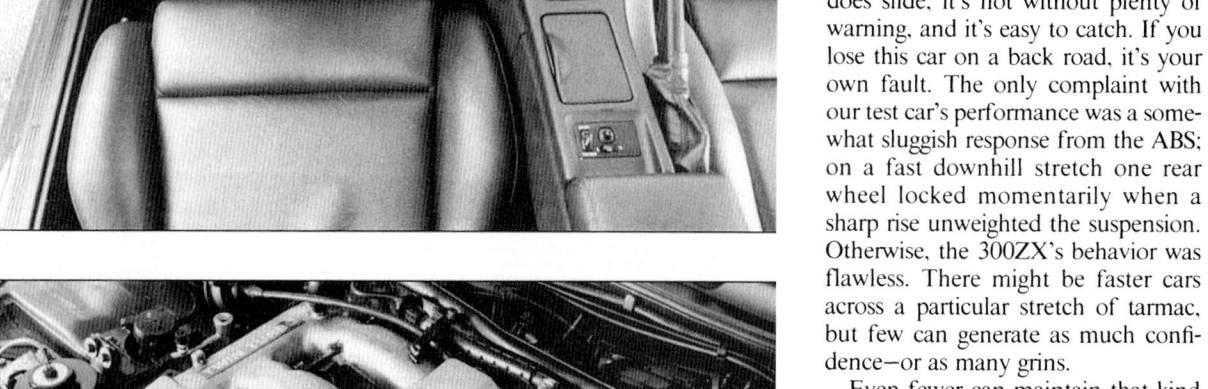

At almost 3500 lb, the Turbo won't qualify as lightweight, but its response is cat-quick, and its Michelins stick to the pavement like bubble gum to a couch. Between turns the turbo V-6 spools up quickly, and responds more like a V-8 to yank distant corners into the foreground.

Moreover, few cars are as competent—or as forgiving. When the 300 does slide, it's not without plenty of warning, and it's easy to catch. If you lose this car on a back road, it's your own fault. The only complaint with our test car's performance was a somewhat sluggish response from the ABS; on a fast downhill stretch one rear wheel locked momentarily when a sharp rise unweighted the suspension. Otherwise, the 300ZX's behavior was flawless. There might be faster cars across a particular stretch of tarmac, but few can generate as much confidence—or as many grins.

Even fewer can maintain that kind of satisfaction in day-to-day living, but in the dullness of everyday use the Nissan shines. Controls provide exceptional feedback without becoming tiresome in traffic; the clutch remains light, the shifter precise, the steering accurate but low in effort. The Turbo

NISSAN

300ZX TWIN TURBO

PRICE

List price, all POE .... $35,890   Price as tested $36,965
Price as tested includes std equip. (T-top, fog lights, tinted windows, elect. adj mirrors, elect. window lifts, central locking, cruise control, air cond, AM/FM stereo/cassette, rear window heat, rear window wiper, anti-theft system, driver's side airbag), leather pkg ($1075)

ENGINE

Type	.turbo dohc 4-valve V-6
Displacement	.2960 cc
Bore x stroke	.87.0 mm x 83.0 mm
Compression ratio	.8.5:1
Horsepower, (SAE)	300 bhp @ 6400 rpm
Torque	283 lb-ft @ 3600 rpm
Maximum engine speed	.7000 rpm
Fuel injection	.electronic port
Fuel requirement	unleaded, 91 pump oct

GENERAL

Curb weight	.3475 lb
Test weight	.3630 lb
Weight dist, f/r, %	.55/45
Wheelbase	.96.5 in.
Track, f/r	.58.9 in./61.2 in.
Length	.169.5 in.
Width	.70.5 in.
Height	.49.2 in.
Trunk space	.23.7 cu ft

DRIVETRAIN

Transmission			.5-sp manual
Gear	Ratio	Overall ratio	(Rpm) Mph
1st	.3.21:1	.11.84:1	.40
2nd	.1.93:1	.7.12:1	.67
3rd	.1.30:1	.4.80:1	.99
4th	.1.00:1	.3.69:1	est 129
5th	.0.75:1	.2.77:1	est 155
Final drive ratio			.3.69:1
Engine rpm @ 60 mph in 5th			.2450 rpm

CHASSIS & BODY

Layout	.front engine/rear drive
Body/frame	.unit steel
Brakes, f/r	.11.0-in. vented discs/ 11.7-in. vented discs, vacuum assist, ABS
Wheels	.cast alloy, 16 x 7.5J f, 16 x 8.5J r
Tires	.Michelin MXX, 225/50ZR-16 f, 245/45ZR-16 r
Steering	.rack & pinion, power assist
Turns, lock to lock	.2.4
Suspension, f/r: angled upper control arms, lower A-arms, third links, coil springs, tube shocks, anti-roll bar/upper lateral links, angled upper links, mid-lateral links, lower angled A-arms, coil springs, tube shocks, anti-roll bar	

ACCELERATION

Time to speed	Seconds
0–30 mph	.2.5
0–40 mph	.3.6
0–50 mph	.5.0
0–60 mph	.6.5
0–70 mph	.8.8
0–80 mph	.11.0
0–90 mph	.13.4
0–100 mph	.16.5
Time to distance	
0–100 ft	.3.2
0–500 ft	.8.2
0–1320 ft (¼ mi)	.15.0 sec @ 96.0 mph

BRAKING

Minimum stopping distance	
From 60 mph	.132 ft
From 80 mph	.231 ft
Control	.excellent
Overall brake rating	.excellent

FUEL ECONOMY

Normal driving	.19.6 mpg
EPA city/highway	.18 mpg/24 mpg
Fuel capacity	.18.7 gal.

HANDLING

Lateral accel (200-ft skidpad)	.0.91g
Speed thru 700-ft slalom	.66.4 mph

Subjective ratings consist of excellent, very good, good, average, poor. na means information is not available.

features 2-position shock damping. There's a noticeable difference in the two modes, but the sport setting feels too stiff, even for fast road work. Through most of the test the selector was set for touring, which provides a firm, but comfortable ride.

It's only heavy traffic that points up the 300ZX's most significant failing: rear visibility. The sharply canted rear window shrinks to mail-slot proportions in the rearview mirror, and the wide C-pillars make lane-changing a tentative, thrust and parry affair. Others might find fault with the wasted dash space above the glove box, but complaints about the interior amount to picking nits. The instrument panel remains a model of clarity for an enthusiast car, and most controls are grouped in pods flanking the instruments, close to the driver's fingertips.

Also at your fingertips in the 300ZX Turbo is one of the finest performance cars ever to turn a wheel. While it might have lost a few points in its claim to "world's best sports car," that can't undercut the ZX's overall ability. Because while Nissan might have designed it one part at a time, the 300ZX is surely far more than the sum of its parts.

—*Jim Miller*

300ZX
CONVERTIBLE
A ragtop-to-riches saga

BY RAY THURSBY

PHOTOS BY DEAN SIRACUSA

formance and almost excessive civility in a single package.

But an enduring classic's most noteworthy features should not be eclipsed by the opposition in the space of two or three years. Yes, the Turbo's performance is still impressive, but the 300-bhp club is gaining new members regularly, and 4ws is available (should you want it) from several sources. Anyway, state-of-the-moment technical marvels are seldom enough to make a car memorable in and of themselves.

Those elements that qualify the 300ZX for the short list of this decade's significant cars are present in any ZX, from Turbo to T-Roof to 2+2: timeless, exciting looks, an interior that is stylish, efficient and comfortable (a rare combination), plus a level of performance and handling that should stand the test of time. And the normally aspirated 300ZX comes closest to being a lineal descendant of the original Datsun 240Z, already accepted by most observers as a classic of the Seventies.

Fine. Assuming you accept this argument so far, you might wonder why the convertible, and not the basic 300ZX 2-seat hardtop, gets my vote. It's a tough call. On the one hand, the tin-top's roof line is very much a part of the ZX "look," a definite asset to the design. On the other hand is a simple, personal, emotional response: Given a choice between open and closed sports cars, I'll take convertibles every time.

Classic cars are chosen by emotion. Explanations and justifications always come later.

When Nissan set out to add an open-air 300ZX to its catalog, the engineers faced a daunting task. Like every other unit-body automobile, the ZX coupe derives much of its rigidity from the roof structure. Merely slicing away the lid would have produced unacceptable results, ranging from cowl shake to doors that creak in their apertures to genuinely spooky handling.

If the act of 300ZX decapitation is not for the backyard enthu-

When all the votes are finally tabulated, when all the experts have had their say, I predict that Nissan's 300ZX grand tourer will be among the cars of the Nineties elevated to classic status. And of all the ZX models eligible, the new convertible, latest addition to the (now) four-model line, is the one that would get my nod.

Others might choose the 300ZX Turbo. On the surface, that seems like sound reasoning. The Turbo created a sensation when introduced: 300 bhp and 4-wheel steering, wrapped in a body that was distinctive as could be. In 1990, it offered staggering per-

siast, neither is the detail work that follows. A deck lid has to be made; so does a top boot, hard or soft. And of course there's the top itself, which should, at the very least, go up and down without major physical or mental trauma to the operator, and protect the car's interior from the elements. It would be nice if it looked reasonably good when raised, too.

Nissan's topless 300ZX scores on all points. A very few people (not me) might quibble about the retention of the B-pillar and its added transverse brace, but it really doesn't hurt the car's appearance, and does wonders for strength. Chassis flex is not a problem; on all but the worst road surfaces, the convertible feels plenty solid and handles just like any other ZX. In fact, the open ZX does not suffer from one of my few gripes about the coupe, an annoying low-speed, low-frequency resonance from somewhere in the rear compartment. A new trunk lid turns the small but well-shaped luggage bin into a secure storage space. All of the major convertible-specific pieces are quality items, and the necessary cut-and-shut work of removing metal and reinforcing what's left has been performed to the same high standards that characterize the rest of the car.

The fabric-and-sticks part of the conversion is handled equally well. Two manual latches hold the top snug against the windshield; at the back, it is secured to the plastic-trimmed metal top boot by solenoid-operated latches. Thus the up/down operation is reduced to a level that's about as simple as it can be: You release the front retainers by hand, push two buttons (one releases the back of the top, the other opens the boot), lift the boot lid, lower the top into its well, close the lid, drive away. It takes less time to perform this drill than to read about it.

And how nice the resulting sensations! In the open 300ZX, you can hear the music of the silky 3.0-liter V-6 to best advantage, and enjoy the Great Outdoors—if there is any nearby—without having to endure excessive buffeting around A- or B-pillars.

Despite a nearly 300-lb weight penalty incurred by necessary chassis reinforcements, the convertible has lost nothing in subjective performance. Normally aspirated 300ZXs have always been a little slow off the line unless revs are kept high (with torque and horsepower peaks at 4800 and 6400 rpm, respectively, there's not much happening down low) but both engine and gearbox encourage you to do just that. Beyond 3000 rpm or so, there's plenty of urge available. The shift linkage merits special praise for precise, easy operation. A 4-speed automatic transmission is optional, by the way, but why deny yourself the pleasure of the manual box?

Like the rest of the non-Turbo 300ZXs, the convertible does without Nissan's Super-HICAS 4-wheel steering. I see that as a plus. Subjectively (again), the convertible takes to the hills with a nimbleness I find lacking in its more muscular brother. Both are more fun to herd along at speed than most of their newer rivals, but the convertible chassis seems more responsive to driver commands.

Two disappointments in this area: The steering, though reasonably light and precise, is devoid of feel, turning (no pun intended) the instinctive process of placing the car for entry into a corner into a deliberate, conscious operation. And the brakes couldn't complete a hard run through the local canyons without going into the smell/fade mode.

Top marks, as ever, for the attractive 300ZX interior. The seats are comfortable, the driving position excellent (though an adjustable steering column would be a plus), and the instrument panel with its sensible switch pods flanking big, clear gauges still sets the standard by which sports-car interiors should be judged.

What more can I say? If the elements described don't add up to justification for terming the 300ZX convertible a classic—and I maintain they do—they still add up to one heckuva great sports car. On that basis alone, the open-air ZX deserves your serious consideration.

N I S S A N

300ZX CONVERTIBLE

PRICE

List price, all POE	$37,570
Price as tested	$37,570

Price as tested includes std equip. (driver airbag, alloy wheels, ABS, leather seats, air cond, pwr windows, door locks, mirrors, AM/FM-cassette, theft alarm), cloth seats (n/c).

GENERAL DATA

Curb weight	3432 lb
Test weight	est 3600 lb
Weight distribution, f/r, %	est 53/47
Wheelbase	96.5 in.
Track, f/r	58.9/60.4 in.
Length	169.5 in.
Width	70.5 in.
Height	49.5 in.
Trunk space	5.8 cu ft

ENGINE

Type	dohc 24-valve V-6
Displacement	2960 cc
Bore x stroke	87.0 x 83.0 mm
Compression ratio	10.5:1
Horsepower, SAE net	222 bhp @ 6400 rpm
Torque	198 lb-ft @ 4800 rpm
Maximum engine speed	7000 rpm
Fuel injection	electronic port
Fuel requirement	premium unleaded

DRIVETRAIN

Transmission	5-sp manual

Gear	Ratio	Overall Ratio	(Rpm) Mph
1st	3.21:1	13.10:1	(6500) 37
2nd	1.93:1	7.87:1	(6500) 62
3rd	1.30:1	5.30:1	(6500) 92
4th	1.00:1	4.08:1	(6500) 120
5th	0.75:1	3.06:1	(5300) 130

Final-drive ratio	4.08:1
Engine rpm @ 60 mph, top gear	2700 rpm

CHASSIS & BODY

Layout	front engine/rear drive
Body/frame	unit steel
Brakes, f/r	11.0-in. vented discs/ 11.7-in. vented discs, vacuum assist, ABS
Wheels	cast-alloy, 16 x 7.5
Tires	P225/50VR-16
Steering	rack & pinion, power assist
Turns, lock to lock	2.4
Suspension, f/r	angled upper control arms, lower A-arms, third links, coil springs, tube shocks, anti-roll bar/upper lateral links, angled upper links, mid-lateral links, lower angled A-arms, coil springs, tube shocks, anti-roll bar

ACCELERATION

Time to speed	seconds
0-30 mph	2.7
0-40 mph	4.0
0-50 mph	5.6
0-60 mph	7.4
0-70 mph	9.8
0-80 mph	12.6
0-90 mph	15.3
Time to distance	
0-100 ft	3.3
0-500 ft	8.6
0-1320 ft (1/4 mile)	15.7 sec @ 90.5 mph

BRAKING

Minimum stopping distance	
From 60 mph	128 ft
From 80 mph	213 ft
Control	excellent
Overall brake rating	excellent

HANDLING

Lateral accel (200-ft skidpad)	0.85g
Speed thru 700-ft slalom	62.8 mph

FUEL ECONOMY

Normal driving	na
Fuel economy (EPA city/highway)	18/24 mpg
Fuel capacity	18.2 gal.

Subjective ratings consist of excellent, very good, good, average, poor, est estimated, na means information not available

Nissan 300ZX Turbo

MY PHILOSOPHY OF cars is simple: A car ought to be able to do what it looks like it can do. Within that plea for honesty, under the heading of Sports Cars, two paths lead to the same definition.

I imagine an idyllic road laid out along the natural contour of blossoming hill country. It runs through a meadow, curves around a pond and then carves a path through a forest up to the timberline. Now there are two sporting ways for me to effectively appreciate such a feast without wasting a crumb or spilling a drop. The first is to join in the natural universe by dropping the top on a coltish-yet-benign roadster: Mazda's Miata. The other path to sports-car nirvana is to challenge the road in a performance car that fits my driving style like a co-conspirator: Nissan's 300ZX Turbo. These two cars have separate, distinct personalities, but both possess that libertine spirit of fun essential to pegging an automobile as a sports car.

For this trip to Bodega Bay, I chose to attack, so I picked the 300ZX.

Three hundred horsepower is a nice, round number for a nice, quick car. The twin-turbo 3.0-liter V-6's peak torque—283 lb.-ft.—is mustered down at 3600 rpm. Yet the 300ZX's dohc 24-valve V-6 doesn't have the "off-or-on" power delivery of many turbos, but a smooth, affirmative transition.

The 300ZX Turbo fulfills its co-conspirator function faithfully, reading the road and sending inputs back through the quick steering and firm suspension. Its Super HICAS 4-wheel steering system helps make the ZX an extremely competent, controllable hit-the-apex/point-and-shoot sports car, its tail resistant to straying and responsive to course corrections.

Do the ZX's looks match up to its performance? Absolutely. This Nissan has been easy on our eyes for three years now, and it still looks like it belongs in *Blade Runner*. In white, it's an athletic friend; in black with chromed wheels, it's a sinister wonder.

And like all good sports cars, the 300ZX Turbo reflects its time. These are the "let-me-check-with-my-accountant" Nineties we live in, so a reasonable price tag for services rendered and relatively good gasoline mileage are much appreciated. The Nissan 300ZX Turbo has both, along with a roomy interior and two snug, comfortable bucket seats ready to throw a sporty leather arm around your shoulders as if to say, in unison with the rest of the car, "Let's drive!"

—*Richard Homan*

Going to the beach circa 1968: With my older sister's friend Gloria punching out the beat to "Build Me Up, Buttercup" on the accelerator of her white Mustang convertible, life was good and getting better. Combine cars with music, and all shall be well.

—Richard Homan, Executive Editor

Nissan created a wave of tsunami proportions with its original 240Z back in 1970, showing Americans that the Japanese took a back seat to no one when it came to designing and building sports cars. In the intervening years, the Z-car (as it's affectionately known to its admirers) got heavier and more sluggish, and lost much of its original styling purity. But with the debut of the 1990 300ZX, Nissan was riding the crest of that wave again, with a toned-up, powerful, beautifully shaped Z that was philosophically aligned with the original car.

Heading the roster for 1994 is the convertible model which, owing to the good rigidity of the T-top model, needed little in the way of structural reinforcements. In the end, thicker panels were used in the doorsills and floor, and key crossmembers were also strengthened.

When the urge for open-air motoring calls, you lower the top manually, after releasing the windshield header latches. When stowed, the top is covered by a hard plastic cover that's essentially flush with the bodywork. But of questionable esthetic merit is the protruding roof bar that remains in place. Its function is twofold: to increase the body's rigidity further, and to serve as an attachment point for the shoulder-belt anchors. (It's worth noting here that the rest of the 300ZX line this year gets dual airbags and manual 3-point seatbelts that replace rather fussy door-mounted belts.)

The convertible shares its specifications with the normally aspirated 2-seater and 2+2 models, which can be ordered in fixed roof or T-top configurations. All have the 222-bhp 4-cam 24-valve 3.0-liter V-6, a choice of a 5-speed manual or electronically controlled 4-speed automatic transmission (the latter unavailable on the base, fixed-roof 2-seater, however), P225/50VR-16 tires on alloy wheels and 4-wheel vented disc brakes with ABS.

If you're willing to trade wind-in-the-face for kick-in-the-pants, the Turbo model is for you. Three hundred horsepower await the command of your right foot, provided by the same basic V-6, fortified with twin turbochargers and intercoolers. To handle the extra power, Turbos get 1-in.-wider rear wheels (16 x 8.5) and commensurately wider tires (P245/45ZR-16), Super HICAS rear-wheel steering, and a cockpit-adjustable variable shock-damping system. Turbos can be spotted by their distinctive horizontal slots below the front bumper (to feed the intercoolers) and by the rear wing, which has been revised slightly this year.

Whatever the seating accommodations, top configuration or state of engine tune, the rejuvenated 300ZX remains a great-looking, capable sports car with dynamic capabilities that can please the most demanding drivers. The days of the 300-bhp supercar may be numbered. If you're in the market for an example of the genre, you'd do well to look closely at what Nissan has to offer.

SPECIFICATIONS

Base price, base model . . . . est $32,000	Curb weight . . . . 3185 lb	Suspension, f/r . . . . ind/ind
Base price, premium model . . . . . . est $40,000	Fuel capacity . . . . 19.0 gal.	Brakes, f/r . . . . disc/disc, ABS
Country of origin/assembly . . . . Japan	Fuel economy (EPA), city/highway. . . 18/24 mpg	Tires P225/50VR-16
Body/seats. . . . . 3D*/2, 2+2, conv/2	Base engine . . . . 222-bhp dohc 24V V-6	Steering type. . . . . rack & pinion (p)
Layout . . . . F/R	Bore x stroke. . . . . 87.0 x 83.0 mm	Turning circle . . . . 34.1 ft
Wheelbase . . . . 95.6 in.	Displacement . . . . 2960 cc	Warranty, years/miles:
Track, f/r . . . . 58.9/60.4 in.	Compression ratio 10.5:1	Bumper-to-bumper 3/36,000
Length . . . . 169.5 in.	Horsepower, SAE net. . . . 222 bhp @ 6400 rpm	Powertrain 5/60,000
Width . . . . 70.5 in.	Torque . . . . 198 lb-ft @ 4800 rpm	Rust-through 5/unlimited
Height . . . . 49.2 in.	Optional engine. . . 300-bhp dohc 24V twin-turbo V-6	Passive restraint, driver's side . . . . airbag[1]
Luggage capacity . . . . 21.8 cu ft	Transmission 5M, 4A	Front passenger's side . . . . airbag[1]

est estimated, *indicates model described in specifications, [1]door belt on convertible

NISSAN

300ZX
CONVERTIBLE

Vive la différence!

BY JIM MILLER
PHOTOS BY RON PERRY

The typical sports car takes to decapitation about as well as the average French revolutionary, which is to say, not at all. After all, while it's not quite as critical as the human noggin, the steel in an automobile's top represents a significant portion of a car's torsional and bending strength, and peeling it away is usually a surefire way to transform an exceptionally solid coupe into an incurably shaky convertible.

So it's understandable that some enthusiasts had severe misgivings about the 300ZX ending up like some automotive Robespierre when Nissan decided to lop off its top two years ago. Not to worry, however, because the ZX came through the surgery with its integrity—and its reputation—intact.

Maintaining the performance of Nissan's premier sportster meant the operation involved more than an industrial can opener. For starters, the cabrio features thicker sheet metal in the door sills and floor, as well as a reinforced rear crossmember. All told, Nissan added or modified more than 50 parts in the car's transformation, yet kept the weight difference between the T-top coupe and the cabrio to less than 100 lb. Tying both sides together, the existing coupe's B-pillar remains as a basket-handle brace behind the seats that's apparent only with the top down. While some might consider the buttressing as an obvious compromise in the design, it helps ensure that the 300's stellar chassis performance remains intact.

It only takes a quick pass across a twisty road to see that Nissan's efforts paid off. While twisty roads can make some convertibles as unruly as a French mob, the 300ZX retains the closed car's secure, controllable character. The sophisticated chassis—fully independent, multi-link suspension front and rear—can still

The convertible boasts the kinds of accouterments that could make even Louis XVI envious.

fill in for even the most inept driver's shortcomings. Though the steering loses some precision in fast, hard corners, it's only in comparison with the coupe that the difference becomes apparent. Of the few convertibles that can match the Nissan's solid feel, most of them—notably Mazda's Miata and Mercedes' regally priced SL—are built from the ground up as roadsters.

Despite the added reinforcement in the car's design, however, Nissan offers the topless ZX only in naturally aspirated form; the powers that be deemed the twin turbo's added 78 horsepower and 85 lb-ft of torque too much for the convertible's trimmed chassis. Instead, owners must content themselves with the standard ZX's 222-bhp V-6.

Nonetheless, that engine is far from a Hobson's choice when it comes to performance. Though it no longer qualifies as cutting edge, it's still well up on the blade. The 3.0-liter powerplant features dual overhead cams, four

nothing between you and the sky but a low-lying cloud bank, and you'll understand the reasoning behind Nissan's thinking. Two years ago when the company performed its operation, the ZX got a new lease on life. Which is certainly more than you can say for Robespierre.

valves per cylinder, variable valve timing, direct ignition and sequential fuel injection. More important, it spins up its power as effortlessly and smoothly as ever, though the same changes that transformed the Maxima's V-6 into such a smooth, quick-revving performer would be welcome here, too.

Our test car came equipped with the optional 4-speed electronic automatic, not necessarily the first choice for an enthusiast, but perfectly in keeping with the convertible's intent. Still, before you assume that this combination makes the droptop some kind of *zaftig* boulevardier, remember this: The ZX convertible can still no doubt manage 0–60 comfortably under 8 sec, so when the need arises—say, outrunning an unruly mob of peasants—the Nissan can get you out of trouble before you can say "let them eat cake." Further, under full power the transmission snaps off upshifts right at redline, and downshifts eagerly when you prompt it with your right foot.

The convertible also boasts the kinds of accouterments that could make even Louis XVI envious. The standard equipment list boasts the usual ZX items, such as limited-slip differential, ABS, air conditioning and power assists for windows, door locks and mirrors, then includes power-adjusted leather seats and an electronically tuned AM/FM-stereo/cassette.

Oddly, if there's a fly in the ointment, it's with the ZX's top mechanism. In this enlightened age, when the typical luxury cabrio features a one-touch power top, the Nissan's multi-step manual arrangement seems unnecessarily fussy. To be fair, the top stows beautifully under an attractive hard tonneau. And with its cloth chapeau raised the drop-top 300 looks as trim as its coupe cousin.

Better still, open it up so that there's

NISSAN

300ZX CONVERTIBLE

PRICE

List price, all POE $43,189
Price as tested $45,297
Price as tested includes std equip. (dual airbags, vari-assist pwr steering, 4-wheel disc brakes, ABS, lim-slip diff, 4-speed auto trans, cast-alloy wheels, foglamps, pwr windows, mirrors & door locks, remote keyless entry, anti-theft alarm, pwr seats, air cond, cruise cont, tilt wheel, leather-wrapped steering wheel & shifter knob, leather seats, AM/FM-stereo/cassette), CD player ($450), Calif emissions ($150), pearlescent teal paint ($359) dest charge ($390), luxury tax ($1209).

ENGINE

Type	dohc 24-valve V-6
Displacement	2960 cc
Bore x stroke	87.0 x 83.0 mm
Compression ratio	10.5:1
Horsepower, SAE net	222 bhp @ 6400 rpm
Torque	198 lb-ft @ 4800 rpm
Maximum engine speed	7000 rpm
Fuel injection	electronic port
Fuel requirement	premium unleaded

GENERAL DATA

Curb weight	3432 lb
Weight distribution, f/r, %	53/47
Wheelbase	96.5 in.
Track, f/r	58.9/60.4 in.
Length	169.5 in.
Width	70.5 in.
Height	49.5 in.
Trunk space	5.8 cu ft

CHASSIS & BODY

Layout	front engine/rear drive
Body/frame	unit steel
Brakes, f/r	11.0-in. vented discs/11.7-in. vented discs, vacuum assist, ABS
Wheels	cast-alloy, 16 x 7.5
Tires	P225/50VR-16
Steering	rack & pinion, power assist
Turns, lock to lock	2.4
Suspension, f/r	angled upper control arms, lower control arms, third links, coil springs, tube shocks, anti-roll bar/upper lateral links, angle upper links, mid-lateral links, lower angled control arms, coil springs, tube shocks, anti-roll bar

DRIVETRAIN

Transmission			4-sp automatic

Gear	Ratio	Overall Ratio	(Rpm)	Mph
1st	2.79:1	11.39:1	(6500)	43
2nd	1.55:1	6.33:1	(6500)	77
3rd	1.00:1	4.08:1	(6500)	120
4th	0.69:1	2.82:1	(4900)	130

Final-drive ratio .4.08:1
Engine rpm @ 60 mph, top gear . . . . .2490 rpm

ACCELERATION

Time to speed	seconds
0-30 mph	2.7
0-40 mph	4.0
0-50 mph	5.6
0-60 mph	7.4
0-70 mph	9.8
0-80 mph	12.6
0-90 mph	15.3
Time to distance	
0-100 ft	3.3
0-500 ft	8.6
0-1320 ft (1/4 mile)	15.7 sec @ 90.5 mph

BRAKING

Minimum stopping distance	
From 60 mph	128 ft
From 80 mph	213 ft
Control	excellent
Overall brake rating	excellent

HANDLING

Lateral accel (200-ft skidpad)	0.85g
Speed thru 700-ft slalom	62.8 mph

FUEL ECONOMY

Normal driving	19.4 mpg
Fuel economy (EPA city/highway)	18/24 mpg
Fuel capacity	18.2 gal.

Performance figures are for 5-speed 300ZX convertible.
est estimated
na means information not available

FIRST DRIVE

PHOTO BY JEFF ALLEN

SMZ

Steve Millen's 300ZX-based celebration of the Z's silver anniversary

BY DOUGLAS KOTT

YOU WANT TO talk commemorative stamps? Hot dawg! Admire them, trade 'em with your friends, lick 'em, stick 'em—and forget 'em. A commemorative coin set? Hooo-wheeee! Those Susan B. Anthonys are *real* shiny. Put them in a drawer next to the combination bottle-opener/fish-scaler/metronome that Aunt Dunderhead gave you last Christmas.

Where am I going with all this? The point is that commemorative things need not be yawn-inducing, dust-gathering paperweights—observe the SMZ, a 365-bhp 13.9-second fat-tired bespoilered, modified 300ZX Turbo that hails from the workshops of Championship-winning IMSA driver Steve Millen. In the words of Nissan public relations spokesmen, the SMZ is built "in celebration of the 25th anniversary of the Z," though the car receives no official endorsement from Nissan. We say it's an anniversary piece that will show its 3½-in. exhaust tips to Z28s and Mustang GTs quicker than you can slip your Aunt's gift into that drawer.

So $55,000 buys you a new 300ZX Turbo (listing at $41,409) and a whole slew of enhancements, starting with the engine. The stock internals of Nissan's 4-cam 24-valve V-6 (with an output of 300 bhp) are deemed sturdy enough to withstand the rigors of extra boost, bumped roughly 2 psi to 11.9. And the good air now goes in through Millen's low-restriction induction setup; the bad, out through an aluminized 3½-in.-bore system extending aft of the stock catalytic converters, resulting in an easily tapped 365 bhp.

That power is most efficiently put to the ground via 265/35ZR-18 Yokohama Advan Nexus tires (fronts are size 255/40ZR-17), which have unusual angled grooves in the shape of long, thin triangles. Wheels (9.0 in. wide in front, 9.5 in. rear), also by Yoko-hama, have spider-thin spokes that remind me of the wheels on Ferrari's 512TR. Stopping power is enhanced with thicker, larger-diameter cross-drilled discs and commensurately hefty calipers from Nissan's Skyline GT-R. And front and rear suspensions receive stiffer variable-rate springs that drop the car a sensible ¾ in., plus a set of thicker adjustable anti-roll bars.

All of which results in grip (0.91g), slalom speed (64.5 mph), zero-to-sixty (5.4 sec.) and quarter mile (13.9 sec. at 101.7 mph) that significantly better the stock car's performance without ravishing your kidneys or unduly pounding your eardrums. Body roll is virtually nil, and corners that would take the stock car to the edge of adhesion can now be taken in serene drama-free arcs. Ride quality deteriorates

only slightly, and excellent driveability remains, with a glass-smooth idle, crisp throttle response and remarkably low noise levels. The SMZ even seems to shift better, with the substitution of a great-feeling faux-carbon-fiber shift knob for the standard lever, complementing the genuine carbon-fiber overlays for the stereo-system surround and window switch plates—touches that lend the Z's interior a race-car ambiance.

And bodywork picks up where the interior bits leave off, with tight-fitting urethane pieces that evoke some of the excitement of Steve Millen's race-winning 300ZX GTS IMSA car. The rear wing, which cleverly bolts up to the stock holes, actually allows for excellent straight-back vision—you can see beneath it, while you have to look over the top of the stock piece.

Millen plans to produce 300 examples of the SMZ, fully backed by Nissan's three-year/36,000-mile warranty and sold through Nissan dealers. By all indications, it's a hot collectible, one that should gather a bare minimum of dust. ◉

When someone finally gets around to drawing up a list of the finest GT cars of the 1990s, the Nissan 300ZX will surely be included. By any measure—performance, appearance and quality come immediately to mind—Nissan's Z-car has been a standout since its 1990 introduction. It's a measure of how effective the basic concept was that the same car is equally appealing six years later.

On the other hand, it's a measure of how small the market for cars like the Z has become that Nissan is rumored to be ready to replace it within the next couple of years with a less-sporty mainstream vehicle. Money talks, and the ZX walks. It's as simple as that.

For now, you can still buy a new ZX in one of four forms: 300ZX, ZX 2+2, ZX Turbo and ZX convertible. Each has its own strengths, and each has its own personality.

The ZX, 2+2 and convertible are all powered by the same 3.0-liter normally aspirated V-6 engine. Hardly underpowered at 222 bhp, this 24-valve dohc unit is smooth as silk and ready to play. As the name implies, the Turbo adds a pair of turbochargers and intercoolers that raise the engine's output to a brawny 300 bhp. A nice 4-speed automatic transmission is available to replace the 5-speed manual in the 2+2 and convertible.

All ZXs ride on a sophisticated, independent multi-link suspension, have four large disc brakes and ABS, limited-slip differential, exceptionally precise steering, and revel in being driven hard. Ride quality is on the firm side, though not as harsh as an RX-7.

Nissan adds some chassis mods to deal with the Turbo's extra performance potential, including Super HI-CAS rear-wheel steering, wider rear wheels and tires and adjustable shock absorbers. Appropriately, the fastest Z-car is also the best-handling.

No ZX is exactly austere inside. All have practically every luxury-car touch that fits into their cozy cabins, with little more than leather upholstery as an option.

For a serious enthusiast, the only question is which ZX to consider first. The ZX is superb, the 2+2 is good for bringing a couple of small children along for the ride, the convertible adds open-air fun, and the Turbo is just plain fast. Whichever you choose, however, you'll be buying a classic, guaranteed.

QUIKFACTS

MODEL	MSRP	ENGINE	TRANS	ABS	AIRBAG	A/C
Coupe	$37,439	V-6	5M	STD	DUAL	STD
2+2	$40,189	V-6	5M	STD	DUAL	STD
Conv	$44,679	V-6	5M	STD	DUAL	STD
Turbo	$43,979	V-6T	5M	STD	DUAL	STD

SPECIFICATIONS

Layout	rwd
Wheelbase	95.6 in.
Track, f/r	58.9/60.4 in.
Length	189.5 in.
Width	70.5 in.
Height	49.2 in.
Curb weight	3299 lb
Base engine	222-bhp dohc 24V V-6
Bore x stroke	87.0 x 83.0 mm
Displacement	2960 cc
Compression ratio	10.5:1
Horsepower, SAE net	222 bhp @ 6400 rpm
Torque	198 lb-ft @ 4800 rpm
Fuel econ, city/hwy	18/24 mpg

Optional engine(s)	300-bhp turbocharged dohc 24V V-6
Transmission	5M, 4A
Suspension, f/r	ind/ind
Brakes, f/r	disc/disc, ABS
Tires	P225/50VR-16
Luggage capacity	23.7 cu ft
Fuel capacity	18.7 gal.
Warranty, years/miles:	
Bumper-to-bumper	3/36,000
Powertrain	5/60,000
Rust-through	5/unlimited

Farewell scenes are big in the movies. Everybody remembers a favorite, from the airport finale in "Casablanca" to the new Don Corleone leaving his family home for the glitter of Las Vegas in "The Godfather." Great emotional stuff, with plenty of tugs at the heartstrings.

But what about real life? How does it feel to look at a car you know is going away after a brilliant 26-year run? In the case of Nissan's legendary 300ZX, it was for me a bittersweet moment that played out in pure Hollywood style, complete with flashbacks.

Yes, the ZX has reached the end of its road and, despite rumors that have the name cropping up on a new, smaller 2-seat sports car, it's certain that the end of the current model's production sometime this year will bring the Z-car saga to an end. A steep decline in sales over the past few seasons is the determining factor; there's no good reason for Nissan to tool up a fourth-generation Z—one that can meet upcoming federal safety standards, which today's version will not—if not enough buyers are willing to lay down their money for it.

But what a road! From the beginning—the first Datsun 240Z of 1970, a bargain-priced ($3526) grand tourer with a refined sohc inline-6, sleek styling penned by Albrecht Goertz and an exceptional blend of straight-line speed and back-road ability—through the dog days of bloated

NISSAN
300ZX
2+2

Not with a whimper ...

BY RAY THURSBY
PHOTOS BY BRIAN BLADES

280ZX 2+2s and better early 300ZXs, and up to the ultimate, and final, 4-model lineup of today. Whichever flavor you fancy, be it basic ZX, 2+2 (an ideal way to take a companion and two small pets on the road with you), convertible or road-burning Turbo, you'll be driving a classic. And enjoying every mile of your own little high-performance movie.

For me, the first scene is a morning in the fall of 1989. I was in Arizona to drive the as-yet unreleased 1990 300ZX for an early test report. Before I'd even cranked up the ZX's sweet dohc 24-valve V-6, I was taken by the car's unusual shape. It looked low and purposeful, from its then-unusual glassed-in headlights to arching roofline to reverse-angle tail. At the time, my impression was that the ZX had a "pleasing organic appearance that will wear well as the years pass." Time has passed, and I see no reason to amend that opinion.

The snug cabin was equally stylish and very comfortable. Functional, too, with pods that flank the steering wheel putting major controls within easy reach of the driver. Photos taken that day show an airbag-free interior; that's about all that has changed inside the ZX between then and now.

Still, it was the ZX's performance that was most impressive. The 3.0-liter V-6 was smooth and willing, making its 222 bhp at well past 6000 rpm. The gearbox had ratios well-suited to keeping the revs up, and a slick linkage. Handling?

On the highway the ZX displayed near-perfect balance, with initial understeer that could be exchanged for mild oversteer at the driver's command. No brake problems; they simply stopped the car again and again.

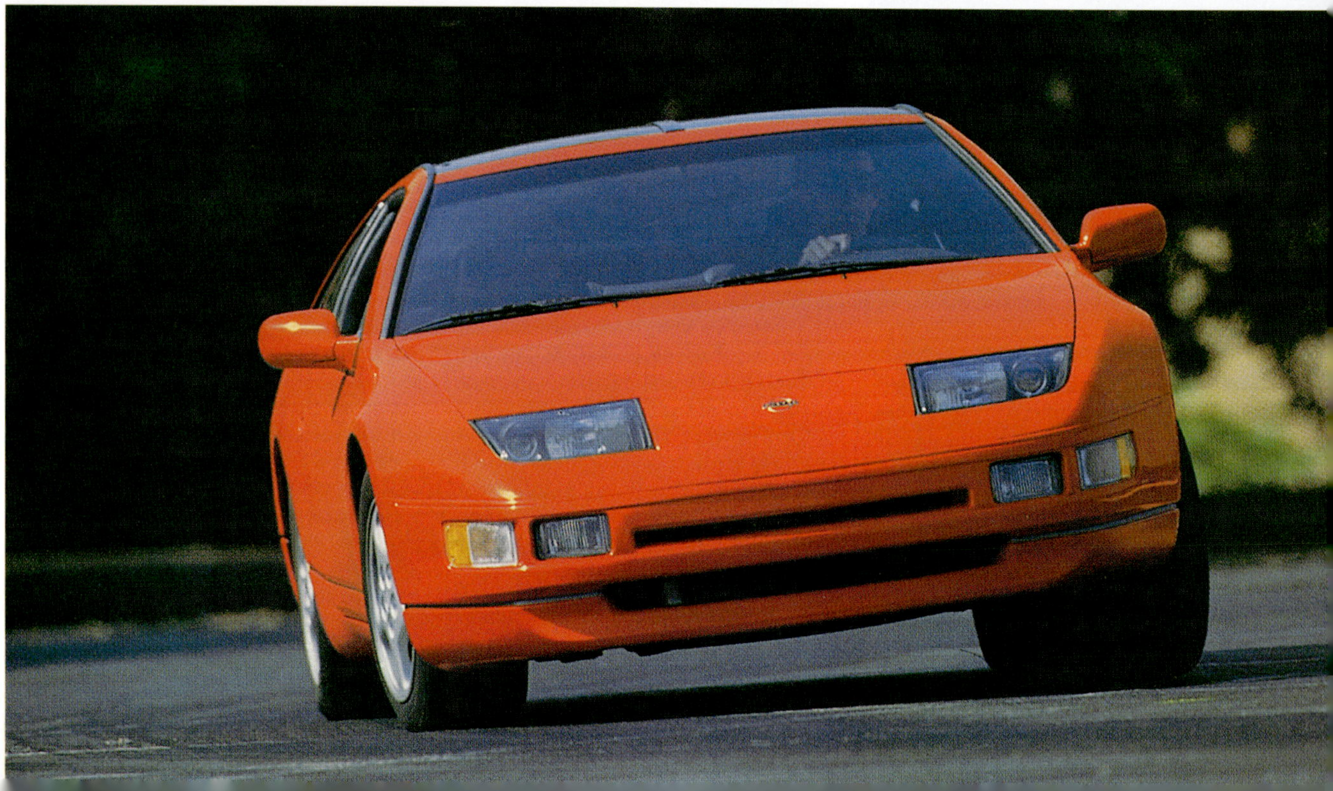

And that was only the base ZX. The Turbo's pair of pinwheels raised horsepower to 300 while chassis upgrades—driver-adjustable shock absorbers, wider rear tires and Super HICAS rear-wheel steering—ensured that the extra ponies

were usable. If ever a Z-car deserved the "ultimate" tag, this was it.

Nothing has changed. Today's ZXs are still stylish, still refined, still exciting performers, exactly as they were in 1990. The 2+2 in particular is a fine all-around grand tourer, beautiful, well-equipped, comfortable and fast, with the added space in back adding a dash of practicality. It's docile too, capable of dealing with traffic tie-ups and gentle turn-up-the-a/c-and-radio cruising.

For all that, the ZX—in any form—is at its best when let loose. The 24-valve V-6 still packs a wallop, even if it is marginally slower than some newer rivals. The sensation of speed is more impressive than the actual velocity in any case; if numbers matter to you, note that the normally aspirated ZX isn't all that much slower than its force-fed brother until you reach 3-digit range. The optional 4-speed automatic transmission (as installed in our test car) doesn't hinder performance all that much, though my choice remains the slick 5-speed manual. Zipping through sweepers and switchbacks in the nimble Nissan—which feels a half-ton lighter than its 3400-lb curb weight would suggest—is just plain fun,

and you can use early throttle application and razor-sharp steering to put it into an easily controllable drift.

Nissan went to some length (an extra 8.5-in. overall) to make the 2+2 an

attractive proposition to buyers with either ride-along animal companions or families. Kids will fit in back—and wouldn't they rather be in the ZX than in, say, a Sentra?—as will short-legged adults, as long as the ride is of short duration. Removing the standard T-roof panels adds infinite head room, and lots of fresh air without much wind buffeting.

Not all is perfect in ZX-land. Rearward vision continues to be a problem, particularly for tall drivers; you just can't see very much through the back or side quarter windows. And every current-generation ZX I've driven (excluding the convertible) has suffered from a peculiar low-frequency resonance in back, probably caused by road noise being amplified in the open cavity below the hatch.

Complaints are not the stuff of lasting memories, though. Warts and all, the ZX is a lovely car that makes its driver feel good in any situation.

Back in 1990, Nissan called the ZX the "best sports car of the Nineties." Maybe it was, maybe it wasn't. The sad truth, however, is that fewer people are buying sophisticated, costly sports cars today. Good as the ZX is, it is simply not what most enthusiasts are looking for.

Judging by the success of the Mazda Miata and the interest being generated by new, simpler, smaller sports cars from Mercedes-Benz, BMW and Porsche, the trend seems to be shifting. When these new machines, more like the original 240Z in character, finally arrive they won't have a Nissan Z-car to contend with.

And that seems a shame.

> *Back in 1990, Nissan called the ZX the "best sports car of the Nineties." Maybe it was, maybe it wasn't.*

NISSAN

300ZX 2+2

PRICE

List price, all POE	$41,089
Price as tested	$44,037

Price as tested includes std equip. (Dual airbags, vari-assist pwr steering, 4-speed auto. trans., ABS, limited-slip diff., cast alloy wheels, pwr windows, mirrors and door locks, remote keyless entry, pwr seats, air cond, AM/FM/cassette stereo, anti-theft alarm, tilt/leather-wrapped steering wheel, leather shift knob, cruise control), leather seating ($1299), Calif emissions ($150), luxury tax ($1094), dest charge ($405)

ENGINE

Type	dohc 24-valve V-6
Displacement	2960 cc
Bore x stroke	87.0 x 83.0 mm
Compression ratio	10.5:1
Horsepower, SAE net	222 bhp @ 6400 rpm
Torque	198 lb-ft @ 4800 rpm
Maximum engine speed	7000 rpm
Fuel injection	sequential elect. port
Fuel requirement	premium unleaded

GENERAL DATA

Curb weight	3401 lb
Weight distribution, f/r, %	53/47
Wheelbase	101.2 in.
Track, f/r	58.9/60.4 in.
Length	178.0 in.
Width	70.9 in.
Height	48.1 in.
Trunk space	11.5 cu ft

CHASSIS & BODY

Layout	front engine/rear drive
Body/frame	unit steel
Brakes, f/r	11.1 in. vented discs/-11.8 in. vented discs, vacuum assist, ABS
Wheels	16 x 7.5
Tires	P225/50VR-16
Steering	rack & pinion, power assist
Turns, lock to lock	2.7

Suspension, f/r . . . . upper & lower A-arms, coil springs, adjustable tube shocks, anti-roll bar/upper lateral links, mid-lateral links, lower a-arms, coil springs, adjustable tube shocks, anti-roll bar

DRIVETRAIN

Transmission			4-sp automatic	
Gear	Ratio	Overall Ratio	(Rpm)	Mph
1st	2.79:1	11.39:1	(6500)	43
2nd	1.55:1	6.33:1	(6500)	77
3rd	1.00:1	4.08:1	(6500)	120
4th	0.69:1	2.82:1	(4900)	130
Final-drive ratio				4.08:1
Engine rpm @ 60 mph, top gear				2490 rpm

ACCELERATION

Time to speed	seconds
0-30 mph	2.7
0-40 mph	4.0
0-50 mph	5.6
0-60 mph	7.4
0-70 mph	9.8
0-80 mph	12.6
0-90 mph	15.3
0-100 mph	na
Time to distance	
0-100 ft	3.3
0-500 ft	8.6
0-1320 ft (1/4 mile)	15.7 sec @ 90.5 mph

BRAKING

Minimum stopping distance	
From 60 mph	128 ft
From 80 mph	213 ft
Control	excellent
Overall brake rating	excellent

HANDLING

Lateral accel (200-ft skidpad)	0.85g
Speed thru 700-ft slalom	62.8 mph

FUEL ECONOMY

Normal driving	19.4 mpg
Fuel economy (EPA city/hwy)	18/24 mpg
Fuel capacity	18.7 gal.

Subjective ratings consist of excellent, very good, good, average, poor
na means information not available

The Turbo's Super HICAS rear-wheel steering made it a joy to hold in long, lurid drifts for the photographer.

1990-1996 Nissan 300ZX

These Zs are real enthusiast bargains

BY PETER BOHR
PHOTO BY DEAN SIRACUSA

THE Z IS DEAD. AMERICAN DRIV-ing enthusiasts could feel only a tinge of sadness when Nissan officials made the announcement. After 27 years of Z-cars, the 1996 300ZX would be the end of the line for the famed Japanese sports car.

The first of the breed, the 1970 240Z, had established the Z-car as an attractive, sophisticated and affordable alternative to European sports and GT cars. Americans bought them in droves; at the height of the car's popularity, sales approached 100,000 cars annually. By the mid-1990s, however, Z-car sales had dwindled to fewer than 5000 a year.

Some attributed the car's downfall to the times. In recent years, sports cars—Japanese sports cars in particular—appeared to fall into disfavor. Consider the casualties: Mazda's RX-7, Mitsubishi's 3000GT and Toyota's Supra were all sent to the graveyard, keeping the Z-car company.

But in retrospect, the Z-car probably was not so much a victim of sports-car malaise as it was of its own excesses. After all, modest sporting machines like Mazda's Miata and Mitsubishi's Eclipse flourished during the 1990s. At some point along the way between boom and

bust, the Z-car had simply lost its edge.

In hindsight, some aficionados of Nissan's sports car place the blame on the first generation of 300ZX, the series that ran from 1984 to 1989. As we once wrote, "For a car to become a '300ZX' meant it was becoming loathsome and technically senile." We also called it "the automotive equivalent of a couch potato." From the snappy 240, the Z-car had devolved into a sloppy-handling personal-luxury car. Moreover, it was not the paragon of reliability that Americans had come to expect of Japanese cars. Plagued with annoying problems, it was difficult to repair.

And then came a new 300ZX for 1990. In a dramatic about-face, Nissan's engineers designed a state-of-the-art GT that, a decade later, still seems as up to date as tomorrow's news. A clean-sheet design, the second-iteration 300ZX retained only the V-6 engine block from the first-generation car. The engine was reworked with new 4-valve heads, variable intake-valve timing and sparkplugs fired by individual computer-directed coils. Beneath an enticingly sleek new body, there was an exceptionally stiff chassis and a multilink suspension setup that

made the new 300ZX one of the finest-handling cars around. And it was filled with worthwhile extras, from anti-lock brakes to a theft-deterrent system.

Alas, the car was too much, too late—too much money, that is. In a sharp departure from the legacy of the original, affordable 240Z, Nissan's new supercar carried a price tag that was well beyond the reach of most enthusiasts. By 1996, a top-'o-the-line 300-bhp turbo or a convertible Z approached $45,000.

But if the 300ZX was pricey then, it certainly isn't now. Less than five years later, that same 1996 will fetch little more than 45 or 50 cents on the dollar. Earlier Zs are even greater bargains. For instance, a 1990 or 1991 300ZX coupe will sell for under $10,000—in good shape. And that, friends, makes the last in the series of Z-cars a sports-car lover's dream. The Z may be dead, but long live the Z.

300ZX selection

CHOOSING A USED SECOND-GENERA-tion 300ZX should be a relatively easy process. Nissan got the car right from the git-go, and thus needed to make few changes over the six-year production run. But the 300ZX does come in an assortment of flavors. There were three editions during the first year: A base model 2-seat coupe, a 2+2 with rear jump seats and the flagship 2-seat turbocharged model. Besides twin turbos and intercoolers, the turbocharged Z has the bonus feature of Super HICAS, a mid-to-high-speed rear-wheel steering system. Buyers had a choice of either a 5-speed manual gearbox or a 4-speed automatic transmission. But removable T-top roof panels were standard on all three versions.

A "Slicktop" 2-seater was added for 1991. For those who preferred the Z's silhouette free from distractions, it dispensed with the T-tops. And the Z-car got a driver's-side airbag—optional in 1991, made standard in 1992. For 1993, a fully topless edition joined the lineup; the new 300ZX 2-place convertible, available only with the naturally aspirated V-6, has a basket-handle chassis-stiffening bar behind the seats, a manually operated canvas top and a neat plastic cover to hide the top when it's stowed. A passenger-side airbag was the notable addition for 1994. For 1995 and its swan-song year, 1996, the 300ZX carried on virtually unchanged.

Is there a preferable year among the lot? Not really, according to the two Z-car experts we consulted for this Used Car Classic. Pierre Perrot, owner of Pierre'Z Service Center in Hawthorne, California, played a key role in Nissan's recent, highly publicized Z-car restoration program. Perrot restored several 240Zs to as-new condition, which were later sold in selected Nissan dealerships as a sort of tribute to the memory of the Z-car series. In addition to restoration, Perrot's shop provides service on Z-cars of any year.

And on the other coast is Mike McGinnis, who's been repairing Z-cars since their introduction in 1970. Today, he's the owner of Banzai Motorworks in Beltsville, Maryland. Neither Perrot nor McGinnis strongly recommends one year of the second-generation 300ZX over another, as long as a car

has been well maintained.

But each has his favorites among the various 300ZX models. Perrot is inclined to the 2+2 with an automatic transmission. He cites the extra interior room and a slightly better ride (because of the longer wheelbase) as advantages. And he finds the larger 300ZX's proportions more visually pleasing—in sharp contrast, by the way, to the bulbous shapes of Nissan's earlier attempts at 2+2 Z-cars. He likes the automatic because of its smooth operation and robust nature.

McGinnis, on the other hand, is the sports-car purist; he selects a normally aspirated 2-place car with a manual gearbox as his favorite 300ZX. But what may come as a surprise to some gung-ho enthusiasts, neither Perrot nor McGinnis is enamored with the twin-turbo version. Says McGinnis, "Because of all their power, they tend to go through transmissions and clutches. The turbocharged cars are also more difficult to repair. And they're difficult to drive at speed—it's too easy to break the tires loose." Adds Perrot, "One clogged oil line, and a turbocharger is ruined."

SPECIFICATIONS

	1990 300ZX Turbo	1996 300ZX 2+2
Curb weight	3480 lb	3400 lb
Wheelbase	96.5 in.	101.2 in.
Track, f/r	58.9/61.2 in.	58.9/60.4 in.
Length	169.5 in.	178.0 in.
Width	70.5 in.	70.9 in.
Height	49.2 in.	48.1 in.
Engine type	dohc twin-turbo V-6	dohc V-6
Bore x stroke	87.0 x 83.0 mm	87.0 x 83.0 mm
Displacement	2960 cc	2960 cc
Bhp	300 @ 6400 rpm	222 @ 6400 rpm
Torque, lb-ft	283 @ 3600 rpm	198 @ 4800 rpm
Transmission	5-speed manual	4-speed automatic
Suspension, f/r	ind/ind	ind/ind
Brakes, f/r	discs/discs	discs/discs
Steering type	rack & pinion	rack & pinion

PERFORMANCE DATA

0-60 mph, sec.	6.5	7.4
Standing ¼ mile, sec	15.0	15.7
EPA city/highway	18/24 mpg	18/24 mpg
Road Test date	12/89	1996 R&T Sports & GT Cars Guide

TYPICAL REPAIR PRICES*

Replace power window switch	$125
Brake job, including turned rotors, per axle	$130
60,000-mile tuneup (see also "timing belt")	$175
Replace power window motor	$305
Replace leaking brake master cylinder	$350
Replace clutch	$600
Replace driveshaft U-joint	$600
Replace timing belt, water pump, pulleys	$850
Replace one turbo	$1500
Rebuild automatic or manual transmission	$2100
Rebuild normally aspirated engine	$7000
Rebuild turbocharged engine	$8000

*Prices include parts and labor at $60 an hour. Sources: Mike McGinnis, Banzai Motorworks, 6735 Midcities Ave., Beltsville, Md. 20705; Pierre Perrot, Pierre'Z Service Center, 12579 Crenshaw Blvd., Hawthorne, Calif. 90250

Buyer's checklist

FRIGHT-PIGS ARE RELATIVELY RARE among this generation of 300ZX cars. The cars are still young enough so that many are still owned by their original buyers. And because they were pricey when new, the cars were purchased by folks who could afford to maintain them. Moreover, many of these Z-cars—especially ones on the East Coast, according

■ A fixed hoop added chassis stiffness and roll-over safety to the convertible 300ZX, introduced in 1993. Only 3556 were built from 1993 to 1996.

■ **300ZX Turbo's 300-bhp V-6 engine. Note twin throttle bodies, and plumbing to dual intercoolers in the nose.**

THE MARKET

Typical prices for cars in fair to excellent condition:

1990 300ZX coupe/2+2	$6500–$11,300
300ZX Turbo	$7350–$14,200
1991 300ZX coupe/2+2	$8275–$13,200
300ZX Turbo	$9075–$16,125
1992 300ZX coupe/2+2	$9175–$13,700
300ZX Turbo	$10,425–$16,500
1993 300ZX coupe/2+2	$11,500–$16,900
300ZX Turbo	$12,375–$18,775
300ZX convertible	$13,750–$19,675
1994 300ZX coupe/2+2	$12,575–$18,175
300ZX Turbo	$14,625–$21,575
300ZX convertible	$16,625–$23,100
1995 300ZX coupe/2+2	$16,075–$22,250
300ZX Turbo	$17,200–$24,400
300ZX convertible	$20,625–$26,825
1996 300ZX coupe/2+2	$19,500–$26,000
300ZX Turbo	$20,950–$28,550
300ZX convertible	$24,200–$30,600

Source: *CPI Value Guide*, P.O. Box 3190, Laurel, Md. 20709

to McGinnis—see duty as second or third cars, not as everyday drivers, and are apt to be low-mileage cars. And perhaps most important, the cars are inherently reliable; Nissan seems to have rectified many of the problems of the earlier cars. All this is, of course, good news for a prospective buyer of a used 300ZX.

Nevertheless, it's prudent to take care when buying any used car. A Z-car that comes with a complete set of repair receipts will allow you to judge its service history and verify its odometer mileage reading. Be sure to have the car inspected by a mechanic familiar with Z-cars before you buy. In addition to the usual checks for engine compression, accident damage and obvious cosmetic problems, here are some special points to keep in mind when examining a 300ZX:

1. Check service records for regular oil and oil filter changes—every 3000 miles, recommend Perrot and McGinnis. Frequent oil changes are particularly critical to the good health of the hard-working turbocharged engines. If well maintained, the normally aspirated 300ZX V-6 should be good for 200,000 to 300,000 miles before needing major repair. A well-maintained twin-turbo V-6 should last 150,000 to 200,000 miles. The turbos themselves are fairly long-lived—especially if the driver is religious about letting the engine idle for a minute or two after every high-speed run, allowing the turbos to wind down, before switching off the ignition.

2. Look over the records to see if the timing belt was replaced at 60,000 miles. The engine is freewheeling; that is, valves won't collide with pistons should the belt break. But a busted belt will leave the car immobile. Perrot and McGinnis also recommend changing the water pump, idler pulleys and thermostat along with the belt, while the front of the engine is apart. "Cheap insurance," says Perrot.

3. Check the records for tuneups and fluid changes. Beyond oil changes, the second-generation 300ZX cars require surprisingly little routine attention. The sparkplugs (platinum-tipped), PCV valves and the serpentine belt should be replaced every 60,000 miles. Air filters should be changed at 60,000 miles as well; McGinnis warns that poor-quality air filters can shred, causing problems with the mass airflow sensor. McGinnis also recommends changing the automatic transmission and brake fluids every 30,000 miles. The cooling system should be flushed every year or so.

4. Note oil leaks. The 300ZX V-6 engine isn't particularly known for leakage. But valve covers are prone to minor seepage; tightening the covers usually stops any leak. Rear main seals may also develop minor leaks, but both of our experts recommend waiting until a clutch is required before replacing the seal.

5. Check the operation of the transmission. The automatic is near-bulletproof. The 5-speed manual transmission is generally long-lived as well. But if it's going to fail, it's likely to be the fault of a bearing or synchro. Close the windows, and while the engine idles, listen for worn bearings. If a bearing is worn, the noise will stop when you depress the clutch. To check for worn synchros, be sure to *down-shift* through the gears. Clutch life is highly dependent on the driver's skills, but 60,000–80,000 miles is the norm.

6. Note unusual vibration or rumbles at speed. The driveshaft is, in fact, two shafts connected by a U-joint. The U-joint often wears, causing the entire car to shake. A rumbling noise may indicate a bad transmission mount; the mount typically deteriorates after becoming soaked with oil.

7. Inspect the brake system. Brake pads typically last 30,000 to 35,000 miles. Both experts recommend factory brake pads. Warped rotors are common (you'll feel a pulsing brake pedal)—not because of heat damage, but because the lug nuts were improperly tightened at some time. The lug nuts should always be tightened by hand, to an even 70 lb. all the way around, says

Perrot. Be aware that the wheels are not interchangeable from side to side; for proper brake cooling, the right-side wheels should be mounted on the right and the left-side wheels mounted on the left. Leaky brake master cylinders are also common; look for fluid underneath the joint where the master cylinder and booster come together.

8. Glance at the side windows during high-speed driving. The 300ZX has no side window frames. If the glass bows out, moving away from the seal, the windows can be adjusted—though it requires taking apart much of the door. Power window motors and switches are generally durable, but can be ruined if rainwater manages to penetrate their casings. T-tops may leak, though not usually because of worn seals. Adjusting the catch will often stop the leak.

9. Examine the oilpan, the front bodywork and air dam for damage. The low-slung stance of the 300ZX can cause problems for the careless driver. "Things often get banged up in front," says Perrot. But a bashed oilpan may cause more than a cosmetic problem. The engine's oil pickup is near the front of the pan, and dents may restrict the oil flow, possibly damaging the engine. Be sure the pan is straight. Leaves and road debris can get into the air-conditioner condenser, diminishing its performance.

10. Inspect the tires for uneven wear. If there are no problems with front suspension components, yet the tires show abnormal inside-edge wear, there may be too much negative camber. The camber is not adjustable as the car comes from the factory. However, there is a retrofit kit available for the upper control arm that allows for camber adjustment. ◎

ROAD&TRACK

World Exclusive First Drive!

Nissan 350Z

The legendary

Z-Car returns...

for under

$30,000

December 2001 $3.99

Canada $4.99   UK £2.95
www.roadandtrack.com
aol keyword: road

03920

0 274111

WORLD EXCLUSIVE FIRST DRIVE

2003 NISSAN

350Z

A star is reborn

BY SAM MITANI · PHOTOS BY KOICHI OHTANI

"YOU CAN LIKEN IT TO SOMEONE RIPPING THE HEART OUT OF YOUR BODY," CONFIDED A Nissan official when his company announced in 1996 that it would discontinue marketing the 300ZX in the U.S. "And without a heart, the body cannot survive."

Those words turned out to be hauntingly prophetic; the ensuing years saw the Japanese carmaker's fortunes plummet to near-bankruptcy. Many pointed to bad decision-making, while others criticized the company's advertising strategy. Some, including me, attributed part of the downfall to the absence of the Z. Like a Hollywood movie without a strong lead actor, Nissan lacked that larger-than-life component to draw people in and create excitement.

> "Our performance target is the Porsche Boxster S, while our price target is keeping it **below $30,000.**"

In early 1998, I got wind of a special project headed by then president of Nissan Design International (now called Nissan Design America) Jerry Hirshberg. The rumor was that he was working on a concept sports car, a new Z, no less.

"Nissan was becoming a faceless corporation," said Hirshberg. "Out of frustration, we convened a meeting at NDA to consider what we designers could do to turn the company around. My suggestion was that we desperately needed to reintroduce the Z. Everyone rallied around this idea and although we had a full slate of projects at the time, the entire staff jumped into this task with vigor. Within three months, we had a full-size clay prototype."

The styling theme of this unofficial Z was retro, with cues taken from the original 240Z. Hirshberg decided on this route because he wanted the car to be unmistakably identified as a Z. It drew enough attention around the offices of Nissan North America for executives there to give the car the green light to become a running prototype.

As soon as it was ready, we drove it (the only ones to do so) and put it on the cover of our March 1999 issue. According to Hirshberg, that exposure helped sway the opinions of those high up in the corporate hierarchy. And at the New York motor show later that year, Nissan officially announced it would produce the new Z, hoping to bring it to market sometime in 2002 or 2003.

But would this be a case of too little too late? Nissan was mired in such financial troubles that some doubted the company would be around after 2000. Just when it

seemed that the end was imminent, Renault came to the rescue. Hardly had the ink dried on the merger documents when the French car company took drastic and immediate action, transplanting its financial whiz, Carlos Ghosn (pronounced *gōn*) as Nissan's chief operating officer. Ghosn announced at a press conference before the 1999 Tokyo Motor Show that head count at Nissan would be drastically reduced, a number of longtime suppliers dumped and two main assembling plants shut down. It was *risutora* (Japanese for restructuring)

on a scale that the Japanese had never seen before. My biggest concern? That the Z would be either put on the back burner or abandoned. Then Ghosn uttered the following words: "We will build the Z. And we will make it profitable."

THE ROAD TO PRODUCTION

Hirshberg's concept got the proverbial wheels rolling by rekindling Z awareness. However, in terms of styling, the bright orange 2-seater missed the mark. "The car doesn't have the visual impact of the last

Z," said some. Others cried, "We don't want another 240SX, we want a real sports car."

So it was back to the drawing board for NDA. But this time, the company's design studios from Japan and Europe became involved. The powers that be at Nissan headquarters decided to hold a competition to see which camp could create the best-looking Z. To make things even more interesting, Lotus was asked to participate. The U.S. team's reins were handed over to Diane Allen.

"The most important facet was to put 'Z-ness' into the car, so we started by tak-

■ These sketches show the direction Nissan originally wanted to go with the 350Z. As you can see, some aspects of the design didn't make it, most notably the front air dam. The rear retains its original theme dominated by its triangular taillights. After these design proposals were made, the stylists went to work fine-tuning the details to produce the car you see on these pages.

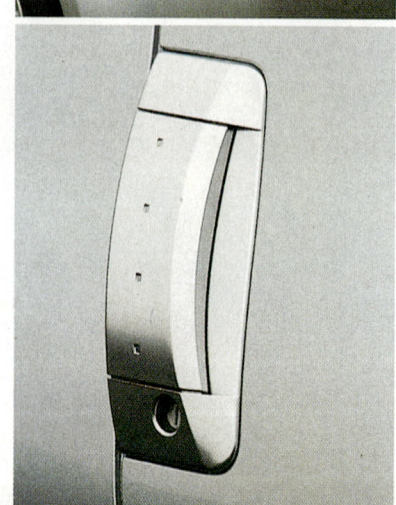

ing the best of the 240Z and the latest version of the 300ZX and throwing away the worst. But above all we wanted it to represent our vision of the future sports car. Therefore, we didn't want anything retro about our design," she said.

NDA won the contest, edging out the team from Japan. Allen and her crew took responsibility for the overall styling of the car, while the Japanese team was assigned to provide the finishing touches. The car you see here is the result of their collaborative efforts.

As the styling of the car evolved, so too did the mechanical side of the equation. Nissan was determined not to fall into the trap of the last 300ZX, whose high-tech theme resulted in a price tag that far exceeded the means of its primary audience. But the question remained: Should a low price (a target of less than $25,000) be the priority, or should the company just "go for it" and then try to keep the price reasonable?

It was a simple decision for John Yukawa, designated as the car's project leader. Soon after his appointment, he told me which path he would take. "There is no way I am going to hold back on the performance aspect of the Z. I feel that the Z should be a car that equals or bests more expensive entries from Europe. Our performance target is the Porsche Boxster S, while our price target is keeping it below $30,000."

An almost impossible challenge? Perhaps. But Yukawa had an ace up his sleeve: the VQ powerplant in the Maxima. It was receiving rave reviews in virtually every automotive publication around, and this V-6 was capable of producing so much more than the 2001 Maxima's 222 bhp and 217 lb.-ft. of torque.

"There was never any doubt about which engine I wanted to go with; the VQ was our primary choice from the start. I also wanted to go the naturally-aspirated route—I felt that the acceleration behavior of a naturally-aspirated engine is much more linear and rewarding than a supercharged or turbocharged engine's," Yukawa said.

For the 350Z, the 3.5-liter 24-valve V-6 has been tuned to produce about 280 bhp at 6500 rpm and 253 lb.-ft. of torque at 4500. These not-yet-final figures are largely the result of breathing improvements, including a new intake system and freer-flowing exhaust. The aluminum-block powerplant also features continuously variable valve timing and probably a revised compression ratio.

When it came to the 350Z's handling, Yukawa went the conservative route, not wanting to create a car with a bone-crunching ride: "My primary goal was to create a car that corners elegantly and effortlessly. I didn't want something that darted into corners like a go kart, but one that stepped into them in a predictable manner. I wanted the handling feel to be more mature than that of, say, a Honda S2000," he said. "And since we were designing the car primarily for the North American market, we wanted to make sure it was a comfortable tourer."

Yukawa felt that the best suspension for this was a multilink setup both front and rear because of its excellent load adaptability that "consistently keeps the tires firmly planted to the tarmac while maintaining an ideal balance and a nice ride."

The 350Z is scheduled to go on sale in the summer of next year as a 2003 model, Yukawa reiterating that the price will be in the neighborhood of $29,000.

■ Interesting details abound in the 350Z's styling, but the most eye-catching of them all are the car's triangular taillights and geo-mechanical door handles. These elements were part of the original design study car that made it all the way to production. Nissan's highly-praised VQ powerplant, mounted longitudinally, ensures optimal performance.

NISSAN 350Z SPECIFICATIONS

Curb weight	est 3150 lb
Weight distribution	52/48
Wheelbase	104.3 in.
Track, f/r	60.4 in./60.4 in.
Length	169.7 in.
Width	71.5 in.
Height	51.6 in.

ENGINE & DRIVETRAIN

Type	aluminum block & heads, V-6
Valvetrain	dohc, 4-valve/cyl
Displacement	3498 cc
Bore x stroke	95.5 mm x 81.4 mm
Horsepower	est 280 bhp @ 6500 rpm
Torque	est 253 lb-ft @ 4500 rpm
Transmission	6-speed manual

CHASSIS & BODY

Layout	front engine/rear drive
Body/frame	unit steel
Suspension, f/r	multilink/multilink
Brakes	12.8-in. vented discs/ 12.7-in. discs
Steering	rack & pinion
Wheels	cast alloy, 18 x 8JJ
Tires	225/45R-18 f, 245/45R-18 r

ESTIMATED PERFORMANCE

0-60 mph	6.0 sec
0-1320 ft (¼ mile)	14.0 sec

DRIVING IMPRESSIONS

It was late spring when I saw three versions of the 350Z tucked away in an old garage on Nissan's Tochigi proving grounds. One wore the finalized body contours (but was not mechanically representative of the production car), while the other two were test mules that represented the car's driving dynamics.

I went to the "design" car first. It appeared slightly different from the last version I saw in Arizona earlier this year (see cover story, March 2001). The front end of this car looked better than that of the prototype; it had a smaller more conventional-looking grille and larger headlights that ran deeper into the color-keyed bumpers. The production Z is also sleeker, with a slimmer profile and a lower beltline. That said, the 2-seater retains its aggressive stance by way of bulging flared fenders, both front and rear, and sporty 18-in. 6-spoke alloy wheels. The rear carries over unchanged from the last prototype, characterized by drooping triangular taillights that are visible from the sides and a Porsche 911-style sloping roofline. The production 350Z's exterior dimensions remain relatively unchanged with an overall length, width and height of 169.7, 71.5 and 51.6 in., respectively.

The car's interior has a few retro cues, but its overall design is quite fresh. Directly in front of the driver is a large tachometer, flanked by a speedometer and the temperature/fuel gauge. On top of the center dash are three smaller gauges a la 240Z. The cabin may appear somewhat cramped at first glance, but once you slide into the bucket seats, you'll find there's quite a bit of head room. The rear cargo area is large for a 2-seat sports car, with more luggage space than most anything in its class, but there's a fat strut tower brace that gets in the way of fitting large items like a full-size suitcase or a golf bag.

Next I jumped into one of the test mules and turned the ignition. A deep raspy exhaust note filled the cabin; it was immediately evident this wasn't the same engine I was used to in the Maxima. The shifter slides into 1st gear with a reassuring *snick*. The car shoots off the line like a dart from a blowgun, the V-6 demonstrating its propensity for low- and midrange torque, dishing out extra helpings of it the moment the tachometer needle brushes past 3000.

Shift the 6-speed manual gearbox to 2nd, stay on the throttle and you're treated to another wonderful forward surge as the g-forces build impressively. According to my chronograph, the 350Z runs to 60 mph in a tick less than 6 seconds. The 350Z's top end promises to be just as impressive. I hit 120 mph on a long straightaway and the car wasn't even breathing hard.

Through the twisty sections of the track, the 350Z exhibited near-neutral balance through all types of turns, with minimal understeer. And when I tried to slide the rear out, it took a mammoth effort because the rear tires stay planted to the ground. The steering felt precise and communicative, exhibiting a nice on-center feel. My only complaint was that the body leaned a bit through the tight stuff and floated over rises.

"We're still fine-tuning the suspension, and the final version will be firmer than the one you drove today," Yukawa said.

Overall, the 350Z possesses the same spirit as the 240Z back in 1970. It has the look and the feel of Europe's best sports cars, while promising a considerably lower price. I learned after my brief drive that not only will the 350Z give the likes of BMW's M Coupe and Porsche Boxster S a run for their money, but that the heart is back in Nissan, and it's pumping as strongly as ever.

■ Inside the new Z, you'll find a genuine driver's environment, highlighted by supportive bucket-type seats and a gearbox with a short-throw linkage and a large easy-to-grab shift knob. The main gauges—tachometer, speedometer and fuel/temperature readout—are clustered prominently in front of the driver while three smaller ones grace the top of the center dash a la the 240Z. And while the rear strut bar looks nice and helps increase handling precision, it does complicate loading and unloading large pieces of luggage. For enthusiasts, however, this is a tradeoff that's easy to accept.

2003 Nissan 350Z

Rebirth of an icon

BY DOUGLAS KOTT • PHOTOS BY GUY SPANGENBERG

IT TOOK THE FIRM HAND OF Carlos Ghosn to bring Nissan back from the brink of financial disaster. But it has taken the Z-car's much-publicized return to recapture our imagination. For the first time since 1996 in America, Nissan is counterbalancing its line of sporty sedans by offering a true, red-blooded, apex-devouring, kidney-thumping, practicality-be-damned sports car. One that, Nissan hopes, will recall the elemental simplicity of the much-revered 240Z, mark a return to affordability, and compete on a dynamic level with some of the world's best 2-seaters. Luckily for us, the new 350Z succeeds powerfully on all three counts.

Much as the 240Z did in 1970 (when, in an R&T comparison test titled "The $3500 GT," the vastly more powerful Datsun effectively pummeled the Fiat 124 Sport Coupe, MGB GT, Opel GT and Triumph GT6 Mk 3), the 350Z offers crème brûlée performance for a Jell-O pudding price. Getting slightly ahead of ourselves, consider that the new Z will match a Porsche Boxster S in the 0–60 sprint (5.6 seconds) and lose by only a few car-lengths in the quarter mile (14.3 sec., versus the Boxster's 14.0). Then mull over the following: The base 350Z, which features the same 287-bhp V-6, 6-speed transmission and forged aluminum multilink suspension as our "Track Model" test car, comes in at slightly more than half the cost of Porsche's *Mittelmotor*. That's $26,269 for the base, with our test car listing at $34,079 fitted with a limited-slip differential, xenon lights, yaw and traction control, amply sized Brembo brakes, wider Bridgestones (225s front, 245s rear), and forged 18-in. Rays Engineering wheels.

Economies of scale make it possible. The 350Z utilizes a version of Nissan's FM (front mid-engine) platform that underpins the new Infiniti G35, albeit now with a tidier, near-Corvette-size wheelbase (104.3

in , versus the G35's 112.2). Its VQ35DE V-6, placed behind the front axle as the chassis designation suggests, can also be found in lesser tune beneath the hoods of the Nissan Maxima and Altima, and the Infiniti G35, I35 and QX4.

For sports-car duty, less restrictive intake and exhaust plumbing work with the variable-phase intake cams to help the steel-sleeved, aluminum-block engine stomp out 287 bhp at 6200 rpm and 274 lb.-ft. of torque at 4800 rpm. Of course, the engine drives the rear wheels, through a 6-speed transmission, a carbon-fiber-reinforced plastic driveshaft and, for all models other than the base car, a viscous limited-slip differential.

Fire up the Z and you're greeted by a mellifluous, quasi-exotic rip from the dual exhausts. Select 1st, and you'll notice the robust, unbreakable feel of the short shift lever that slots from gear to gear with rifle-bolt precision. Clutch effort is fairly light considering the power being transmitted, and the torque is impressive—there's 200 lb.-ft. even at a lowly 1200 rpm, when the electronic throttle's motor is just starting to crack open the butterfly.

Leave the windows down, though, because the buttery exhaust soundtrack helps to balance the considerable moan and boom that make it through the firewall at high revs. This powerplant does like to spin, and each upshift is rewarded with a forceful punt of acceleration with a minimum of squat, a nasty trait of older 300ZXs with semi-trailing arms at the rear. There's flexibility galore, so even the 1.00:1 5th gear is an effective passing ratio at higher speeds.

Lean on the middle pedal, and the big Brembos—4-piston calipers working on 12.8-in. rotors up front, with rear 2-piston units acting on 12.7-in. discs—scrub off speed with utter confidence, and aren't the least bit touchy or noisy, even when cold. And the Z corners with the same "Let's go faster" eagerness, carving precise arcs with no mid-corner corrections needed from the well-weighted rack-and-pinion steering, which, though precise, can't quite muster the Boxster's near-telepathic feedback.

Press harder and the fun is tempered with resolute understeer, although it's happening at a high enough grip level that most won't experience it, short of a track day or super-spirited canyon run. Dropping throttle in mid-bend reduces the understeer, but the chassis is rear-grip-biased enough to remain stable in a panic situation. If there's a criticism to levy, it's that the Track Model should wear Bridgestone's top performance tire, the Potenza S-03 Pole Position, instead of the Potenza RE 040.

Driving the Z is big fun, and its super-

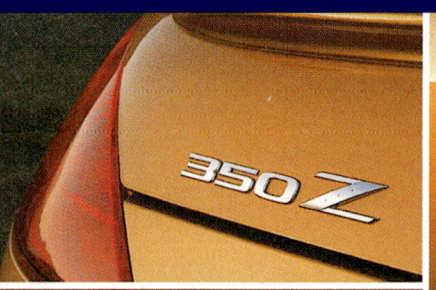

■ **Clockwise from below:** The 350Z corners with little roll and high predictability; partial engine cutaway reveals cam chain drives for the VQ35DE engine, the coil-on-plug ignition and the stout shifter truss at the rear of the 6-speed transmission; rear three-quarter view shows off the burly tailpipes, considerable flares and high beltline; xenon headlights come on all but base 350Z; artsy emblem shot; and the Track Model's 4-piston Brembo fixed calipers behind the 6-spoke 18-in. forged wheels—considerably lighter than optional 18-inchers available on other 350Z models.

rigid chassis that allows the suspension to work so well is a key part of that. Some efforts here do compromise utility, though. A rear suspension brace that looks like a miniature version of the St. Louis Arch bisects the load area beneath the rear hatch, and the structure-packed C-pillars are quite thick, offering only a porthole view out of the rear quarter windows. The ride is quite firm and sometimes thumpy—and every Z model comes with the same spring rates, shock valving and anti-roll bar diameters, but we're told the slightly taller sidewalls of the base model's 17-in. tires add some comfort. But this is a sports car, remember?

With a proper sports-car interior, we might add. The ambience here is racy and a little austere, with plenty of enticing bits such as the thick-rimmed 3-spoke steering wheel with just-so silver accents, and a motorcycle-pod gauge cluster that tilts with the steering column, a la Porsche 928. There are three hooded ancillary gauges atop the center dash, angled toward the driver, with the nearest containing a multifunction display that offers everything

■ **The Z's 2-seat interior is refreshingly straightforward, with torso-hugging seats, intuitively placed controls and a gauge pod that tilts with the steering wheel. Shifter connects to 6-speed gearbox, and has ultra-sturdy feel; rear chassis brace also helps in the rigidity department, at the expense of effectively dividing the cargo area.**

from tire pressures to rpm settings for a blinking upshift light in the tach face. The manually adjustable seats are excellent, with the driver's offering a subtle extra amount of shoulder and torso bolstering, and there's head, leg and elbow room aplenty, even for the vertically gifted. Somewhat amorphous door panels, covered in what looks like textured wetsuit material, are the starkest expanses, but neat cast aluminum door latches integrated with the side air vents provide some relief.

Nits to pick? Well, quality of some of the plastics, especially the "reptile skin" center dash, falls short of Audi or Honda levels, and there's no conventional glovebox; several storage bins are provided in the panel behind the seats, the largest of which re-

quires tilting the passenger seat forward to access. And the "carbon-fiber weave" upholstery does look a bit prone to wear.

Yet, in the words of one editor, when the price of the 350Z is considered, "the criticisms simply vaporize." This is a fantastic car, with the money spent in all the right places. You be the judge of its styling; but it was universally admired by our staff for its wide, powerful lower body, tidy greenhouse that's evocative of the Audi TT, and tapering roofline that hints at Porsche 911. A convertible version, available in six months to a year from now, can only heighten its appeal. Fans of the Z had very high expectations for this new car, and the consensus around here is that Nissan has delivered the goods.

THE COMPETITION

Chevrolet Corvette 50th Anniversary
Tested: 8/02

Porsche Boxster S
Tested: 9/00

■ We're comparing the 350Z to a Vette? Yes—the wheelbases and weights are nearly identical—but the Chevy's brash 350-bhp V-8 gives it a 0.7-second advantage to 60 mph. Porsche's mid-engine roadster matches the Z's 0-60, but pulls harder in the quarter mile and delivers better steering feel. It's certainly hard to overlook the Nissan's value.

	Nissan 350Z	Chevrolet Corvette 50th Anniversary	Porsche Boxster S
Current list price	$34,079*	est $48,000	$51,600
Engine	dohc 3.5-liter V-6	ohv 5.7-liter V-8	dohc 3.2-liter flat-6
Horsepower	287 bhp @ 6200 rpm	350 bhp @ 5600 rpm	250 bhp @ 6250 rpm
Torque	274 lb-ft @ 4800 rpm	375 lb-ft @ 4400 rpm	225 lb-ft @ 4500 rpm
Transmission	6-speed manual	6-speed manual	6-speed manual
0–60 mph	5.6 sec	4.9 sec	5.6 sec
Braking, 60–0 mph	119 ft	134 ft	125 ft
Lateral accel (200-ft skidpad)	0.89g	0.89g	0.93g
EPA city/highway	est 20/26 mpg	19/28 mpg	18/26 mpg
Length	169.6 in.	179.7 in.	171.0 in.
Width	71.5 in.	73.6 in.	70.1 in.
Height	51.9 in.	47.7 in.	50.8 in.
Wheelbase	104.3 in.	104.5 in.	95.2 in.
Track, f/r	60.4 in./60.8 in.	62.0 in./62.0 in.	57.3 in./59.4 in.
Curb weight	3290 lb	est. 3230 lb	3020 lb

*Track Model tested.

2003 Nissan 350Z "Track"

Nissan North America, Inc., 18501 S. Figueroa, Gardena, Calif. 90248; www.nissandriven.com

At a Glance

0–60 mph	5.6 sec
0–¼ mile	14.3 sec
Top speed	est 155 mph'
Skidpad	0.89g
Slalom	65.6 mph
Brake rating	very good

List Price: $34,079
Price as Tested: $34,619

Price as tested incl std equip. (dual front airbags, ABS, yaw and traction control, cruise control, auto. air cond, AM/FM/CD sound system, tilt steering wheel, anti-theft system, keyless entry; pwr mirrors, windows & door locks, 18-in. wheels and tires w/pressure monitoring, Brembo brake rotors and calipers, limited-slip diff, front & rear spoilers), dest charge ($540).

SCALE: 10 IN.(254mm) DIVISIONS
DRAWING BY TIM BARKER

SPECIFICATIONS

Engine

Type	aluminum block & heads, V-6
Valvetrain	dohc 4-valve/cyl
Displacement	213 cu in./3498 cc
Bore x stroke	3.76 x 3.20 in./95.5 x 81.4 mm
Compression ratio	10.3:1
Horsepower (SAE)	287 bhp @ 6200 rpm
Bhp/liter	82.0
Torque	274 lb-ft @ 4800 rpm
Redline	6600 rpm
Fuel injection	elect. sequential port
Fuel	premium unleaded, 91 pump octane

Warranty

Basic warranty	3 years/36,000 miles
Powertrain	5 years/60,000 miles
Rust-through	5 years/60,000 miles

Chassis & Body

Layout	front engine/rear drive
Body/frame	unit steel, alum. hood
Brakes: Front	12.8-in. vented discs
Rear	12.7-in. vented discs
Assist type	vacuum, ABS
Total swept area	533 sq in.
Swept area/ton	310 sq in.
Wheels	cast alloy; 18 x 8f, 18 x 8½ r
Tires	Bridgestone Potenza RE 040; 225/45ZR-18 91W f, 245/45ZR-18 96W r
Steering	rack & pinion, vari pwr asst
Overall ratio	15.9:1
Turns, lock to lock	2.6
Turning circle	35.3 ft

Suspension
Front: multilink, coil springs, tube shocks, anti-roll bar
Rear: multilink, coil springs, tube shocks, anti-roll bar

General Data

Curb weight	3290 lb
Test weight	3435 lb
Weight dist (with driver), f/r, %	55/45
Wheelbase	104.3 in.
Track, f/r	60.4 in./60.8 in.
Length	169.6 in.
Width	71.5 in.
Height	51.9 in.
Ground clearance	4.7 in.
Trunk space	6.8 cu ft

Accommodations

Seating capacity	2
Head room	36.5 in.
Seat width	2 x 18.0 in.
Leg room	43.0 in.
Seatback adjustment	10 deg
Seat travel	9.0 in.

Drivetrain

Transmission: 6-speed manual

Gear	Ratio	Overall ratio	(Rpm)	Mph
1st	3.79:1	13.42:1	(6600)	38
2nd	2.32:1	8.22:1	(6600)	61
3rd	1.62:1	5.74:1	(6600)	88
4th	1.27:1	4.50:1	(6600)	112
5th	1.00:1	3.54:1	(6600)	142
6th	0.79:1	2.81:1	est (5700)	155*

Final drive ratio.........3.54:1
Engine rpm @ 60 mph in top gear.........2150
*Electronically limited.

Instrumentation

160-mph speedometer, 8000-rpm tachometer, coolant temp, fuel level, oil pressure, volts

Safety

dual front airbags, anti-lock braking, yaw and traction control (all standard equip.)

PERFORMANCE

Acceleration

Time to speed	Seconds
0–30 mph	2.1
0–40 mph	3.3
0–50 mph	4.4
0–60 mph	5.6
0–70 mph	7.6
0–80 mph	9.3
0–90 mph	11.7
0–100 mph	14.2

Time to distance	
0–100 ft	3.0
0–500 ft	7.8
0–900 ft	11.2
0–1320 ft (¼ mile)	14.3 @ 100.2 mph

2003 NISSAN 350Z "TRACK"
¼ mile: 14.3 sec. @ 100.2 mph

2003 CHEVROLET CORVETTE 50th ANNIVERSARY
¼ mile: 13.4 sec. @ 101.1 mph

2000 PORSCHE BOXSTER S
¼ mile: 14.0 sec. @ 100.5 mph

Braking

Minimum stopping distance
From 60 mph	119 ft
From 80 mph	217 ft
Control	excellent
Brake feel	very good
Overall brake rating	very good

Subjective ratings consist of excellent, very good, good, average, poor; na means information is not available.

Fuel Economy

Our driving	18.6 mpg
EPA city/highway	est 20/26 mpg
Cruise range	353 miles
Fuel capacity	20.0 gal.

Handling

Lateral acceleration (200-ft skidpad)	0.89g
Balance	moderate understeer
Speed through 700-ft slalom	65.6 mph
Balance	mild understeer
Lateral seat support	very good

Interior Noise

Idle in neutral	49 dBA
Maximum in 1st gear	82 dBA
Constant 50 mph	75 dBA
70 mph	78 dBA

Test Notes:

At the drag strip, the 350Z scoots off the line with modest wheelspin. Best standing starts are accomplished with drop-clutch launches while holding the engine at 2000 rpm. The gearbox feels a bit notchy, but the shifter has nice short throws. The brake pedal actuation is linear, corresponding well to how much stopping power is applied to the rotors. • Through the slalom the Z likes to be tossed, but the rear stays in check. • Around the skidpad, more steering feedback is needed.

Test Conditions:

Temperature	Humidity	Elevation	Wind
75° F	45%	350 ft	calm

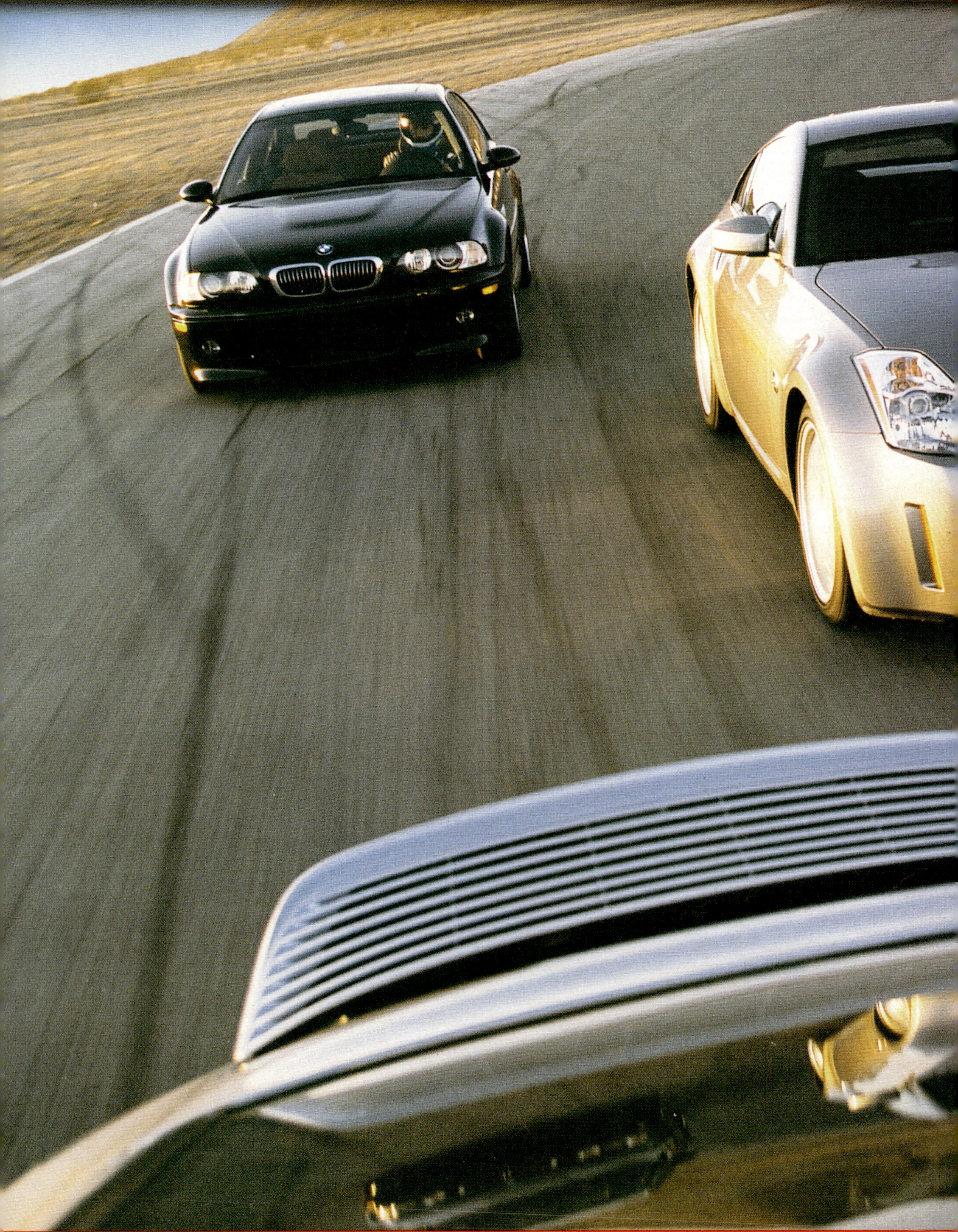

DAVID AND THE GOLIATHS

With a sling full of value and performance, the Nissan 350Z takes aim at three sports-car giants

BY KIM WOLFKILL • PHOTOS BY JEFF ALLEN & MARC URBANO

EVER SINCE NISSAN FIRST TALKED about bringing back the Z-car at the 1999 North American International Auto Show, sports-car fans have been wondering just how good it will be. Now that it's here, the 350Z has shown itself to be a fun, fast and genuinely enjoyable sports car. And priced between $26,269 and $34,079, it has also turned out to be a refreshingly affordable one. Just as its progenitor did more than 30 years ago, the new Z shows that impressively high levels of performance can be had without breaking the bank.

Having already tested the 350Z on its own and found it to be the real deal (see our full road test, September 2002), it's only fitting that we bring in some competition to see what it's made of. With that in mind, we've assembled three highly seasoned sports cars to measure the 350Z against: the BMW M3, Chevrolet Corvette Z06 and Porsche 911. They cover a relatively wide price spectrum, but with similar performance objectives. The M3 offers a sports-car experience with room for four, the Corvette enjoys unrivaled bang for the buck, while the 911, well, is a 911. The benchmark.

Unlike previous comparison tests, there won't be the usual 1-2-3-4 ranking, but instead an examination of all four cars focusing on how well the new kid on the block compares with each of the other three (we'll call it the "Z Factor"). Performance and personality will certainly be instrumental to our evaluation, but given the range of prices for this foursome, so will overall value. In addition to logging laps and collecting data, we're also crunching numbers to see how the Nissan fares from a price-versus-performance standpoint relative to the M3, Z06 and 911. The other three may cost more, but how much (if any) extra performance do those thousands of dollars buy? Does the difference manifest itself in the form of better acceleration, handling and braking or a more satisfying driving experience? Where does price help the Z and where does it hurt?

NISSAN 350Z— CAPABLE NEW CONTENDER

On paper, our 350Z Track model has all the makings of a modern sports car: a quick-revving 3.5-liter 24-valve V-6, short-throw 6-speed manual gearbox, independent multilink front/rear suspension and sure-stopping Brembo brakes. Power is a respectable 287 bhp at 6200 rpm with 274 lb.-ft. of torque. These are solid sports-car credentials wrapped in suitably racy sheet metal.

On the road, the new Z does its best to satisfy the expectations its spec sheet quietly hints at. Fire it up and a quick spin

"The 350Z **inspires confidence** because it doesn't feel like it will ever bite you."

around the block tells you pretty much what the 350Z has to offer. The cockpit feels almost instantly accommodating, albeit heavy on the plastic, and the controls do everything they're asked. The Track model's cloth sport seats provide necessary support during hard cornering without feeling overly confining around the thighs or shoulders.

Lean on the throttle and a satisfying wave of linear acceleration accompanies the quick, mechanical throws of the compact shift lever. The V-6 pulls smartly from midrange to its 6600-rpm redline, yet seems to lack the top-end snap some of us were expecting from nearly 290 bhp. Still, it's fast enough to blast the 350Z to 60

■ **Despite being the least powerful of the group at 287 bhp, the Nissan 350Z's 3.5-liter V-6 (top left) delivers plenty of low-end torque, making the car feel quick off the line. The BMW M3's 333-bhp 3.2-liter inline-6 (far left) loves to rev, and possesses the best top-end song of the group. The Chevrolet Corvette's 5.7-liter pushrod V-8 (middle left) pumps out 405 bhp, and it serves as a testament to the adage "There's no replacement for displacement." There's little to fault with the Porsche 911 Targa's 3.6-liter flat-6 (left); its 320 bhp comes on smooth and linearly from idle to its 7000-rpm redline.**

mph in a scant 5.8 seconds and through the quarter mile in 14.4 sec. at 99.7 mph. As revs climb higher, the cabin takes on a decidedly boomier tone, contrasting sharply with the pleasing growl emitted by its twin exhaust pipes.

Dynamically, there are few cars so immediately comfortable to drive quickly. Thoughtful chassis and suspension tuning have made it relatively easy (and hugely satisfying) to hustle the Z around offramps and racetracks alike. Excellent overall balance allows it to seamlessly process braking, steering and throttle inputs without unduly upsetting the chassis. Fore-to-aft weight transfer has a minimal effect on the car's composure, allowing the driver to transition from braking to power more quickly when cornering.

At street-legal speeds, it seems there's very little a driver can do to upset the Z's composure. Overly enthusiastic corner entries result in a benign dose of understeer, while mid-turn throttle lift merely causes the nose to tighten its line. For those who really go overboard, Nissan's Vehicle Dynamic Control (VDC) uses the standard complement of speed/yaw sensors and selective brake intervention to effectively re-

store order. Adding to this sense of security are the Track model's Brembo brakes, which deliver consistent, fade-free performance in all conditions.

Even at the high speeds we encountered driving on the 2.5-mile "Big Track" at Willow Springs International Raceway, getting the 350Z to rotate its tail takes a concerted effort. Its natural tendency is toward a slight turn-in/mid-turn push that gives way to a balanced corner exit drift. The result is a car whose considerable limits are fun to explore without venturing too far into the unknown. Senior Editor Andy Bornhop said it best following his first hot laps in the Nissan, "The 350Z inspires confidence because it doesn't feel like it will ever bite you." This confidence is most evident in the lap times, where the 350Z turned a fast lap just marginally faster than both the M3 and 911. Being able to push the Z comfortably right up to the limit contributed substantially to its surprising pace around the track.

Now that we know the Nissan 350Z has the goods to be considered a genuine sports car, let's see how it stacks up against three of the hardest-hitting veterans in the game.

The handling differences among our quartet became obvious after several lapping sessions on Willow Spring's 2.5-mile "Big Track." The Nissan 350Z felt the most graceful and predictable of the group. Its overall handling balance is reassuringly stable; with steadfast rear grip and mild, steady-state understeer, it's easy to drive quickly right away. The BMW M3 exhibited a heavier dose of understeer, especially through Turn 2, a 3rd-gear right-hand sweeper. Despite the patience required before picking up the throttle here, the M3 is fast and rewarding, with excellent steering precision and tracking. As far as cornering speed and grip are concerned, the Chevrolet Corvette Z06 is simply in a class by itself. Its near-neutral handling and massive Goodyear F1 Supercar tires—265/40ZR-17s up front and 295/35ZR-18s at rear—allowed us to attack all the corners with abandon. The Porsche 911 Targa, like the Z, was easy to drive quickly right away. Its rear weight bias does, however, command an extra measure of respect—and a little flick of opposite lock cresting Turn 6, where the tail can step out and really get your attention. Most of the cars showed even tire wear after each had completed 25 laps or so—with the exception of the M3's Michelins, which showed noticeable cupping on the fronts, especially on the outer tread blocks. A few suspension changes to reduce the M3's push would no doubt prevent this.

Nissan 350Z.

BMW M3 SMG II.

Chevrolet Corvette Z06.

Porsche 911 Targa.

BMW M3 WITH SMG II— EVERYDAY PERFORMANCE MADE EASY

One trip through the gears and it's readily apparent why people are so enamored of this car. With their latest iteration of the venerable inline-6, BMW's engineers have produced one of the sweetest running 6-cylinder engines ever built. Thanks to an abundance of technology—Double VANOS valve operation, six electronically controlled throttles, high compression and an 8000-rpm redline—the M3's 3.2-liter engine possesses an uncannily smooth power delivery.

Not only smooth, but also flexible, the M3's six has a wide, usable powerband. Midrange punch is already good, but once above 4000 rpm, the engine adopts an even more menacing snarl as it pulls strongly right up to redline. "It begs to be wound out," said Executive Editor Doug Kott. "Where the Corvette and 911 are content to be short-shifted, the M3 likes to rev." It turns out 333 bhp at 7900 rpm and 269 lb.-ft. of torque.

Chassis control is managed by an M-tuned MacPherson-strut front and multilink rear suspension mated to an M Variable limited-slip differential. Providing the necessary grip are 18-in. wheels and tires, while heavy-duty brakes keep all this speed in check. Also stepping in to offer occasional spin control is BMW's Dynamic Stability Control (DSC) system. For this test, our car is equipped with the optional Sequential Manual Gearbox (SMG) that uses electrohydraulic actuators to facilitate ultra-fast shifts of the 6-speed manual transmission via steering wheel-mounted paddles.

Under street driving conditions, the M3 doesn't seem that different from a stiffly sprung 3 Series. The seating position feels natural, lines of sight are clear and the interior switchgear is first-rate. Grab a footful of throttle, however, and the engine springs to life, urging the car forward with a new sense of enthusiasm. Bend into a turn and the reward is a flat, stable cornering attitude with just enough understeer to advise caution toward the limit. Roll out of the throttle mid-turn and the rear rotates predictably until throttle is smoothly reapplied. With plenty of grip and near-instantaneous power, the M3

"Where the Corvette and 911 are content to be short-shifted, **the M3 likes to rev.**"

proves fun and exciting to drive quickly.

Hit the track and it's much of the same. Similar to the 350Z, it can simply be jumped into and driven. It does what it's asked and accepts driver inputs comfortably and with little fuss. Balance is good and the car's cornering attitude can be easily altered with minor throttle and steering changes. As cornering speeds climb, the understeering safety net carried over from the street becomes more pronounced, costing a small measure of mid-corner speed. Rotating the car with throttle changes gets around some of this, but for serious track enthusiasts, an adjustment to the M3's wheel alignment would likely eliminate this situation.

Those same track enthusiasts might also like the lightning-quick shifts of the SMG transmission. With paddle-actuated shifts performed faster than any human could do, the Formula 1-derived system takes some of the thinking out of driving fast. Do-it-yourself stalwarts may still prefer the satisfaction of performing their own gearchanges, but there's no denying the system's speed and convenience at the track. Around town, our crew's opinions were mixed. International Editor Sam Mitani was enamored of SMG in all conditions, while the rest of us still prefer the 6-speed manual for street use.

Factor: BMW M3

▶▶ **The Z's V-6 lacks some of the M3's inline-6 smoothness and horsepower, yet enjoys more torque at slightly lower revs. The result is an engine that's nearly as powerful at the racetrack, but feels less satisfying and refined around town, where it matters more.**

▶▶ **Inside, the $20,000 price difference becomes most apparent in the quality of the materials. The BMW's cabin doesn't work $20K better, but it's a more pleasant, sophisticated place to spend your daily commute. Poor outward views and little usable space also hurt the Z especially compared with the M3's four seats and trunk.**

▶▶ **Dynamically, it's tough to fault the Nissan's unflappable handling. It's more confidence-inspiring than the M3 (which is saying a lot) with less at-limit understeer and none of the M3's off-throttle oversteer. A little oversteer would actually be welcome at the track, but the current setup increases the safety margin for the average driver around town.**

▶▶ **The braking edge goes to the Nissan, whose Brembo stoppers posted the exact same braking numbers as the M3, but**

were more fade-resistant during high-speed use.

▶▶ **BOTTOM LINE: Similar to the Z in performance, the M3 delivers a more sophisticated driving experience, but at a price premium.**

CHEVROLET CORVETTE Z06— TRACK TUNED, STREET CIVILIZED

From the moment pricing was first announced, the Corvette Z06 has been the best performance buy in modern sports cars. It's hard to argue with 405 bhp, 400 lb.-ft. of torque, 0–60 mph in 4.5 sec. and a 171-mph top speed all for a shade over $50,000. What's more, after years of evolution and well-executed chassis tuning, this latest Corvette also offers refreshing levels of refinement to go with its searing performance.

Drive a new Z06 on your favorite stretch of bad highway and the ride is light-years ahead of previous iterations. It's still firmer than many sports cars, but not nearly as harsh as its extreme speed potential would lead you to expect. Even more surprising is that, among our foursome, the Z06 actually delivers the most compliant ride in daily driving conditions. Few doubted the Vette would trounce all comers at the racetrack, but would it also be the most comfortable?

Instrumental to its dizzying speed is the Z06's ability to generate huge amounts of acceleration and grip. With the lightest weight (3110 lb.) and highest horsepower of the bunch, it comes as little surprise the Corvette powers away like it does. The 5.7-liter LS6 engine produces prodigious amounts of thrust from 3500–6500 rpm and then starts all over again with each shift of the 6-speed manual transmission. Even in higher gears, acceleration continues unabated until the speedo climbs above 140 mph after which speed gain tapers off slightly.

Keeping this terrestrial rocket on the ground is a combination of 17/18-in. wheels/tires and a well-sorted suspension. Track-tuned bits like a thick 30.0-mm front anti-roll bar, specially tuned shock absorbers, stiff transverse rear leaf spring and a half degree more negative camber at all four corners combine to grace the Z06 with unparalleled high-speed grip. At low-

er speeds, a deft right foot (and traction control) is the only thing keeping the rear tires from lighting up.

Balance remains impressively neutral at speed with neither the front nor rear end itching to step out before the other. At the track, transitioning from braking to turning to accelerating takes some practice as the body has a tendency to seemingly hover over the wheels for a moment until the chassis has had a chance to take a set. Once loaded, the chassis responds well to throttle inputs and rewards the driver with increasing levels of grip. Just as impressive are the brakes, which serve up excellent initial bite, predictable control and the shortest stopping distances of our group.

Performance aside, the Corvette suffers from some of the same interior cost-cutting issues that plague the 350Z. While delivering a perfectly comfortable seating position

and sound ergonomics, the Z06's cockpit still lacks the higher-quality feel of its more expensive competition. Some of the plastics would better suit a Camaro and for a car with such a high level of lateral grip, the seats don't offer nearly enough lateral support.

Despite these quibbles there's still no denying the Z06's amazing bang-for-buck factor. It delivers the kind of performance expected from cars costing two to three times as much yet walks away from cars in its immediate price vicinity.

Z Factor: CHEVROLET CORVETTE Z06

>> There's little the Z or any other car in this test can do against the Z06's monstrous V-8. Its unrelenting power and bottomless torque make it hard to beat.

>> The Corvette requires a careful period of acclimatization before its full performance potential can be realized. The 350Z is almost immediately easy to drive quickly

and doesn't demand nearly the same seat time to get comfortably up to speed.

▶▶ Both cars share interiors that can't compete with other high-end sports cars. This certainly doesn't affect the performance of either car, but plays a role in the quality of the overall driving experience. At their price points something had to give, and better the interior than the mechanicals.

▶▶ Under hard acceleration, both cars create quite an interior racket, but in different ways. The 350Z's overly mechanical engine sounds drown out the much more pleasing exhaust note, while the Z06's engine and exhaust work in concert to produce a loud but intoxicating roar.

▶▶ *BOTTOM LINE:* Brothers in arms from a performance versus price standpoint, each delivers impressive performance for the money without the frills of more expensive competitors.

PORSCHE 911 TARGA—
ULTIMATE REAR-ENGINE REFINEMENT

No one said it would work in a sports car, but Porsche has continued to baffle physicists for more than 40 years with its nonstop improvement of the rear-engine layout. The latest-generation 996 platform has gone the furthest at refining the 911 so effectively that the tail-happy behavior of past 911s is all but a myth.

Due to end-of-the-year availability issues, we were unable to secure a Sport Chassis-equipped 911 Carrera 2 for testing, so instead we went with a 911 Targa. Initially there were concerns over its torsional rigidity versus a coupe's, but as it turned out, the Targa felt every bit as stiff as previous coupes we've driven and did an excellent job of representing the 911 line. The only real performance difference is that the Targa weighs about 150 lb. more than the coupe.

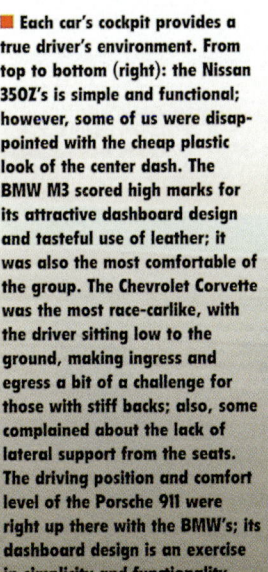

■ Each car's cockpit provides a true driver's environment. From top to bottom (right): the Nissan 350Z's is simple and functional; however, some of us were disappointed with the cheap plastic look of the center dash. The BMW M3 scored high marks for its attractive dashboard design and tasteful use of leather; it was also the most comfortable of the group. The Chevrolet Corvette was the most race-carlike, with the driver sitting low to the ground, making ingress and egress a bit of a challenge for those with stiff backs; also, some complained about the lack of lateral support from the seats. The driving position and comfort level of the Porsche 911 were right up there with the BMW's; its dashboard design is an exercise in simplicity and functionality.

2002 BMW M3 SMG II

BMW of North America, Inc.,
P.O. Box 1227, Westwood, N.J. 07675; www.bmwusa.com

List Price: $45,900 **Price as Tested: $55,695**

2003 Chevrolet Corvette Z06

Chevrolet Motor Division,
30007 Van Dyke Rd., Warren, Mich. 48090; www.chevrolet.com

List Price: $50,485 **Price as Tested: $51,450**

Price as tested incl std equip. (ABS, front, side and head airbags, yaw & traction control, limited-slip differential, cruise control, keyless entry, pwr windows, mirrors & door locks), premium package (moonroof, leather, power seats w/memory, auto. adjust headlights, and rain sensing wipers) $3200, cold weather package (heated seats and headlight washers) $700, sequential manual gearbox SMG II ($2400), bi-xenon headlights ($700), Harman Kardon sound system ($675), Carbon Black metallic paint ($475), gas-guzzler tax ($1000), dest charge ($645).

Price as tested incl std equip. (ABS, dual airbags, yaw & traction control, limited-slip differential, cruise control, alloy wheels, dual-zone climate control, leather seats and steering wheel, AM/FM radio/CD player, keyless entry; pwr driver's seat, pwr windows, mirrors & door locks), memory functions ($175), electrochromic mirror ($120), dest charge ($670).

	BMW M3 SMG II	Chevrolet Corvette Z06	Nissan 350Z Track	Porsche 911 Targa
General Data				
Curb weight.	**3450 lb**	**3110 lb**	**3310 lb**	**3340 lb**
Test weight	3580 lb	3270 lb	3430 lb	3470 lb
Weight dist (with driver), f/r, %. .	50/50	53/47	53/47	37/63
Wheelbase	107.5 in.	104.5 in.	104.3 in.	92.6 in.
Track, f/r.	59.4 in./60.0 in.	62.4 in./62.6 in.	60.4 in./60.8 in.	57.7 in./58.3 in.
Length	176.9 in.	179.7 in.	169.6 in.	174.5 in.
Width	70.0 in.	73.6 in.	71.5 in.	69.7 in.
Height	54.0 in.	47.7 in.	51.9 in.	51.4 in.
Engine				
Type	dohc 4-valve/cyl **inline-6**	ohv 2-valve/cyl **V-8**	dohc 4-valve/cyl **V-6**	dohc 4-valve/cyl **flat-6**
Displacement	3245 cc	5665 cc	3498 cc	3596 cc
Bore x stroke.	87.0 x 91.0 mm	99.0 x 92.0 mm	95.5 x 81.4 mm	96.0 x 82.8 mm
Compression ratio.	11.5:1	10.5:1	10.3:1	11.3:1
Horsepower (SAE)	**333 bhp @ 7900 rpm**	**405 bhp @ 6000 rpm**	**287 bhp @ 6200 rpm**	**320 bhp @ 6800 rpm**
Torque	**269 lb-ft @ 4900 rpm**	**400 lb-ft @ 4800 rpm**	**274 lb-ft @ 4800 rpm**	**258 lb-ft @ 4250 rpm**
Redline.	8000 rpm	6500 rpm	6600 rpm	7000 rpm
Fuel injection	elect. sequential port	elect. sequential port	elect. sequential port	elect. sequential port
Rec. fuel	prem unleaded, 91 pump oct	prem unleaded, 91 pump oct	prem unleaded, 91 pump oct	prem unleaded, 91 pump oct
Chassis & Body				
Layout	**front engine/rear drive**	**front engine/rear drive**	**front engine/rear drive**	**rear engine/rear drive**
Body/frame	unit steel w/alum. hood	fiberglass/unit steel	unit steel w/alum. hood	unit steel w/alum. hood
Brakes, f/r	**12.8-in. vented discs/** **12.9-in. vented discs**; vac asst, ABS	**12.6-in. vented discs/** **11.8-in. discs**; vac asst, ABS	**12.8-in. vented discs/** **12.7-in. vented discs**; vac asst, ABS	**12.5-in. vented discs/** **11.8-in. discs**; vac asst, ABS
Wheels	cast alum.; **18 x 8J f, 18 x 9J r**	cast alum.; **17 x 9½ f, 18 x 10½ r**	forged alloy; **18 x 8 f, 18 x 8½ r**	cast alum.; **18 x 8 f, 18 x 10 r**
Tires.	Michelin Pilot Sport; **225/45ZR-18 f, 255/40ZR-18 r**	Goodyear F1 Supercar; **P265/40ZR-17 91Y f, P295/35ZR-18 91Y r**	Bridgestone Potenza RE 040; **225/45ZR-18 91W f, 245/45ZR-18 96W r**	Continental SportContact 2; **225/40ZR-18 f, 285/30ZR-18 r**
Steering	**rack & pinion,** power assist	**rack & pinion,** power assist	**rack & pinion,** vari power assist	**rack & pinion,** power assist
Overall ratio	15.4:1	16.1:1	15.9:1	16.9:1
Turns lock to lock	3.2	2.7	2.6	3.0
Suspension, f/r	**MacPherson struts,** double-pivot lower L-arms, coil springs, tube shocks, anti-roll bar/**multilink,** coil springs, tube shocks, anti-roll bar	**upper & lower A-arms,** transverse composite spring, tube shocks, anti-roll bar/**upper & lower A-arms,** toe links, transverse composite spring, tube shocks, anti-roll bar	**multilink,** coil springs, tube shocks, anti-roll bar/**multilink,** coil springs, tube shocks, anti-roll bar	**MacPherson struts,** lower A-arms, coil springs, tube shocks, anti-roll bar/**multilink,** coil springs, tube shocks, anti-roll bar
Accommodations				
Seating capacity	**5**	**2**	**2**	**2+2**
Head room, f/r	38.5 in./35.0 in.	37.0 in.	36.5 in.	37.3 in./30.8 in.
Front-seat leg room.	46.5 in.	43.0 in.	43.0 in.	43.5 in.
Rear-seat knee room.	21.5 in.	na	na	18.5 in.
Trunk space	14.5 cu ft	13.3 cu ft	6.8 cu ft	4.6 cu ft

Subjective ratings consist of excellent, very good, good, average, poor; na means information is not available.

2003 Nissan 350Z Track

Nissan North America, Inc.,
18501 S. Figueroa, Gardena, Calif. 90248; www.nissanusa.com

List Price: $34,079   Price as Tested: $34,688

Price as tested incl std equip. (ABS, dual airbags, yaw & traction control, cruise control, auto. air conditioning, AM/FM radio/CD player, tilt steering wheel, anti-theft system, keyless entry; pwr windows, mirrors & door locks, 18-in. wheels and tires w/pressure monitoring, Brembo brake rotors and calipers, limited-slip differential, front & rear spoilers), floormats ($69), dest charge ($540).

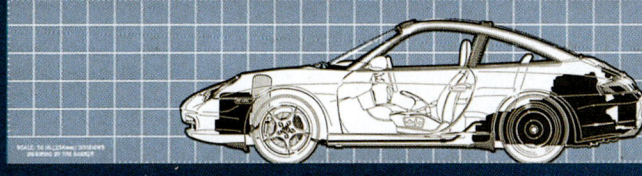

2002 Porsche 911 Targa

Porsche Cars of North America, Inc.,
980 Hammond Dr., Suite 1000, Atlanta, Ga. 30328; www.porsche.com

List Price: $75,200   Price as Tested: $84,975

Price as tested incl std equip. (ABS, dual front and side airbags, speed-activated rear spoiler, cruise control, integrated fog lamps, auto. climate control, AM/FM radio/CD player, keyless entry; leather interior, pwr seats, windows, mirrors & door locks), advanced touring package ($3240), comfort package ($2100), 18-in. wheels ($1325), stability control ($1230), metallic paint ($825), wheel caps w/colored crests ($175), floormats with Porsche lettering ($115), dest charge ($765).

	BMW M3 SMG II	Chevrolet Corvette Z06	Nissan 350Z Track	Porsche 911 Targa
Acceleration				
Time to speed, sec				
0–20 mph	1.1	1.3	1.4	1.1
0–40 mph	2.9	2.7	3.4	2.6
0–60 mph	4.9	4.5	5.8	5.0
0–80 mph	8.1	7.0	9.5	8.2
0–100 mph	12.3	9.9	14.5	12.0
Time to distance				
0–1320 ft (¼ mile)	13.5 @ 104.2 mph	12.8 @ 113.5 mph	14.4 @ 99.7 mph	13.5 @ 104.9 mph
Braking				
Minimum stopping distance				
From 60 mph	122 ft	114 ft	122 ft	120 ft
From 80 mph	213 ft	204 ft	213 ft	208 ft
Control	excellent	excellent	excellent	excellent
Brake feel	good	very good	very good	very good
Overall brake rating	very good	excellent	excellent	excellent
Handling				
Lateral accel (200-ft skidpad)	0.89g	0.98g	0.88g	0.92g
Balance	moderate understeer	mild understeer	moderate understeer	mild understeer
Speed thru 700-ft slalom	68.8 mph	67.6 mph	67.3 mph	65.5 mph
Balance	mild understeer	mild understeer	mild understeer	mild understeer
Drivetrain				
Transmission	**6-speed sequential w/paddles**	**6-speed manual**	**6-speed manual**	**6-speed manual**
Gear/Ratio/Overall/(Rpm) Mph				
1st, :1	4.23/15.30/(8000) 40	2.97/10.16/(6500) 48	3.79/13.42/(6600) 38	3.82/13.56/(7300) 39
2nd, :1	2.53/9.15/(8000) 66	2.07/7.08/(6500) 69	2.32/8.22/(6600) 61	2.20/7.81/(7300) 68
3rd, :1	1.67/6.04/(8000) 100	1.43/4.89/(6500) 100	1.62/5.74/(6600) 88	1.52/5.40/(7300) 98
4th, :1	1.23/4.44/est (8000) 136	1.00/3.42/(6500) 143	1.27/4.50/(6600) 112	1.22/4.33/(7300) 122
5th, :1	1.00/3.62/est (7250) 155*	0.84/2.87/(6500) 170	1.00/3.54/(6600) 142	1.02/3.62/(7300) 146
6th, :1	0.83/3.00/est (6000) 155*	0.56/2.45/est (4280) 171	0.79/2.81/est (5700) 155*	0.84/2.45/est (6175) 177
Final drive ratio	3.62:1	3.42:1	3.54:1	3.44:1
Engine rpm @ 60 mph in top gear	2400 rpm	1500 rpm	2150 rpm	2300 rpm
*Electronically limited.				
Fuel Economy				
Our driving	est 17.0 mpg	est 20.0 mpg	est 21.0 mpg	est 19.0 mpg
EPA city/highway	16/23 mpg	19/28 mpg	20/26 mpg	18/26 mpg
Cruise range	est 265 miles	est 350 miles	est 399 miles	est 302 miles
Fuel capacity	16.6 gal.	18.5 gal.	20.0 gal.	16.9 gal.
Interior Noise				
Idle in neutral	54 dBA	59 dBA	47 dBA	56 dBA
Maximum, 1st gear	84 dBA	84 dBA	85 dBA	79 dBA
70 mph	74 dBA	79 dBA	78 dBA	76 dBA

> **"The 350Z gives away very little performance relative to its more costly competitors."**

Underway, it's tough to tell the difference as the 911's signature flat-6 works its melodious magic in back. Displacing 3.6 liters and putting out 320 bhp, this latest engine is the quietest and smoothest-revving Porsche powerplant to date. Combining increased displacement (over the 2001 models' 3.4 liters) with VarioCam Plus variable valve timing has produced improved midrange torque. Performance from the 6-speed manual transmission is typically Porsche. It doesn't draw attention to itself with any glaring strengths or weaknesses, quietly getting the job done shift after shift, lap after lap.

Given its unorthodox configuration, the 911's chassis never ceases to amaze with its ability to go fast. At lower speeds, the MacPherson-strut front and multilink rear suspension does a commendable job of keeping the chassis settled and the car pointed in the right direction. As speeds climb, weight transfer becomes more pronounced and the 911 occasionally hints at its former self. A fair bit of vertical suspension movement reminds drivers to keep their inputs smooth and a mild dose of mid-turn/exit understeer prevents too much in the way of tail-out shenanigans. "Wide rear tires and decades of tuning haven't completely tamed this car's rear bias," commented Kott. "You learn to respect it and modify your driving accordingly."

Like all Porsches, steering feel is nearly telepathic with a slight lightening under acceleration. Braking performance is also typically 911 with a very communicative

pedal, good power and excellent modulation. The brakes on our test Targa feel a little softer than on other 911s we've driven, though braking distances are not adversely affected. Fade is a non-issue and directional control under braking is the most stable of our group.

Given its considerably steeper price tag, finding where the money goes is a case of looking in a lot of small places rather than a couple of big ones. Interior appointments are on a similar level to the M3's and considerably more elegant than in the 350Z or Corvette. Fit and finish also appear just a touch better than in the value twins, as does overall build quality. And then there's the Targa top that costs an extra $7000 over the standard 911 coupe. But add it all up and there's still a huge difference that can be justified only by the simple fact that the 911 is a Porsche. Purchasing a 911 not only buys you a car, but a small slice of automotive history mixed with ample quantities of performance and prestige.

Z Factor: PORSCHE 911 TARGA

» As with the Corvette, driving the 911 takes patience and a period of adjustment. Once mastered, there are few cars as satisfying to drive quickly. The Z suffers from no such waiting period, as it's instantly easy to drive near its limits.

» Its interior may not be nearly as plush as the Porsche's, but for enthusiastic driving, the 350Z's well-bolstered

seats, rifle-bolt shifter and idiot-proof handling take the thinking out of logging some fast miles.

▶▶ Logging longer, faster miles are right up the 911's alley, where a pleasing driving environment is of greatest importance. Over time, the Z's choppy highway ride and droning engine are no match for the Porsche's proven long-haul credentials.

▶▶ If you can afford a 911, odds are good you're not shopping for a Z. But if you are, it's amusing to know you can own a car with nearly the performance of a high-dollar Porsche for about half the cost.

▶▶ *BOTTOM LINE:* Very different cars for very different buyers, but given their respective audiences, each delivers the goods.

FINAL THOUGHTS

Our Z Factor notes reveal that the 350Z gives away very little performance relative to its more costly competitors. What's not shown in the numbers is the overall ease with which the Z can be driven. Thanks to a willing engine and capable chassis, the 350Z makes it possible for impressive levels of performance to be accessed with minimal fuss.

Z buyers probably won't cross-shop M3s or 911s, but at least they can feel confident in knowing they're paying way less and still getting a whole lot for their money. As for buyers of these more expensive sports cars? It's hard not to respect Nissan's accomplishment, but they're probably fine with spending the extra cash for the added refinement their particular cars possess.

As with the original 240Z, this newest incarnation is as affordable today as its predecessor was back in 1970. Costing around $35,000 with all the bells and whistles, the 350Z represents a serious sports-car value. Not only does it offer performance rivaling cars costing thousands more, but also it signals the arrival of a capable new contender in a market that can always use a fresh face. Is it as good as its more costly counterparts? In some ways yes, in some ways no. When we assigned a "performance per dollar" value to the cars, it was the venerable Corvette that took top honors, not the Nissan. But regardless of how you look at it, the 350Z is clearly car enough to put up a good fight no matter who the challenger is.

Putting it all together...

PRICE

NISSAN 350Z TRACK	$34,688
BMW M3 SMG II	$55,695
CHEVROLET CORVETTE Z06	$51,450
PORSCHE 911 TARGA	$84,975

0-60 MPH

NISSAN 350Z TRACK	5.8 sec.
BMW M3 SMG II	4.9 sec.
CHEVROLET CORVETTE Z06	4.5 sec.
PORSCHE 911 TARGA	5.0 sec.

1/4 MILE

NISSAN 350Z TRACK	14.4 sec.
BMW M3 SMG II	13.5 sec.
CHEVROLET CORVETTE Z06	12.8 sec.
PORSCHE 911 TARGA	13.5 sec.

LAP TIME

NISSAN 350Z TRACK	01:40.06
BMW M3 SMG II	01:40.09
CHEVROLET CORVETTE Z06	01:36.50
PORSCHE 911 TARGA	01:40.79

SKIDPAD

NISSAN 350Z TRACK	0.88g
BMW M3 SMG II	0.89g
CHEVROLET CORVETTE Z06	0.98g
PORSCHE 911 TARGA	0.92g

SLALOM

NISSAN 350Z TRACK	67.3 mph
BMW M3 SMG II	68.8 mph
CHEVROLET CORVETTE Z06	67.6 mph
PORSCHE 911 TARGA	65.5 mph

BRAKING: 80-0 MPH

NISSAN 350Z TRACK	213 ft.
BMW M3 SMG II	213 ft.
CHEVROLET CORVETTE Z06	204 ft.
PORSCHE 911 TARGA	208 ft.

Z Factor

We derived a way to compare Performance Per Dollar of our varied group, in a sense another Z-Factor: In the expression:

$$(A \times B \times SL \times SK \times L)/\sqrt{P}$$

A, acceleration to 60 mph; B, braking; SL, slalom; SK, skidpad; L, lap time; and P, price, are normalized on 10-point scales. The final values are normalized as well so the cars can be rated on a 10-point scale, 10 being best.

PERFORMANCE PER DOLLAR

NISSAN 350Z TRACK	7.8
BMW M3 SMG II	7.6
CHEVROLET CORVETTE Z06	10.0
PORSCHE 911 TARGA	6.1

Long-Term TEST

By Jim Hall

2003 NISSAN 350Z TOURING

A sports car for the real world

THE WAIT IS OVER. AFTER WHAT SEEMED like an entire lifetime, the Z is back. And, in retrospect, the sabbatical was a good thing. After all, the last-generation 300ZX was a very good car—fun to drive, on top of being a looker. But over the years, the Z had lost sight of the single most important attribute that had made it so successful: It was no longer an affordable, everyman's sports car.

Enter the 350Z.

The designers have penned an exciting body, as the new 350Z is a thoroughly modern-looking sports car while simultaneously being instantly recognizable as a Z car. Head-on, I find the wide and muscular lines of the front fender/wheel arches particularly appealing as they remind me of the slick-looking bodywork on the current DTM German touring-car racers.

A 3.5-liter dohc 24-valve V-6 with CVTCS (Continuously Variable Valve Timing Control System), mated to a 6-speed close-ratio manual and rated at 287 horsepower, is the standard drivetrain for all 350Zs (a 5-speed automatic with manual mode is available on all but the Base model). Independent multilink aluminum suspension, 4-wheel vented disc brakes, electronic drive-by-wire throttle and 17-in. aluminum-alloy wheels with low-profile all-season tires, combined with this engine and rigid chassis, are at the heart of what is a very enjoyable sports car for both the old-school Z-car fans and the next generation.

Other standard equipment consists of automatic climate control, alarm with remote keyless entry; leather-covered shift lever and steering wheel; power windows, mirrors, and door locks; and a 6-speaker 160-watt AM/FM/CD player. There are also ABS and dual airbags.

With performance on a level of sports cars costing almost twice as much (see "David vs. the Goliaths," pg. 82), the 350Z is truly a bargain. The cost-to-performance ratio begins to look really good when you consider this: In a conversation a few months ago with Road Test Assistant Shaun Bailey, compiler of the Road Test Summary, I was dumbstruck when he said the average as-tested car price listed in the summary

PHOTOS BY JOE RUSZ

works out to more than $80,000.

Here are the numbers for the various Z car versions:

A 350Z Base is the entry-level version (as described above) and has an MSRP of $26,269.

Next up is the Enthusiast model that adds cruise control, aluminum pedals, a viscous limited-slip differential, traction control, HomeLink, a day/night auto rearview mirror and xenon headlamps—a significant amount of additional content for this model's $28,249 sticker price.

The next level is the Performance model, which adds a larger 18-in. wheel/tire package along with tire air pressure monitoring and Vehicle Dynamic Control (VDC) stability control for $30,429.

The Touring model adds more passenger comfort and pleasantries with heated leather power seats, heated mirrors and a 240-watt Bose 7-speaker AM/FM/cassette/CD with a 6-disc in-dash sound system. Price: $33,179.

For the owner who's looking to race or autocross, or just wants the ultimate performance 350Z, there's the Track model at $34,079 that includes a front and rear spoiler, lighter forged 18-in. wheels and Brembo brakes at all four corners. There are no suspension tweaks on this version—it's the same firmly sprung system found on all models.

We've opted for a Touring version with the 6-speed stick along with one of the only two options available, side and side-curtain airbags, at a cost of $569 for our extended stay to 50,000 miles (the remaining option is a DVD-based navigation system that runs $1999). Add in destination charges of $540 and you arrive at our 350Z's $34,288 total.

■ **Fun in Z sun: hip looks and 0–60 mph in the mid-5s, beginning at less than $27,000.**

We learned much about the driving characteristics of our 350Z out at the test track. For starters, we had difficulty finding the optimal shift points on acceleration runs as we were encountering the engine's rev limiter about a hundred rpm shy of the 6600-rpm indicated redline on the tachometer. One really has to keep an eye on the tach to know when to change gears as the engine's sound and feel never change or diminish—talk about pulling-power all the way to redline.

Something else that caught our attention was the car's handling around the skidpad. In counterclockwise laps, it displayed good balance overall with just a slight touch of understeer. But in-car weight changes its demeanor considerably. Rounding the circle clockwise, with the driver now positioned on the outside, the car demonstrated noticeably greater understeer. There is hardly any body roll in either direction.

Quantitative and qualitative data derived from track testing are well and good as they allow us to derive a performance baseline in a controlled setting. But the real test will come with how this 350Z Touring edition performs in the real world.

A lot is riding on this new Z as it has some very big shoes to fill, what with the successful lineage that began some three decades ago. This should be an interesting long-termer. ◈

2003 NISSAN 350Z TOURING SPECIFICS	
Total miles	2874
Miles since last report	na
Average mpg to date	16.6
Best mpg (avg of 3)	17.5
Worst mpg (avg of 3)	15.5
Repair costs to date	0
Maintenance costs to date	0
Delivered price	$34,288

TEST TRACK DATA	
Acceleration, 0–60	5.6 sec
1/4 mile	14.3 sec @ 99.4 mph
Braking, from 60 mph	115 ft
from 80 mph	206 ft
Skidpad	0.87g

Nissan 350Z

THE WAIT IS FINALLY OVER. NISSAN'S Z car returns this year, and does so in dramatic fashion, splashing onto the world stage with all the splendor of a newly discovered supermodel. At first glance, it's immediately evident that the 350Z is a pure sports car, with head-turning styling highlighted by Teutonic overtones, seats for two and a powerful 287-bhp engine.

The 350Z is the ideal sports-car size, measuring 169.6 in. from bumper to bumper, putting it in the neighborhood of its primary competitors, the Porsche Boxster and Audi TT. The styling of the new Japanese sports car also reflects who Nissan is targeting with the Z: the Germans, the likes of BMW, Porsche and Audi. With a TT-like roofline, and Porsche 911-like rear-end, the styling of the 350Z is aggressive and unique for a Japanese sports car. Still, there's enough "Z DNA" (as Nissan's designers call it) to make it instantly recognizable as a Z.

The rear-drive sports car is powered by Nissan's highly touted 3.5-liter VQ engine. This 24-valve V-6 has been tuned to produce 287 bhp at 6200 rpm and 274 lb.-ft. of torque at 4800. What this means for the 3290-lb. car is a 0-to-60-mph sprint of 5.6 seconds and a quarter-mile blast in a scant 14.3. The handling of the 350Z is also world-class. Thanks to a rigid structure, a quick and precise steering system and a finely tuned suspension—multilink at both front and rear—the 350Z exhibits crisp turn-in response and near-neutral balance. What's more, the car displays an even ride on the Interstate, so a long multi-hour session behind the Z's steering wheel isn't an unpleasant affair. In fact, it's quite refreshing because the cabin stays relatively quiet.

But the most astounding aspect of the 350Z is its price. With the base model starting at a tad more than $26,000, it holds the upper hand against its significantly more expensive Europeans.

The 350Z comes in five trim levels: Standard, Enthusiast, Performance, Touring and Track. The base model comes with a long list of standard items, including a 6-speed manual gearbox, 17-in. alloy wheels, vented front and rear disc brakes with ABS, dual stage airbags, keyless entry and a 160-watt AM/FM/CD with 6 speakers. The next grade up, the Enthusiast Model, gets you xenon headlights, traction control, viscous limited-slip differential and the choice of a 5-speed automatic transmission. With the Touring Model, you get a 240-watt Bose stereo system and leather heated seats. Our choice is the top-of-the-line Track Model that comes only with a 6-speed manual transmission. Among other things, it comes with 18-in. alloy wheels, Brembo brakes, Vehicle Dynamics Control and tire air-pressure monitor.

So, you can see that Nissan pulled no punches when it came to its new sports-car's performance, and it took an incredibly aggressive stand concerning the car's price. With the new Z, the Japanese sports car is back, and this time it looks like Nissan is here to stay.

SPECIFICATIONS:

Layout	rwd
Wheelbase	104.3 in.
Track, f/r	60.4/60.8 in.
Length	169.6 in.
Width	71.5 in.
Height	51.9 in.
Curb weight	3290 lb
Base engine	3.5-liter dohc 24V V-6
Bore x stroke	95.5 x 81.4 mm
Displacement	3498 cc
Horsepower	287 bhp @ 6200 rpm
Torque	274 lb-ft @ 4800 rpm
EPA city/highway	20/26 mpg
Optional engine(s)	none
Transmission	6M, 5A
Suspension, f/r	ind/ind
Brakes, f/r	disc/disc, ABS
Tires	225/45ZR-18 f, 245/45ZR-18 r
Luggage capacity	6.8 cu ft
Fuel capacity	20.0 gal.

WARRANTY:

Bumper-to-bumper	3 years/36,000 miles
Powertrain	5 years/60,000 miles
Rust-through	5 years/60,000 miles

www.nissandriven.com

AT A GLANCE:

MODEL	MSRP	ENG	TRAN	ABS	SEATS	A/C
Standard	$26,269	V-6	6M	STD	2	STD
Enthusiast	$28,249	V-6	6M	STD	2	STD
Performance	$36,429	V-6	6M	STD	2	STD
Touring	$33,179	V-6	6M	STD	2	STD
Track	$34,079	V-6	6M	STD	2	STD

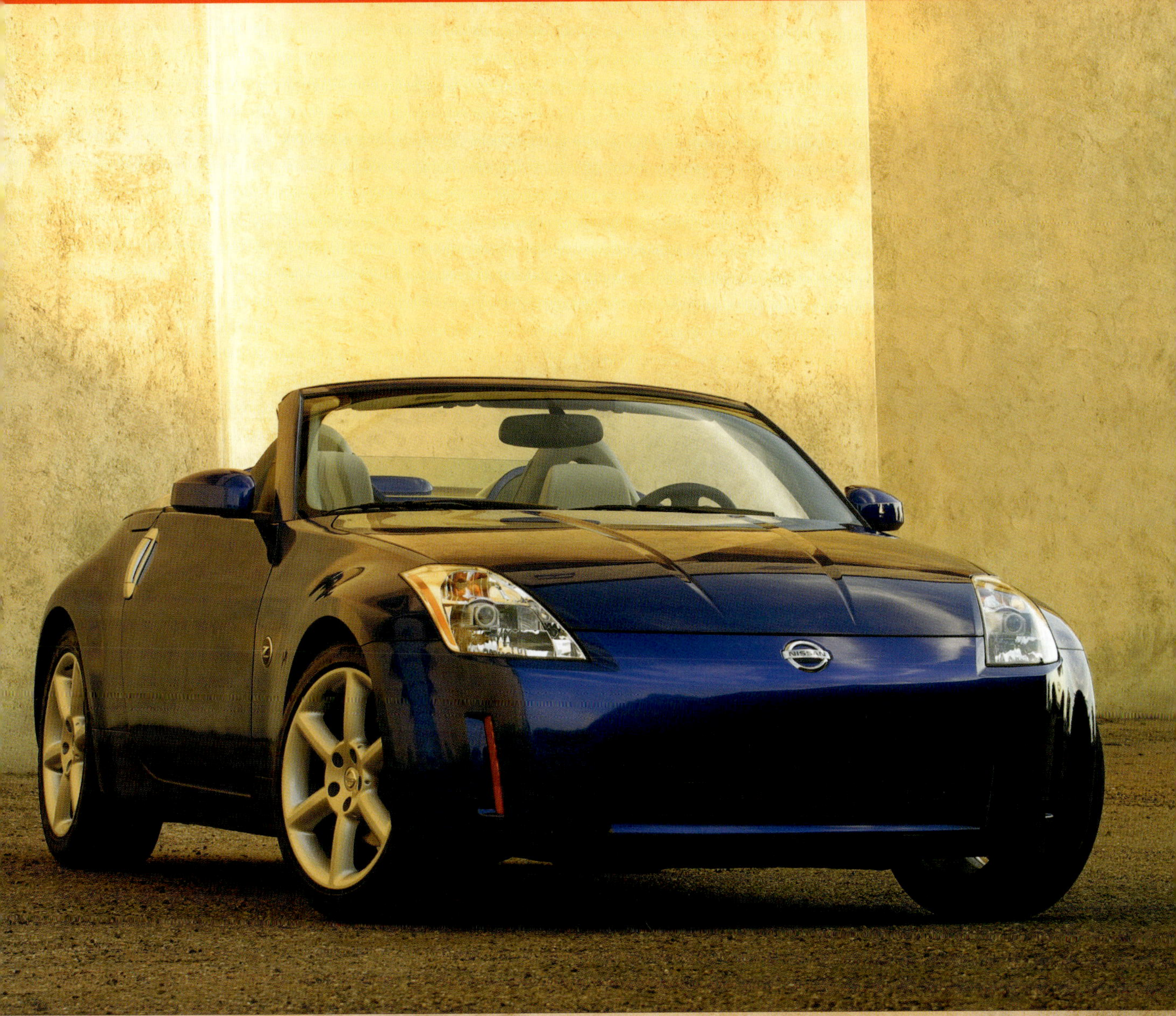

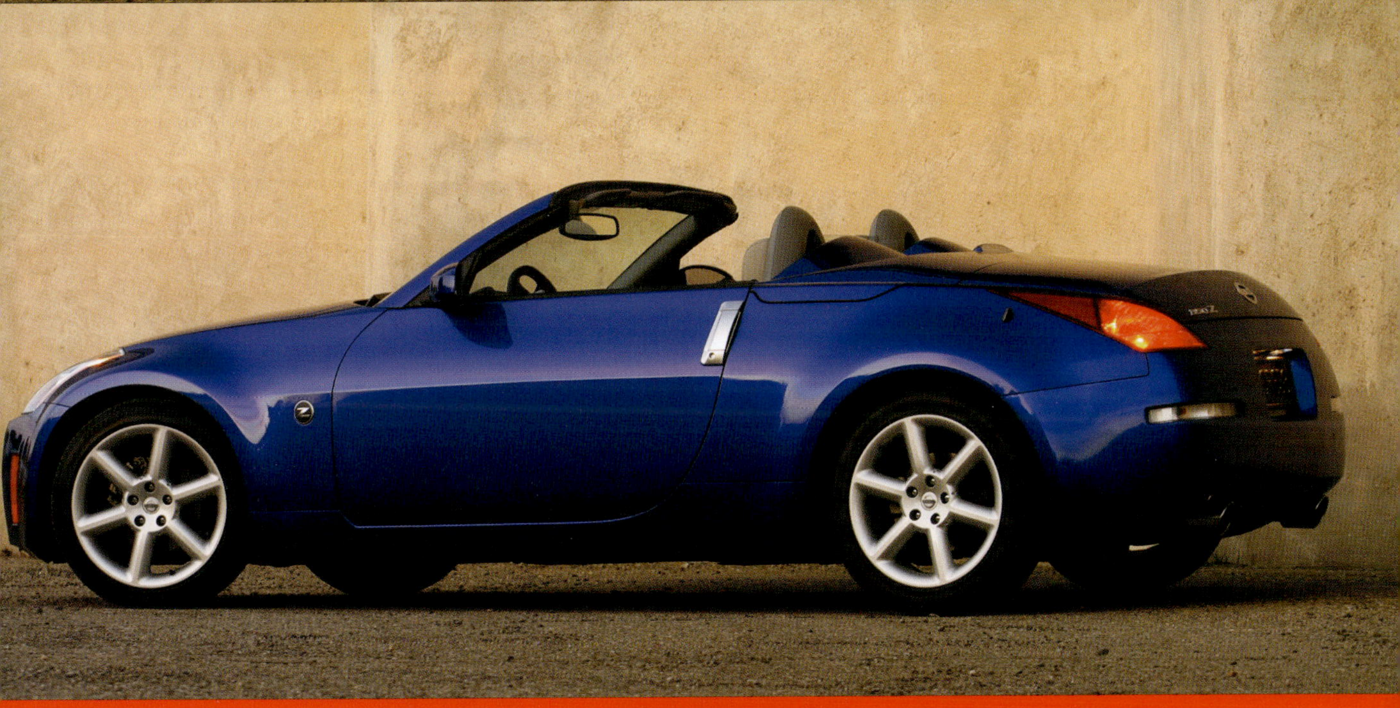